ESCAPE

MY LIFELONG WAR AGAINST CULTS

BY: PAUL MORANTZ
WITH HAL LANCASTER

ESCAPE: MY LIFELONG WAR AGAINST CULTS

by Paul Morantz and Hal Lancaster

is published by
Cresta Publications
P.O.Box 545
Pacific Palisades, California 90272
crestapublications@hotmail.com

Title page layout design by Mitchell Lancaster
Printed in the United States of America

2nd Edition Copyright © 2013 by Paul Morantz and Hal Lancaster

Library of Congress Cataloguing-in-Publication Data
Paul Morantz and Hal Lancaster
ESCAPE: MY LIFELONG WAR AGAINST CULTS
ISBN-13: 978-0-615848-69-3
ISBN-10: 0-615848-69-9
Library of Congress Control Number: 2012937398

DEDICATION

This book is dedicated to Charles Dederich. Besides providing a mountain of rich source material, he made the critical decision to rescind the allocation of $10,000 to hire a professional assassin to kill me. Fortunately for me, he put his faith in the Imperial Marines he had trained to perform just such a task.

I will be forever grateful for that decision. Without it, I wouldn't have been around to write this book.

Table Of Contents

Foreword 7

Introduction: Sympathy for the Disciples? 13

SECTION I: An Unusual Education

Chapter 1: Escape from Mao, or Brainwashing 101 25

Chapter 2: Escape from Innocence 39

Chapter 3: Escape from Cielo Drive 47

Chapter 4: Escape from Nichiren Shoshu and the 13th Century 59

Chapter 5: Escape from Golden State Manor 65

Chapter 6: Escape from the SLA and Tania 75

SECTION II: From Miracle to Madness to Mayhem

Chapter 7: Escape from Synanon

Part 1: Down the Rabbit Hole 93

Part 2: The Rise of Violence 103

Part 3: A Venomous Special Delivery 119

Part 4: A Date with the Devil 137

Part 5: An Act of Betrayal 149

SECTION III: Scoundrels, Charlatans, and False Prophets

Chapter 8: Escape from Jonestown 169

Chapter 9: Escape from est (or How I Saved the LAPD) 181

Chapter 10: Escape from the Cult of Cruelty 199

Chapter 11: Escape from the Moonies 217

Chapter 12: Escape from Rancho Rajneesh 233

SECTION IV: The Beat Goes On

Chapter 13: Escape from L. Ron Hubbard Way

Part 1: From Xenu to Xenophobia 249

Part 2: Anonymous, the Virtual Vigilante 275

Chapter 14: Escape from a Seaside Sect 287

Chapter 15: Escape from the Love Doctor 293

Postscript: Escape from the Present-To What? 309

Acknowledgments 327

Foreword

Imagine a callow and chubby youth suddenly thrust into the maelstrom of college life, desperately seeking a comfortable place in this alien world. For me, that place was the *Daily Trojan*, the campus newspaper of the University of Southern California. It was the only place on that teeming urban campus that made sense to me, where people of like minds and interests gathered to work, schmooze, and even play. I made my first collegiate friends there. Some because they were like me: a bit  shy, uncertain, grasping for something they hadn't quite identified yet. Others because they were my polar opposites: intellectual, cocksure and corrosively funny.

Then there was Paul Morantz. He was everything I aspired to be and like nobody I had ever met. He had an encyclopedic knowledge about sports. He could approach anyone—from the school's imperious football coach to some of its most psychotic athletes—and fearlessly pummel them with confrontational questions. Most of all, women loved him. After all, he was tall, well-built, with thick, wavy dark hair, a leering smile and a sense of humor to match. All of which prompted us to dub him "The Wolf," a nickname he eagerly embraced (and still does).

In those days, Paul had three priorities in life: women, USC football and the beach, generally in that order, except in the fall. During football season, the top two were at least tied, unless USC was in the national championship hunt, in which case everything else was tied for second.

Hardly the profile of a man who would eventually put his heart and soul—and life—on the line in the name of freedom and the rights of the individual, who would spend more than 30 years fighting coercive and violent individuals and organizations, who would be bitten by a rattlesnake put in his mailbox by one of those groups and would survive to become one of the nation's leading authorities on brainwashing and cults.

But if you knew Paul back then—really knew him—you would have seen this coming. For no matter what he sank his teeth into, no matter how profound or insignificant it was, he did it with a fire in his belly, an innate certainty about the righteousness of his quest and a bulldog-like refusal to ever give up.

When Paul became sports editor of the *Daily Trojan* and I its editor in 1967, he came to me complaining of a truly heinous injustice: the university wouldn't pay for a *Daily Trojan* reporter to travel to Michigan State for a USC football game. Like any right-thinking student of the '60s, he wanted to protest, but in a unique, tongue-in-cheek way. So instead of writing about the game, we ran the *Los Angeles Times'* story under a headline proclaiming, "We Were Not There." Opposite, we ran a detailed story on a fraternity flag football game, noting in type of equal size, "We Were There." In between was a large photo of Paul and another reporter, Lance Spiegel, hunched over a radio, ears cupped, with a caption reading, "DT Press Box."

In those days, staid old USC was The Land the Protest Era Forgot. Things like this just weren't done. The president of the university was the publisher of the newspaper, for heaven's sake. Indeed, one of his vice presidents hauled us in to rail against our impertinence, which only amused Paul. *Daily Trojan* reporters have traveled with the team ever since.

After law school, Paul took a job as a public defender, partly because he loved fighting for the underdog and partly because the supervisor who interviewed him for the District Attorney's office advised him he was "too stylish" and directed how he should reshape his haircut to look like one of the "good guys." In clear and un-ambiguous terms, Paul told him what he could do with his styling tips.

It didn't take him long to stir up a hornets nest in the public defender's office, either.

Assigned to Division 40 in the Criminal Courts Building in Los Angeles, Paul soon faced off against Judge Noel Cannon, a legend in Los Angeles jurisprudence lore, and not in a good way. Known as the Pink Lady, Noel Cannon was famous for her pink mini-dresses, the derringer she frequently flashed and the Chihuahua who accompanied her to court. Power-hungry and vindictive—she once threatened to jail a policeman who tried to explain that the motorist she was honking at was merely waiting for a pedestrian to cross—she reveled in ignoring the law when it suited her own agenda. She especially enjoyed jailing public defenders for offenses real and imagined. In 1972, she put seven of them in jail, including Paul. *Time* Magazine noted that most lawyers were loath to cross her. "Good lawyers knew that," Paul wrote in an article about his experiences with Judge Cannon. "Unfortunately, I wasn't that good." (Knowing Paul as I do, I can assure you that he was cackling and leering as he wrote that line.)

The headstrong combatants battled nearly every day. But Judge Cannon made a grave mistake when she took out her ire towards Paul on one of his clients. Kenneth Williams, an 18-year-old black student accused of a gang-related robbery and beating, was arrested because he fit the general description given of one of the attackers by the victim. Because the prosecution neglected to subpoena the victim to testify, the two sides agreed to reschedule his preliminary hearing and release him instead of dismissing the case as the law required and re-arresting him. Judge Cannon rescheduled the hearing, but refused to release Williams on his own recognizance. So Paul prepared a declaration that was filed in a higher court seeking the immediate release of his client. The new judge not only ruled that Williams was being illegally confined, but dismissed the case, noting the investigating officer had cleared Williams of the charges.

Unfortunately, Williams wasn't informed of the dismissal and showed up for his newly scheduled hearing. Spotting him in the courtroom, Judge Cannon, enraged by Paul's legal end run, jailed Williams without explanation. At the end of the day, he was released.

Now it was war. Paul started gathering statements from witnesses involved in the case. The report he compiled detailed Cannon's inappropriate actions in the case and eventually found its way to Kent Richland, a deputy in the state attorney general's office. Based in part on the report, he launched an investigation that would lead to a state Judicial Commission inquiry. Paul testified before the commission and Judge Cannon was found guilty of 21 acts of willful misconduct, among other charges. She was eventually removed from the bench.

So what qualities are you looking for in a defender of the rights of the individual? Passion? Persistence? Courage? An unshakable belief in doing the right thing? I would submit that my friend had exhibited all of those qualities long before he ever took on Synanon, the People's Temple, the Unification Church, Scientology, the Center for Feeling Therapy and a host of other con artists and false prophets.

In the spirit of full disclosure, Paul also has a healthy ego and isn't averse to the occasional bit of grandstanding. I think he would cop to that. It comes with the territory. But Paul is also a true romantic and a dreamer. For all the stories his friends have passed around for years about his libidinous lifestyle, I'll let you in on his dirty little secret: It has all been a quest for true romantic love, that forever-after soul mate. This romantic streak also informs his worldview. He is a true believer in the American Heroic Myth, embodied by such men as Davy Crockett and Serpico. They are his role models, true heroes with a clear-eyed, selfless belief in right and wrong.

Some might call that naïve and there may be some truth to that. On many occasions, Paul has ridden to the rescue of a friend in financial distress—not all have proven worthy of his generosity. How is it that I'm the only one of his friends who didn't know what an easy mark he is? Paul told me he once had a woefully incompetent secretary, but couldn't bring himself to fire her. Why not? "She was so bad, I knew she wouldn't be able to get another job," he explained. "So basically, I was stuck with her."

Fortunately, he has also retained his playfulness, humor and, most passionately, his love of USC football. Otherwise, he'd be way too perfect for a flawed guy like me. Check out his website—PaulMorantz.com, which features all of the feature stories and essays he has penned over the years, divided into various subject categories. The three biggest categories? The Cult Expert, Synanon and USC Football.

His love of his alma mater's pigskin program has endured through some dark times. I don't mean all that cult stuff. I'm talking about the lost years when Paul Hackett coached the team into the doldrums of mediocrity, the crushing moral downfall of O.J. Simpson and Reggie Bush, two great running backs he idolized (Paul may have been the last person on earth to finally admit that O.J. did it), and the excruciating and inexplicable last-minute defeat to Texas in the 2005 national championship game, which derailed USC's quest for an historic third consecutive national title.

This love also has sustained him through the debilitating red blood cell aplasia he has been fighting for the past several years, an affliction that renders his body incapable of producing sufficient red blood cells and subjects him to continual blood transfusions. About a year ago, a visitor found him unconscious in his home. Paramedics were summoned.

Let Paul tell the rest:

"I remember, when jolted from the darkness, that the voices seemed so far away. There were cries about coming back and about how people needed me; they were not having much success. Then it got quiet and finally, a much wiser voice chimed in. 'Paul,' the voice said, calmly, 'it is almost fall.'"

Like many of us, and probably more than most of us, Paul now sees himself closer to the end than the beginning. This book is part of another mission: to leave a legacy that will make his son, Chaz, proud and will remind people that he was here and his presence meant something.

He also wants to pass on this treasure trove of information and opinions about brainwashing and destructive cults, important but little understood topics that have touched his life in so many bizarre and fascinating ways. What you will read here is a whopping good yarn, but only a fraction of the whole story, which is why he has bequeathed his massive collection of documents on cults to USC's Edward L. Doheny Jr. Memorial Library, which has created an archive on his career.

So, mission accomplished. Let's hope USC keeps winning, so he might be able to add a few more chapters to that legacy.

— Hal Lancaster

Introduction: Sympathy for the Disciples?

"Youth is not absolution for treachery, and personal self-discovery is not an excuse to take up arms against one's country."
— *former Atty. Gen. John Ashcroft*

"Pleased to meet you, can you guess my name?"
— *"Sympathy for the Devil" by the Rolling Stones*

In a famous story by Stephen Vincent Benét, a naïve young man is lured into a pact with the devil, only to regret it later. It is left to the great lawyer, Daniel Webster, to deliver a stirring speech that wins sympathy from a jury of spirits, thus saving the young man's soul and freeing him from Beelzebub's clutches.

However, in the last half century there has been little sympathy for the many naïve youths who, in a quest for spirituality and purpose, have succumbed to the manipulative processes of modern-day devils who likewise seek to claim their souls. In several high-profile cases, juries and judges have come down hard on those who have been brainwashed by sociopaths seeking to use them to fulfill some wrathful agenda.

It is one of the most profound issues facing our legal system: How do we balance deterrence and compassion, especially in instances where the perpetrators of crime are also its victims? Consider the many sensationalized cases of brainwashing that have flooded the public's consciousness over the years, from the Manson family, to the mass suicides at Jonestown, to the Patty Hearst kidnapping, and more recently, to the unsettling case of John Walker Lindh, a troubled, 19-year-old American who sought a better world through Islam, but instead became entangled in the destructive web of Osama bin Laden.

When Lindh faced the cameras for the first time after his capture, I saw the ghost of Patty Hearst there: a soulless youth explaining in a monotone that he was a Taliban soldier. Like the priest in *The Exorcist*, I believed I was once again seeing an evil force of nature that I had fought many times before.

*   *   *   *   *   *

Lindh, like many youths since the tremulous 60's, lacked sufficient identity and self-esteem and was searching for spiritual direction. Raised in Marin County, once the capital of hot tubs and the Me Decade, he thought he had found the answer when, at age 16, he read the *Autobiography of Malcolm X*. Not even the murder of the central character—most likely by members of his own religious sect—deterred the boy's new direction. He donned Islamic clothes, learned the language and studied the scriptures. But he wanted more. Neither of his parents had been a guiding force in his life. When they divorced, the teenager took off to find a better world. Unfortunately, his path led to Pakistan and Osama bin Laden.

Bin Laden was one of 54 sons borne by the 22 wives of Mohammed bin Laden, an ex-railroad porter who built the biggest construction company in Saudi Arabia. His success came in large part to the close ties he cultivated with the royal family, to whom he eventually became a trusted consigliere.

Osama, after a youthful bout of Westernized drinking and womanizing, became a born-again Muslim and folk hero who unstintingly offered his wealth and services to help defeat— with American aid—the Russians in Afghanistan. The Arab adulation that followed inflamed his budding megalomania.

Unwilling to accept a return to obscurity when King Fahd of Saudi Arabia chose the U.S. over him and his Mujahideen to save Kuwait from Saddam Hussein, Osama began advocating a holy war against his former ally, a country whose power and active role in the Middle East stood as an obstacle to his voracious appetite for power. He promised would-be followers that if they sacrificed their souls to him, they would reap Allah's reward—the infamous 72 virgins—in the next life. As with all sociopaths, and so clear from his tapes, his followers were nothing more than expendable tools to him, existing primarily to die for his glory.

Bin Laden recruited not just the poor and desperate, but the middle class searching for something more. He established camps that not only trained, but indoctrinated. It was into this world that Lindh innocently walked. And when he met up with bin Laden personally and was asked to fight with the Taliban, one can only imagine Osama smiling at the sight of the converted American, stroking his beard and saying, "Pleased to meet you... can you guess my name?"

If the devil made Lindh do it, he was hardly the first to suffer such a fate. History abounds with examples of brainwashing of varying degrees, from the Inquisition, to the Salem witch-hunts, to Stalin, Nazi Germany, McCarthyism and all of Richard Nixon's men. Was the insular Nixon White House a cult? It certainly echoed some of the characteristics of notorious cults, from a paranoid, us vs. them worldview, to the secret tapings, to the dirty tricks squad and the infamous enemies list.

I have long maintained that the administration of George W. Bush fostered an atmosphere of thought reform fueled by post-9/11 fear and paranoia. Bush and his circle of advisers called for their own holy war against their enemies, twisting the truth into a knowingly false sales pitch to justify extreme actions, indoctrinating followers and ostracizing dissenters as traitors to the great cause. Bush and bin Laden are the products of eerily similar backgrounds: both competed with siblings for their powerful fathers' attention; both spent dissolute youths partying before claiming spiritual rebirth; both claimed a direct line to God; both polarized society with a for-us-or-against-us attitude and both turned political crises into personal triumphs that led to growing popularity and power. Certainly, the actions of each spurred the other to ever-increasing violence, producing thousands of casualties, from the victims of 9/11 to the soldiers and civilians lost in the invasion of Iraq. While Bush survived the polarization, bin Laden ultimately did not. Who knows what would have happened had they switched cultures at birth.

*   *   *   *   *   *

So, what do we make of Mr. Lindh's tale? For perhaps the first time in his life, he was treated as special, and made to feel a welcome member of a new and caring family, a family where each member was dedicated, through common beliefs, to building a purer world. And in this fragile and still infantile psychological state, it's no wonder he was susceptible to the idea that the world must be saved by any means. His story echoes familiar domestic tales of youths long before him who joined communes and sects seeking to take their spiritual quest to the next level and were similarly victimized. These aren't the power-hungry or bloodthirsty people often drawn to terrorist groups, but young idealists who truly believe they are following the path of righteousness to a better world. But time and time again, we have seen that in the right environment, a skillful, charismatic leader can turn innocents into crusading terrorists.

Certainly, brainwashing has its limits. In fictional accounts of the process, brainwashing is depicted as some irresistible hypnotic trick that leads to total mind control. Real-world brainwashing involves a change of beliefs through persistent coercion. The victim still makes his own choices, but makes them based on the new beliefs that have been forced on him.

Equally false is the contention, still voiced by many, that anyone who could succumb to such manipulation must be weak, evil, addled, or all three. These people believe that we cannot be brainwashed unless we want to be. Nobody wants to see themselves as that weak, but the simple truth is that we are all vulnerable to the ministrations of brainwashing; the most fanatical converts often are the most intelligent.

*   *   *   *   *   *

For reasons not entirely clear to me, these issues have consumed me for most of my 40 years as a lawyer. Most of that time has been spent fighting for the freedom and rights of victims of manipulative cults, self-help gurus, abusive psychotherapists and murderous sociopaths. While other attorneys have dabbled in this fringe field, only San Anselmo, Calif., attorney Ford Greene and I, to my knowledge, have devoted our careers to it. And I may be the only lawyer who has qualified to testify as an expert on the characteristics of cults and brainwashing.

I have litigated against or in some other way been involved in combating such disparate groups as the Church of Scientology, the People's Temple, Synanon, Rajneesh, est, sex abuser John Gottuso and the Center for Feeling Therapy. I have interviewed well over a thousand former cult members and have cross-examined many destructive gurus and cult leaders. I have read enough diaries, manifestos and internal cult documents to fill a garage—my garage. I was involved in a suit against the Rev. Sun Myung Moon and the so-called Moonies of his Unification Church that resulted in a landmark 1988 ruling by the California Supreme Court that for the first time clearly acknowledged the existence of brainwashing and the rights of victims to sue for both compensatory and punitive damages. I helped write the current California law establishing citizens' right to sue churches for punitive damages and assisted in creating laws separating sex from therapy and later, abusers from private schools.

When I embarked on my legal career, I had no idea where it would lead. Certainly, it has been a unique and fascinating odyssey, one that has been lucrative at times but more often than not has drained my time, resources and energy. And it has more than once put me in harm's way. As a closet journalist, I have wanted to write about this odyssey for many years. I haven't, for a litany of reasons too boring to relate here. But in the interim, I have gritted my teeth at a string of cult books that presented incomplete and often, just plain wrong information.

Take Synanon, for example. That was my best known and most personal case (the cult did, after all, try to kill me). So I take it personally when people get the story wrong.

In 1965, sociologist Lew Yablonski's book, *The Tunnel Back*, declared Synanon's program a cure for drug addicts. While relating accurately how Synanon used peer pressure to force people to conform to its program, Yablonski made the mistake of participating in Synanon programs and wound up brainwashed into believing the cult's rhetoric about all the enemies seeking its destruction. He lauded Charles Dederich as a charismatic leader producing a new breed of professional people who could rid society of drugs and crimes and transform addicts into all-knowing, all-understanding "super beings."

We all know what happened to the last guy who wanted to create a super race.

Then there was Rod Janzen. In 2003, he called to tell me he was nearly finished with *The Rise and Fall of Synanon Inc.* Since I still harbored hopes of writing the definitive Synanon book, I was obviously disappointed. But I was glad someone was doing it and offered to help. All he needed, he said, was for me to confirm the date I was attacked. "How can you write a book about Synanon without interviewing the man who fought it?" I asked, incredulously. He said his source material was the Synanon document archive at the UCLA library. I told him that was a watered-down version stripped of damaging documents by Synanon. I had all the incriminating documents UCLA did not and I offered them to him; without them, I said, his book would be inaccurate. He declined, saying his publisher didn't want to push back the release date.

The book was an abomination. Janzen said he wanted to emphasize the good things Synanon had done because he was an advocate of communes. As such, he denied the existence of brainwashing, even though he admitted he hadn't researched the subject. His reasoning was bizarre: If brainwashing existed, it could mean that it was used in varying degrees by all communes and religions, something he didn't want to consider because it might then have affected him.

He also claimed that the allegations of violence had been greatly exaggerated by the media and insisted that no one inside Synanon had ever been attacked. After I read his farce, I provided him with information from Synanon's own documents that indicated there were more than 80 attacks. As to beatings inside Synanon, I asked him how many would he like to know about? Even after I sent him 100 pages detailing all the episodes of brutality at the group's various facilities and the attacks on perceived enemies, he offered the public no apology for his misstatements on Synanon violence.

We have the Pulitzer Prize to honor outstanding performance in the written word. We should also present the Janzen Jackpot to acknowledge the author who most flagrantly disregards the truth.

Over the years, it has been frustrating to watch journalists and government officials rely on so-called experts who often had it all wrong. So many lives have been lost because of bad information that led to bad strategies for handling cult crises. And in many of those cases, I felt I could help, but couldn't get access to the decision-makers.

Consider the federal government's bungled attempt to capture Branch Davidian leader David Koresh and rescue his followers. Anyone who knew the strength of the bond between a cult leader and his followers could have predicted the outcome of the government's heavy-handed strategy of surrounding the Waco compound with a show of force. When cornered, cult leaders will choose to die rather than confront their failure. And they will induce their followers to die with them, so convinced are they that these deaths fulfill some divine commandment. Jim Jones did it; so did Donald DeFreeze. By surrounding the compound and humiliating Koresh in front of his followers, the government only ensured a bloody ending. And like Jonestown, children died as a result.

The government's mishandling of the incident made me angry. With all of America watching, Attorney General Janet Reno apparently felt she had to show strength and resolve. It was a bad call. Had they sent a select squad of trained operatives there and laid low, an unaware Koresh would eventually have left the compound, where he could easily have been grabbed.

That no one thought to seek my counsel always upset me. It occurs to me, of course, that this is at least partially my fault. Had I written this book and others that I had contemplated over the years, perhaps I would have been on Ms. Reno's speed dial.

So now I want to make up for lost time and contribute to the knowledge base on this little-understood subject. In these pages, I hope to offer as true and complete a picture as I can of the development and characteristics of cults in our society as well as as to record a strange life spent helping victims "Escape." Hopefully, this will lead to a broader understanding of this strange phenomenon. My aim was to make this the only book you'll ever need to read on the subject.

But don't mistake me for some cliché bleeding heart. Despite all the time I've spent defending cult victims, despite all the knowledge I've gained about the power of charismatic leaders to manipulate the vulnerable into committing unconscionable acts, I do not advocate some magic get-out-of-jail-free card for their victims. There must be accountability and there must be punishment to deter those who feel justified in taking the law into their own hands in the name of some twisted political or spiritual master. The Constitution guarantees us the freedom to believe what we want; it doesn't entitle us to commit criminal acts in support of those beliefs, even when convinced they serve a higher purpose. And it makes no difference whether the beliefs are adopted voluntarily or through coercion. Not all who are forced to accept new beliefs commit criminal acts and when they do, they know they are breaking the law.

But I do advocate understanding and compassion. We must temper our fear and outrage against those who might have lived, or could resume living, ordinary lives absent the exposure to destructive cult leaders. Persuasive evidence exists that the effects of brainwashing dissipate quickly when the victim is removed from the influence of the group.

There have been wide disparities in the application of justice in cases involving brainwashing. Mr. Lindh, his young mind inflamed by bin Laden's seductive, if phony, sales pitch, might certainly have attacked an American in defense of his new Taliban "family," but no evidence has been presented that he ever did. Yet, he was sentenced to

20 years in prison without parole for aiding the Taliban, five years more than anyone who actually participated in the 9/11 massacre.

Is that justice or vengeance? Now that we have finally executed bin Laden, the true culprit, should we consider parole for Mr. Lindh, even though he espoused beliefs alien to American culture and ideals? In juggling the interests of the individual and society during a time of mass fear and paranoia, did we miss the sometimes obscure line that separates an evildoer from a victim?

What do we do with Leslie Van Houten, persuaded by drugs and the powerful influence of the murderous Charles Manson to help cleanse the world in a whirlpool of victims' blood. Now serving a life sentence in prison more than 40 years later, she has been, reportedly, a model prisoner; yet, she was turned down for parole a 20th time in 2013. Is 40 years enough time to provide a deterrence factor? Is it time to reconsider our position on Ms. Van Houten, who had the misfortune of accepting a ride from a Manson follower while hitchhiking?

What about the lesser-known case of Scott Anderson?

As told in a book by crime writer Aphrodite Jones, who I met at an art gallery, Rick and Ruth Wendorf of Eustis, Fla., were bludgeoned to death with a tire iron wielded by 16-year-old cult leader Rod Ferrell in 1996. A self-proclaimed antichrist, Ferrell enticed four fellow teenagers into forming a cult of faux vampires who spent their time drinking blood and reading gothic fiction. Ferrell hoped to get enough money from looting the Wendorfs' home to finance the cult's relocation to—where else?—New Orleans.

He was accompanied by Anderson, a confused and vulnerable 16-year-old who idolized the baroque and charismatic Ferrell. But once inside, Anderson froze against a wall and refused to participate in the killings. Nevertheless, he was sentenced to life in prison without the possibility of parole after the group's capture and trial—the same sentence Ferrell received after the commutation of his death sentence. The court ruled that by entering the home with knowledge of the murder-robbery plot, he was guilty of conspiracy to murder. Further, the court said Anderson should have done more to stop the killings.

Once again, it seemed to me, the legal system displayed a complete lack of understanding of the nature of brainwashing and cults. Under the influence of Ferrell, it wasn't surprising that the impressionable teenager could be induced to enter into the plot and even go into the building. But he resisted. He didn't kill anybody. For that, he should be given a gold star. Should he have done more, tried to stop the killings? Perhaps, but in his brainwashed state, it wasn't likely that he was capable of doing so. And it probably would have cost him his own life. Does that mean he should get off scot free? No, but sentencing a teenager in this situation to life in prison constitutes obscene overkill.

Contrast those crimes and punishments with those meted out to Patty Hearst and followers of the Bhagwan Shree Rajneesh.

After being kidnapped in 1974 by the Symbionese Liberation Army, a small, vaguely Marxist band of disgruntled college dropouts and ex-convicts, Hearst declared her allegiance to the group, then joined them on a bloody crime spree and was sentenced to 35 years in prison, later reduced to 7 years. But she was released by then-president Jimmy Carter after only 22 months and granted a full pardon by Pres. Bill Clinton in 2001. Followers of the Bhagwan received relatively light sentences despite being convicted of mass poisonings and the attempted assassination of public officials, all in the name of furthering the guru's cause. All were released long ago.

These are issues we must consider as a society. But in the end, we must all recognize that there is no immunity from the natural human tendencies to be manipulated by guilt and bound by confession. There but for the grace of God...

Keep that in mind as you read the stories that follow. They trace the journey of my life, from innocence and ignorance to a base of knowledge and a host of troubling questions, none of which lend themselves to easy answers. I have expressed my own opinions here, based on the facts as I know them, but I encourage you to read and draw your own conclusions. Some of the names will be familiar to you, others more obscure. In a few cases, I have changed the names of victims who have a psychiatric history or have suffered sexual abuse.

All of the individuals and groups covered in this book have, in some odd way, crossed my path, a lifetime of phantom dots connected by, depending on your beliefs, coincidence or fate.

SECTION I:

An Unusual Education

Chapter 1: Escape From Mao, or Brainwashing 101

In 1953, 21 U.S. military prisoners returning from the Korean War appeared on television spouting Communist doctrine, praising their captors and confessing to war crimes. They said they feared returning to an imperialistic world and spoke of feeling a "great harmony" that they didn't wish to risk for the "pain" of freedom.

Needless to say, Americans were shocked. How could our brave young military men suddenly reject everything this country stood for, the belief system they were sent to defend? What had been done to them?

American journalist Edward Hunter coined the term "brainwashing" after a Chinese informant during the war referred to it as "hsi nao" or cleansing the mind. The correct Chinese term, however, is "tzu hsing kai tsao"—thought reform or ideological molding. But Hunter's term stuck, partly because it was catchy and partly because it put Americans at ease. There was nothing wrong with us; it was those evil Chinese with their drugs and hypnosis and unspeakable torture breaking down our poor boys' will in ways no one could resist.

U.S. researchers, however, found that the process didn't depend on drugs, imprisonment or torture. Not only are we all vulnerable to such ideological conversions, but in various degrees, our own beliefs were shaped in a similar, if less intense, fashion. People subjected to this process certainly aren't like those made to bark like dogs by carnival hypnotists or the zombie-like assassin of *The Manchurian Candidate*. Such control has never been achieved. Victims make their own choices. But if you change beliefs, you change choices.

I define the process as the art of forcing someone to adopt a new belief while convincing him that he has done so voluntarily. The victims of the most persuasive brainwashing feel they have achieved a plateau of enlightenment.

The Chinese communists under Mao Tse-Tung developed this regimen of thought reform in an attempt to "purify" all segments of Chinese society following the revolution. They first tested it in prisons to reform political enemies by immersing them in small groups of other prisoners who had already gone through the process and could testify to the great benefits of the transformation more persuasively than prison officials. By using peer testimony to build a high level of trust, the prisoners were ripe to accept the "higher purpose" of their captors.

Next, they were urged to confess their sins and and criticize others. This made it easier to instill conflict and achieve submission by creating guilt. By continually attacking their former selves and confessing more and more bad deeds, these subjects experienced psychological death and rebirth. For the trainers, the goal was to reduce them to an infantile state, ripe for reprogramming.

The process worked so well, the Chinese expanded it ambitiously to groups of scholars, teachers, artists, writers, politicians, scientists and other professionals, encouraging them to undergo the process as an act of patriotism. This was, said Dr. Robert Lifton, an authority on brainwashing from the Army's Walter Reed Institute of Research, "the most powerful effort at human manipulation ever undertaken."

Thus was created the "struggle group"—an encounter-type group whose indoctrination sessions were similar to many of the self-help programs that flourished in the U.S. in the 1970s, such as Synanon and est. In these Mao-inspired groups, people were persuaded to cast aside all symbols of their former life. The group replaced the family, names were changed, personal wardrobes were discarded in favor of uniforms. The aim was to create a new person who would recognize that the greatest good was to serve the group, as opposed to the group serving the member.

Mao described his program as punishing the past to warn the future. The process of analyzing and criticizing what was undesirable in the past, he explained, is like that of a doctor curing a disease. "If we are to wipe all crimes from their root," he said, we must also "transform the various evil ideological conceptions in the minds of the people so that they may be educated and reformed into new people."

Victims of this kind of "coercive persuasion," the term used by Dr. Edgar Schein, who also studied the Korean War prisoners, were caught in what I call the "double bind." While they were vigorously attacked as dysfunctional and weak and in need of the protection and comfort of the group, they were simultaneously told their allegiance to the group made them special, better than nonbelievers. While obviously contradictory, these two threads were woven into a powerful, binding knot. Continual reproach might eventually have driven people away, while repeated praise might have boosted self-esteem to the point that the group was no longer needed. Battering victims with this double bind kept them confused and scared. That, combined with long, exhausting hours of work, bonding exercises such as singing, confession and lectures, and little sleep, began to break down resistance.

Often, the turning point in the conversion process was an unexpected show of kindness just at the breaking point, providing relief and reward in exchange for acceptance of a new identity. Now the victim not only developed a compulsion to rid himself of all harmful parts but to assist others in making a similar, confession-induced conversion. Denouncing one's father was seen as a sign of successful conversion. Attacks upon family severed past loyalties and brought new commitment. Having effectively emptied himself of his past, the victim rushed to fill the void by accepting a new identity offered by the group in order to avoid a sense of total psychological annihilation.

Eventually, new verbal clichés replaced old beliefs, reducing the world to simplistic equations of black vs. white, good vs. evil, us vs. them and the ends justify the means. War is bad, but holy war is good. Such simplicity certainly appealed to those seeking spiritual clarity, particularly young people plagued by guilt and a negative self-image who gravitated towards all-or-nothing emotional attachments. The new slogans and labels that came with this new identity were believed to expand knowledge. In reality, the new language limited critical thinking by reducing everything to simplistic slogans.

The result was a "zealous convert" with a "duty" to spread this "truth" by any and all means. "Ideological totalism," Dr. Lifton wrote, "may offer a man an intense peak experience, a sense of transcending all that is ordinary and prosaic, of freeing himself from the encumbrances of human ambivalence, of entering a sphere of truth, reality, trust, and sincerity beyond any he had ever known or even imagined."

But brainwashing processes have an expiration date. Without constant reinforcement, brainwashing tends to wear off in about 90 days. This is why Alcoholics Anonymous built its program on lifetime attendance at meetings. When members left a group I was suing, thus becoming a potential witness, it was futile to call them while the experience was still fresh in their minds. Besides, I knew that in about three months, they would invariably call me.

Victims often emerge from their ideological comas angry. After reaching such emotional peaks, Dr. Lifton concluded, the potential exists for an equally intense rebound. The victim of brainwashing might justifiably become an equally zealous opponent, angered over having been controlled. He compared it to the disillusionment the truly religious might feel if they discovered God didn't exist.

*   *   *   *   *   *

These methods gain traction when they fall into the hands of sociopaths and narcissists seeking glory, fame and power. In one form or another, this kind of manipulation has always existed. But in the late '60s, a witch's brew of pop psychology, the quest for spiritual enlightenment and a society on the brink of political and social upheaval created an explosion of destructive cults in America.

The term "cult" has been used almost exclusively by the media to connote a group dedicated to evil. But the word defines a group dedicated to a person or belief, which isn't necessarily a threat. It becomes dangerous when the group seeks to alter its members' beliefs forcefully, when the members exist for the care of the leader instead of the reverse.

I prefer the term "totalist movement," created by Dr. Lifton. A totalist group seeks to grow—and conquer—opposing ideologies. It fosters rigid, black-and-white thinking and a sense that its cause is so just, often directed by God, that any means are justified to achieve its ends, even lying, stealing and terrorism.

Many totalist movements in the U.S., while employing Mao's methods, grew largely from the teachings of such well-known philosophers and psychologists as Ralph Waldo Emerson, B.F. Skinner, Henry David Thoreau, Timothy Leary, and Abraham Maslow. Combined, their beliefs helped shape the atmosphere of civil disobedience, communal living and behavioral design that eventually gave birth to the rebellious youth and societal unrest of the 1960s.

An 1841 essay by Emerson entitled *Self Reliance* would lead to a phrase that would rule pop culture over a century later: "Do your own thing." Unfortunately, many movement leaders used the phrase to convince followers to reject society and follow their twisted lead, which wasn't at all what Emerson had in mind.

Thoreau, Emerson's best friend and protégé, argued in an essay entitled *Civil Disobedience* that people shouldn't permit the government to override their consciences or make them agents of injustice, as in the slave-owning, antebellum South. To end injustice, he advised, refuse to pay taxes, a stand he himself took, leading to his imprisonment.

In *Walden*, a book inspired by his two years living in a cabin on woodlands owned by Emerson, Thoreau extolled the simple life, living in harmony with nature amongst forests and meadows. He derided the education system for wasting precious time teaching students things they would never use instead of pragmatic skills, such as baking bread.

B. F. Skinner took Thoreau's ideas one step further a century later. In his 1948 novel, *Walden 2*, he created a utopian community run not by politicians, but behavioral engineers. Successful social planning, he believed, would allow people to live more productive and contented lives. Labor credits replaced currency and students designed their own curricula based on their interests, which they were free to pursue without grades or regimented classes.

This utopian dream captured the imaginations of many. But a character in the book raises a critical question: "Suppose you suddenly found it possible to control the behavior of men as you wished? My question is, have you the courage to take up and wield the science of behavior for the good of mankind?" An equally important question might be: Do you have the wisdom to know when not to? In totalist groups, that invariably is the sticking point.

The founders of the so-called Humanist Movement, Abraham Maslow and Carl Rogers, largely dismissed such concerns, based on their belief that man was innately good. Curiously, both grew up with domineering mothers; Maslow once wrote that the roots of his philosophy grew from his hatred and revulsion of his mother. So perhaps their utopian views, however illogical, stemmed from some sort of wish fulfillment.

Maslow was heavily influenced by William James, a philosopher/psychologist who was the godson of Ralph Waldo Emerson and the brother of novelist Henry James. James suffered deep bouts of depression in his youth and maintained a life-long interest in mysticism and altered states of consciousness. He believed that religious experiences were more crucial to human development than science.

Maslow took James' beliefs to a new level, insisting that people would, if given a choice, seek to fulfill their highest potential. Anything that interfered with their attaining that potential—and thus, happiness--should be ignored, he contended, including society's rules and mores. Maslow believed that by driving individuals through altered states of consciousness to continual "peak experiences," the resulting moments of extreme joy and excitement would lead mankind to a "transcending unity" and knowledge of a higher truth. Once people achieved this ideal state of psychological health, which he called "self-actualization," he theorized that violence, thievery and sexual exploitation would disappear, because self-actualized people's "true human nature" wouldn't allow them to act in such destructive ways. Maslow believed in Utopia, which he called "Eupsychia." Rogers talked about the "actualizing tendency"—the built-in motivation in every life form—from humans to seaweed—to develop its potential to its fullest extent.

Both also had concerns about the expense of psychotherapy and believed that even laymen could provide therapy. That gave rise to the so-called self-help movement, a concept that flies in the face of most state licensing laws regarding psychotherapy. While it isn't inconceivable that some laymen might prove excellent therapists, Maslow and Rogers never realized there would also be con men and charlatans who would do great harm. Licensing laws assure minimum education requirements for therapists and a platform for pursuing ethics violations.

Many critics—and count me among them—consider these beliefs dangerously naïve, an invitation to the sociopaths who lurk among us to act on their true natures and, perhaps, self-actualize into narcissistic cult leaders.

No wonder that by the unsettling '60s, with these idealistic concepts swimming in their heads and an unpopular war threatening their very existence, young American Baby Boomers began exploring a host of new-age religions and pop psychologies that seemed to bloom like mushrooms on a rainy day, many of a poisonous variety. They sought deep meditation, intense feelings of love, brotherhood and to be one with nature.

But in the euphoric haze of these peak experiences they were vulnerable to the manipulations of certain destructive leaders. Like Mao, these movement leaders understood peak experiences were a key to conversion. The euphoria followers experienced, they were told, resulted from their acceptance of the leader's beliefs. Some of these cults were just love-soaked hippie communes and relatively benign; but others were violent distortions of utopians' hopes and dreams hidden behind the appealing catchphrase "go for it," from the movie *Rocky*. These cult leaders confined their young prey in Skinner-like controlled environments, softened them up with continual activity and denial of sleep, a la Mao, and peppered them with enough of Maslow's language to make it palatable.

Consider the case of Steve Simon, a Harvard-trained psychologist who came to Synanon as an intern at Maslow's suggestion. His Ph.D. dissertation included a glowing report on Synanon, although he conceded that the tumultuous, exciting and chaotic Synanon Game "forces a person to risk his world view and his convictions" if he "over identified" with the game's participants and their message. Those affected would "reach out for the nearest point of stability--the other members of Synanon and Synanon's way of life," he concluded.

His concerns were warranted. Like so many before him, Simon was slammed by other members in a game, then comforted afterwards by none other than Synanon founder Charles Dederich, which made him feel special. He eventually converted, becoming one of Synanon's most devoted members and the group's appointed historian. Years later, he would be convicted of destroying evidence of Synanon's conspiracy to commit terrorism and sentenced to up to five years in prison.

Drugs could also trigger peak experiences. In 1938, Swiss chemist Albert Hofmann was seeking a drug that could control bleeding during childbirth. The compound he synthesized, Lysergic Acid Diethylamide, or LSD, instead produced biochemical changes in the brain that mimicked the symptoms of psychosis. The compound was initially used to study mental illness under controlled conditions, but in the 1950s, Robert Hyde—who did not have an alter ego named Jekyll—tested it on himself and student volunteers, on at least one occasion by spiking a punch bowl at a party. Not surprisingly, his research was funded by the CIA, which thought LSD might be useful for interrogations and brainwashing.

Enter Timothy Leary, who became the spokesman--some would say clown prince—of the 1960's drug subculture. Leary's troubled past included his departure from two colleges, including the U.S. Military

Academy at West Point, for disciplinary reasons, the suicide of the first of his four wives and his resignation as director of the Kaiser Foundation amid a hail of bounced checks. While lecturing at Harvard University, however, Leary believed he had discovered in his experiments with LSD a short cut to Maslow's dream of peak experiences leading to enlightenment. In 1964, he co-authored *The Psychedelic Experience*, which advocated the use of psychedelics as a path to altered states of consciousness that would enlarge mental capacities and spark religious or aesthetic ecstasies with the aid of sensory deprivation, yoga and disciplined meditation. Turn on, tune in and drop out, he crooned to a receptive audience of young people hooked on sex, drugs and rock and roll. He got high with poet Allen Ginsberg and tried, unsuccessfully, to arrange for John F. Kennedy, Nikita Khrushchev and novelist Norman Mailer to get high together.

His controversial experiments with mind-altering drugs eventually got him fired from Harvard. So he took to the lecture circuit to promote his agenda, continued to write books, founded a church, the League for Spiritual Discovery, and even embarked on a brief career as a stand-up comedian.

Alas, the world soon discovered that LSD didn't produce a transcendent state; it just chemically changed the patterns and normal function of the brain and nervous system. While not really necessary to induce the vulnerable to convert, the drug provided brainwashing gurus with a short cut to the destruction of self and opened the mind to external ideological influences.

Even in my youth, I didn't buy the spiritual mumbo-jumbo I was being bombarded with by friends. LSD seemed scary to me—who needed to be chased by pink elephants while driving down the freeway. It didn't seem safe and I suspected mental deterioration was a serious risk.

Still, I was willing to listen, so one day, while still an undergraduate, I decided to go hear Leary at Santa Monica Civic Auditorium. He was greeted with tumultuous applause, but never discussed the medical and psychological issues raised by the use of LSD. Instead, he said things like, "the police do not want you to use LSD because if everyone used LSD there would be no need for the police." The more inane he was, the louder the applause.

I wanted to ask him to stop making a sales pitch and give us the facts, but I feared the fanatical crowd would turn on me. As I left, I was convinced that most of that crowd was doomed and that Leary would be responsible for destroying more lives than your average serial killer. If you kill off the mind, the body will follow.

Even Richard Nixon saw the dangers of Leary's agenda, dubbing him "the most dangerous man in America." Leary once told a reporter that he would fight society's taboos against drugs by resorting to techniques used by religious cults. Fortunately, as his behavior became more and more bizarre, his influence waned. In 1970, after launching a far-fetched California gubernatorial campaign, he was arrested for marijuana possession and sentenced to ten years in prison (at the time, he was appealing a similar conviction in Texas). He staged a daring prison break and escaped overseas, but was eventually captured in Afghanistan and returned to prison. He was freed by government decree in 1976. In his later years, he became a champion for technology. He died in 1996 and his ashes, appropriately, were launched into space along with those of two dozen other space enthusiasts, including *Star Trek* creator Gene Roddenberry.

Another road to enlightenment was the so-called encounter group, which arose as a fashionable, quick-fix alternative to traditional psychotherapy. One form of encounter group—attack therapy—was dangerously familiar. Therapists—and other patients—in a group therapy setting would verbally denounce, abuse or humiliate others in the group until they broke down and confessed past misdeeds. Unwittingly, pied pipers like Maslow and Leary had walked the rebellious youth of that era right into a trap sprung by destructive leaders using Mao's playbook.

To his credit, Maslow wrote in his later years that he realized his ideas were "deeply flawed." There was evil in the world, he acknowledged, theorizing that his quest for a utopian world filled with universal love was a reflection of his unresolved anger towards his mother. During a presentation at the Esalen Institute, the epicenter of the self-help world, Maslow denounced the institute and issued a warning to his former followers: "If you don't use your brain," he said, "you're not fulfilling your potential."

At the time, his comments got little attention—the craving for peak experiences was just too popular. He died in 1970, thus sparing him from witnessing most of the catastrophic rise of a generation of cult demigods spewing distorted versions of his beliefs. Carl Rogers lived to see it all and could only acknowledge that humanist ideas didn't work for everyone.

*   *   *   *   *   *

In 1971, 209 college students participated in a study organized by psychiatrists from Stanford and the University of Chicago, led by Dr. Irvin D. Yalom, to study the effects of encounter groups. After 30 hours in 18 different groups, 16 students were considered casualties of the therapy, defined as "suffering a significant negative outcome." Some became so disturbed they couldn't participate in post-study interviews. Some suffered psychotic episodes. One committed suicide. Most vulnerable were individuals with a low self-concept and unrealistically high expectations of change.

Almost half of the casualties came from the groups with the most confrontational, aggressive and charismatic leaders. Not surprisingly, the most effective and dangerous of these, the testers concluded, came from groups led by members of Synanon, a drug rehab facility with a tough-love approach. These leaders focused on individuals rather than the group and sought firm control over the participants. If a participant didn't cry out, give testimonials or break down, the leader increased the pressure, accusing him or her of being too childish to take responsibility for change.

Even more disturbing was a 1974 study by psychologist Stanley Milgram, who sought to explain the horrors of the Holocaust. Milgram induced volunteers to deliver increasingly heavy electric shocks to other volunteers when they answered questions wrong. In fact they answered wrong intentionally and faked their screams. In reality, the researchers wanted to know how long the volunteers would keep delivering the shocks. Why did they do it? They were convinced that by delivering the shocks to people who exhibited poor recall of details, they were contributing to a study that would improve people's memories under stress. They believed they were contributing to a greater good.

Two-thirds of those tested were categorized as "obedient," and, when placed with others who displayed a willingness to administer lethal doses, a stunning 92% went along. And these subjects weren't feeble or addled; they were drawn from a typical working class pool, including professionals and managers.

But long before Yalom and Milgram, 1940s novelist George Orwell foresaw what the convergence of ideas propounded by Mao, Maslow and Leary would lead to. In *1984* and *Animal Farm*, he accurately described societies where a strong leader with revolutionary ideals imposed his beliefs on the populace, creating a world where only conformists survived.

In reality, *1984* came a decade early in the isolated compounds of Synanon, where another Big Brother droned endlessly over loudspeakers about the fight against the group's enemies.

A budding cult leader, like Synanon's founder Charles Dederich, exhibits signs of fanaticism, intolerance, extremism, megalomania, idealism, excessive self-righteousness, vanity, paranoia and ruth-lessness, wrote Dr. Edgar Schein, who authored a book on the conversion of the Korean war prisoners. The leader, he wrote in *Coercive Persuasion*, has typically failed at a wide variety of endeavors and now seeks to reshape the world to fit his stunted ambitions. He has an unwavering conviction that he has created a new law of social evolution, which he promotes obsessively. His successes foster fear of revenge and rising paranoia. The pressure to fulfill his utopian promises increases his insecurity and willingness to do anything to accomplish his goals.

The leader seeks a security he has never had, power and the favorable judgment of history; many are obsessed with winning a Nobel Prize. Once he convinces followers that terrible things will happen to them if they return to society, the leader can blackmail his flock with threats of excommunication, occasionally purging those he considers unworthy to induce fear of disobedience in those remaining.

Destructive leaders I have encountered have thought nothing of stripping their followers of all of their assets and controlling every aspect of their lives, even to the selection of mates. Mass weddings of couples joined by the leader are common. The message: Your mate is a gift retained only as long as you remain true to the cause. It is all aimed at communicating one concept: commitment to the leader and the group is greater than commitment to any other person.

In every case I've been involved in or studied, the leader's teachings were shaped by traumatic childhood experiences. Most of them felt somehow abandoned, particularly by their mothers--so each sought to create his own family, utilizing his own rules; followers were lab rats, made to do things to reaffirm the leader's beliefs. And if that new utopia crumbled, as it inevitably would, the leader often chose death rather than admit failings. To validate that choice, the "family" was induced to join him in death, as did Jones, Marshall Applewhite and Donald DeFreeze. The most notorious cult leader of all time,

Adolph Hitler, chose that path as the allied forces closed in on his bunker and induced his wife, Eva Braun, to join him. So did loyal lieutenant Joseph Goebbels and his wife, but not before the couple murdered their six children.

Most of these leaders are con men who don't really believe their own scams. It's all a scheme to convince others to do their bidding.

Did Charles Manson really believe in Helter Skelter? Did Donald DeFreeze really think that statues would be built in parks to honor the Symbionese Liberation Army? Both leaders were products of abandonment and the prison system since youth, and sold followers false ideas to motivate them to carry out personal vendettas against society. Each enjoyed exploiting groups of people they hated; for Manson it was women, for DeFreeze it was whites. Did the suicides of Jim Jones and Donald DeFreeze prove their commitment to their cause, or just their willingness to convince others to join them in avoiding responsibility for their failures?

As the inevitable doubts and paranoia creep in, leaders see themselves surrounded by toadies and not fully appreciated. So each concocts bolder, more attention-getting plans and their grip on reality starts to slip. Rejection by outsiders spurs more outrage; the group becomes insular and can take on a lynch-mob mentality.

*   *   *   *   *   *

As the '60s spilled over into the '70s, hippies began trading in their VWs for BMWs and moving to the suburbs to become yuppies. Still, many remained immersed in the humanist teachings of Maslow and others, hoping to free their inner selves through a host of popular self-awareness programs. This wave of self-absorption became known as the "Me Generation."

It was an era of false promises and delusional thinking that paved the way for the abusive totalistic movements and pseudo-psychological programs that also arose. Among the programs that launched the self-help movement was Silva Mind Control, the brainchild of electronics repairman Jose Silva, which claimed that its visualization and self-hypnosis program would help increase one's IQ, develop clairvoyance and allow people to use their minds to heal the body, among other things.

Silva student Alexander Everett created a personal development program called Mind Dynamics and sold it to businessman William Penn Patrick, a member of the ultraconservative John Birch Society who waged a failed campaign for governor of California. Patrick adapted it for use in his Leadership Dynamics Institute, which trained executives at his Holiday Magic cosmetics company. The highly confrontational executive training program subjected participants to beatings, food and sleep deprivation; they were jammed into coffins and cages and forced into performing degrading sexual acts, such as sucking on a dildo in front of the group, acts similar to those committed at the Center For Feeling Therapy, which opened in 1971. Patrick's business empire eventually collapsed in a hail of lawsuits and government investigations into deceptive trade practices and operating without a medical license. He died in a plane crash in 1973.

But Mind Dynamics left its mark as a wellspring of encounter group gurus, including Werner Erhard of est, who pushed the confrontational aspects of the human potential movement even further. A disgruntled former devotee of one Mind Dynamics offspring, Lifespring, told the Washington Post in 1987 that she sought counseling after dropping out of the program. She described a training session where participants were told to strip to skimpy bikinis and bathing suits and then were subjected to taunts about their body shapes and questions about their sexual activities. The participant? Virginia Thomas, wife of Supreme Court Justice Clarence Thomas. Ms. Thomas eventually became an anti-cult activist and organized anti-cult seminars for Congressional staffers.

To me, this was a brainwashed generation built on the false premise that all people were innately good and would do the right thing if allowed to develop to their full potential. This was viewed by more realistic observers as a form of nympholepsy, a state of ecstasy or frenzy caused by a desire for the unattainable. But this delusion created a huge market for wannabe group leaders, false prophets and con artists posing as self-help gurus. They were more than happy to let the psychologically hip in-crowd pay hundreds of dollars each to get what the Korean War prisoners got for free.

The Manson family murder spree had just burst into the public's consciousness and the Jonestown massacre was just a decade away. In between was little lost Patty transformed by peer pressure into gun-toting Tania. And soon, an attempt would be made on my life by acolytes of Synanon, the pioneering drug-rehabilitation program that somehow had gone horribly wrong.

Chapter 2: Escape from Innocence

"Why me?"
— a question I have asked many times.

As a child, I cried when Captain Nemo, one of my early heroes, died at the end of *20,000 Leagues Under the Sea*, Walt Disney's film version of Jules Verne's epic novel.

But when I revisited the movie as an adult, with my son, Chaz, I was shocked at how my life experiences had changed my perspective. By that time, I was well into my career as a cult-fighting lawyer; I had seen first-hand the damage corrupt and manipulative leaders could do to the unfortunates who adored them.

Now, as I watched the saga of my one-time hero, what I saw was a vengeful sociopath who recruited a crew of homeless men and brainwashed them into a state of devotion and servitude. I watched in horror as these mindless drones carried out his orders, including ramming and sinking warships and killing many fellow sailors. Like any cult leader, Nemo had seduced them with a phony sales pitch, convincing them they were protesting the cruelties of war when, in fact, they were carrying out his vengeance against a society that had rejected him. In the end, the mortally-wounded Nemo decides it is time to die and convinces his crew to validate his position by taking the submarine to the bottom of the ocean and dying with him.

Jim Jones couldn't have orchestrated it better.

I left the theater thinking that in the 19th century, unbeknownst to him, Jules Verne had nailed the psychological makeup of a cult leader.

But the world continued to see Capt. Nemo as a hero, demonstrating how little we, as a society, understand about cults. Nemo's popularity with the public forced Verne to resurrect him in *Mysterious Island*. Recently, a heroic and resourceful animated fish was named in his honor, which just proves that you can't keep a good sociopath down.

Of course, experience shapes perception for all of us. I learned this early in my career-long study of cults and cult leaders. It has enabled me to know the psychology of cult leaders so well, it can seem eerie, even to me. A reporter once called to ask about the Heaven's Gate cult and its leader, Marshall Applewhite. This was a day after 39 cult members—including Applewhite and his wife—drank lethal vodka cocktails laced with phenobarbital in an attempt to "shed their containers" so their immortal souls could hitch a ride to a better place aboard a celestial transport that was trailing in the wake of the Hale-Bopp comet.

I had never heard of Applewhite or his cult before that call. But based on my experiences, I told the reporter to look for some sex–related trauma that led him to form the cult and preach that sex is a sin. His relationship with his wife, I predicted, was platonic and the male followers would submit to castration to honor his life choices. Finally, I said, Applewhite didn't really believe his comet tale. He was about to die, or thought he was about to die, from some terminal disease. To validate his decision to end his life, the other members had to join him.

I later learned Applewhite was a married college professor who lost his job and his family after a homosexual affair with a student. After being committed to a mental institution, he entered a sexless marriage with a nurse from the facility and started the cult, where he preached about the evils of sex; he castrated himself and his male followers followed suit. And while the autopsy showed no signs of it, Applewhite had been telling followers that he was about to die from cancer.

Please, no applause.

*   *   *   *   *   *

Several vivid experiences helped shape my perceptions of the world. The first came at a young age, maybe 8, when my father took me to my first USC football game. I was dazzled by the marching band, the galloping white horse, the sea of cardinal and gold in the stands. I was hooked on USC football. It remains the one cult to which I enthusiastically belong.

While I never imagined what I would become growing up, there were hints of it early on. When I was 12, I listened intently during Passover services, as the rabbi explained that wine and matzo should be left outside as a gift for the Angel of Death. Apparently, when the Pharaoh refused to free Jewish slaves in ancient Egypt, God put out a contract on the first-born son of every Egyptian family and sent the Angel of Death to carry out the hit. The angel "passed over" Jewish homes, sparing those children.

That night, my family caught me sneaking outside with a baseball bat. "I can't believe you are all celebrating this," I explained, with all the youthful outrage I could muster. "I can't accept the idea that God would murder innocent children. I'm going outside to hide and when the Angel of Death comes for his wine and matzo I'm going to bash him so he won't ever harm a child again."

Another time, while skulking around the house, looking for clues to the enigma that was my stoic father, I found a secret, members-only Mason pamphlet in his drawer. He was very proud of his acceptance into the Masonic Lodge, but the pamphlet bothered me. If a loyal Mason was on jury duty and the defendant flashed a Mason sign, the literature said, the juror was obligated to work for the defendant's acquittal.

I knew this was wrong and it worried me that such thinking existed in the world.

Even then, I guess, there was a budding lawyer in me, although I didn't see it. I was sure I was going to be a writer. My ambitions were modest at that point. I wanted to go to USC and if I was really lucky, I might get to cover USC football for the school paper. I got that opportunity and when I graduated, the *L.A. Times* offered me a job as a sportswriter.

But by then, my ambitions were changing. Unlike many young people, I had always been drawn to heroes with a clear and unflinching moral purpose: Davy Crockett, the frontiersman who always said, "be sure you are right, then go ahead;" Serpico, who was shunned and threatened by many within the New York Police Department when he persisted in exposing police corruption; and the prosecutor from the political thriller *Z*—which was based on a true story—who ignored 20 death threats to expose an assassination plot hatched by members of the country's ruling party.

The voice of that stern, morally upright little boy plotting to ambush the Angel of Death surfaced. Now I wanted to write big stories, stories that had an impact on people's lives, stories that could change the world, like Truman Capote's *In Cold Blood*.

Fortunately and unfortunately, I listened to my then-girlfriend, who I wanted to marry. She convinced me to go to law school. That was fortunate, because it set me on the road to my eventual career destination. It was also unfortunate, because the girl soon left me for a lawyer.

I had a life-altering experience while in law school. But it had little to do with the study of law.

During my first year of law school, I met someone on campus who talked me into taking a part-time job as a noon duty aide at a predominantly black elementary school near campus. It was a simple job. I watched over them as they ate and played during two lunch periods.

This was my first exposure to a world beyond the campus, beyond my mostly white, middle-class upbringing. And realizing that I was likely the first white person with whom many of the children would spend extended time, I wanted to make a good impression.

I decided the best way to get along was to not treat them like kids. Once, when I spotted a boy climbing the fence to leave, I decided not to lecture him on the importance of school or threaten him with dire consequences. Staying was the right thing to do, I told him, but I wasn't going to try and stop him. "I'm going back to the other kids," I said. "I hope you'll decide to stay." As I walked back, I peeked over my shoulder and saw him climbing back over the fence into the schoolyard.

Events like that were rare. The kids were great. They called me "coach" and treated me like a big brother. Some of the girls once said they knew I had a hot date after school because I had new shoes on. A fifth-grade boy, calling my attention to an attractive woman in shorts, asked me, in a conspiratorial whisper: "Coach, did you catch them legs?"

"Hey," I scolded, "that's somebody's mother."

"Well, she sure ain't mine," he replied.

The fun and games ended Apr. 4, 1968, when news spread of the assassination of Martin Luther King, Jr. It had been only three years since racial unrest lit up Los Angeles during the Watts riots and tensions remained high. Dr. King had spoken at USC a year earlier and when a bomb scare cleared the auditorium, I was too scared to go back in.

I was very nervous as I clocked out that day. My car was several blocks away and I was likely to be the only white man in the vicinity. But when I reached the gate to leave, a large group of fifth and sixth-graders were waiting for me. They stayed after the lunch bell rang instead of returning to class. "Coach," a tall girl with braces said, "we are walking you to your car."

They formed a tight circle, grabbed my hands, and led me to my car. It was a transcendent moment I have never forgotten. At that point in my life, my prime concerns were parties and girls and USC football. But in that instant, I knew it was time to grow up. Those children had honored me that day. Now, I had to go out and earn it.

*   *   *   *   *   *

Another memory visited me recently after years of suppression. It's not one I look back on with fondness and I tell it reluctantly here— for the first time—only because it, too, had a profound influence on me.

I had just graduated high school and, like many young men in that era, I wasn't enthused at the prospect of being drafted and sent to Vietnam. This wasn't a simple decision for me. While I was opposed to the war, I had always wondered whether my heroic aspirations would hold up in the crucible of combat. Since I couldn't bring myself to actually flout the law and flee to Canada, I decided to join the Army Reserves, which exempted me from the draft, and was sent to Fort Ord in Monterey, Calif., for basic training.

I had always thought of myself as an independent sort, who wouldn't succumb to peer pressure. After all, I was a USC fan who lived deep in UCLA territory. I knew nothing of brainwashing, but if someone had told me about it, I would have blithely dismissed it. It couldn't happen to me.

But it could. It did.

While at Fort Ord, I was introduced to an alien concept: homosexuality. Within a short span of time, I was hit on three different times by gay men. Once, while hitchhiking back to the base, I was offered a ride by an older man who put his hand on my knee after I got in the car. In a panic, I jumped out of the car and ran back to the base.

This was 1963. It wasn't a good time to be gay, especially in the macho military. The majority of the men in my unit came from small, rural, Bible Belt communities where gay men were seen as perverts, abominations. When I told the men of these odd incidents, I received no sympathy. What was wrong with me? Why didn't I kick their teeth in? I got a lot of razzing. "Hey, let's go queer-hunting," someone would bray. "We can use Morantz as bait."

The abuse shook my confidence. Why was I being targeted by gays? Was I sending out some subliminal signal I wasn't aware of? I was shunned, in a way, and I didn't like it. I had to do something to reclaim my manhood in front of my peers.

So when a young soldier at the base movie theater put his hand on my thigh one day, I waited for him afterwards and led him to a secluded spot. "Why me?" I demanded. The young man shrugged. He was just taking a shot, as I so often did with women. He offered me oral sex and reached for my zipper. I punched him squarely on the mouth, and as he rolled on the ground, apologizing, I kicked him in the ribs. He scrambled up and ran away.

Flush with macho pride, I hurried back to the barracks to recount my triumph. Needless to say, I was welcomed as a hero, with back slaps and cheers. I was, at last, one of the guys.

But later that night, tossing restlessly in my bunk, I suddenly didn't feel so proud. I imagined him, sobbing into his pillow, a frightened, lonely boy looking for someone like him. I had made his worst nightmare come true.

I realized I had succumbed to peer pressure, a form of what I now know is thought reform. For one awful moment, I had adopted the values of young men who were the products of racist brainwashing in the bigoted communities they grew up in.

This wasn't me. I had never before hit anyone—and I never would again. I vowed to never again let another group tell me what was right or wrong.

I never saw the gay soldier again, so I couldn't apologize. When the gay rights movement started to flourish, I pledged my friendship and support.

Take it from me. Anyone can be brainwashed. It was a lesson I never forgot.

Chapter 3: Escape from Cielo Drive

When you reach the street there is only a left turn; the street is narrow and the sign saying "Cielo Dr." slants downward helter-skeltered. One would expect to see a large black crow on top of it. When my headlights illuminated the sign, I finally remembered why the street name had seemed so eerily familiar.

I met Charles Denton Watson at a job interview in Hollywood in the summer of 1968, when we were both 22 years old. Watson, the product of a staunchly middle-class upbringing in a small Texas town, wore a suit and a string tie on a hot Southern California day and peppered his speech with "yes sirs" and "no ma'ams." It was his first time away from home and he was shy, a blank slate eager to be filled in. For a summer, at least, we became best friends.

The job, as advertised in the *Los Angeles Times*, offered the possibility of making as much as $50 an hour just for talking to young women. It was the summer between graduating from USC and starting law school. All I wanted was to make a little money and do what I enjoyed most—meet girls. It seemed like a dream come true.

Apparently, many others thought so, too, and all those self appointed young studs showed up at the designated hour, preening and posing. The company's four principals prowled up and down this long line, examining the goods as if we were the lineup at a cathouse. They eventually selected Watson, with his Texas football hero good looks, and me for inside sales jobs. The others were sent into the streets in search of gullible young women.

It was, of course, a horrible job, a classic bait-and-switch scheme. But it was my first, and I didn't give much thought to the moral issues involved.

Here's how it worked: The outside reps prowled the streets, chatting up impressionable young women and giving them cards promising a free wiglet from Contessa Creations. For each girl who showed up at the store, the reps got $5. By modeling these wiglets in public, the girls were told, they were providing Contessa with free advertising. But to get the freebie, they had to agree to a short presentation on the company's line of wigs, falls and cascades, so they could answer questions from prospective customers.

Once in the store, the girls were subjected to high-pressure sales tactics worthy of a used-car lot. During the presentation, the salesman would compare the company's cheap, synthetic, machine-made wig with its pricier hand-made wig, fashioned from human hair. The girl was encouraged to stroke the two pieces and to model each. If the salesman sensed interest, he asked some personal questions: Was the girl popular? Did she go out a lot? Was she fashionable? Occasionally, he would explain, the company liked to recruit women to model these more expensive pieces in public. They were too pricey to give away, but for someone pretty enough to serve as a model, the company might sell them at cost.

And throw in the Brooklyn Bridge.

If the girl showed any hesitation, the salesman would confess that he couldn't offer such an outrageous deal without approval from his manager. In would come the closer, to berate the salesman for offering the wigs at such a ridiculously low price. But… since the milk couldn't be put back in the bottle… and the girl did seem like the perfect person to model their products, he would just this once approve it, if we could close the sale right now. Voila! Another happy customer, more often than not.

The job did have its benefits. For example, after a sale, you could ask the customer out. One day, I asked Charles for permission to help one of his customers carry out her purchases. She was a pretty, 18-year-old UCLA coed named Barbara Klein and we ended up dating for a few months, until she auditioned for the *Playboy After Dark* TV show, became Hugh Hefner's girlfriend and changed her name to Barbi Benton.

Then, there were all the parties and the whole Southern California sun and fun scene. Part of the fun of that summer was what some of us called the "bringing out" of Charles. We induced him to ditch the suits in favor of blue jeans, Hawaiian shirts and sandals; we encouraged him to go to parties, indulge in activities that were commonplace in the '60s and most of all, to have fun. But despite our best efforts, I never saw much of a change in Charles. He remained resolutely conservative and polite.

As the summer wore on, the job became more and more depressing. But it seemed only Charles and I asked the *Alfie* question: What's it all about? We used to perform a little skit where we complained about the horrible, hand-sewn human hair and the perfection of the machine-quality alternate. The point was, we knew we could sell whatever we wanted and it began to bother us.

Finally one day, after my hut sales pitch, a girl looked through me and said how about giving her cash for the card. I leaned over and kissed her on the cheek and thanked her for restoring my belief in the intelligence of women. That afternoon I quit and that was the last I ever saw of Charles Watson. As I progressed through law school and my career, my memory of him faded. Who knew that one day, my legal career would center on cults and brainwashing and that my shy, conservative friend Charles Denton Watson would participate in the most famous cult murder spree ever. If ever there was a story that proved the power of brainwashing, it was his.

*   *   *   *   *   *

After that long-ago summer, Charles Watson's life spiraled out of control. He started his own wig business, but it failed. He fell deep into the Hollywood drug scene, not only using, but eventually dealing. One night, he picked up a hitchhiker, who invited him back to his house. It was Dennis Wilson of the Beach Boys, who introduced Watson to a friend: a short, charismatic, wannabe musician named Charles Manson.

Manson, born in Cincinnati in 1934 to a 16-year-old mother, spent most of his childhood with an aunt and uncle after his mother and her boyfriend were convicted of robbing a service station and beating the attendant with Coca-Cola bottles. After her parole, she abandoned him, leading to teen years filled with holdups, foster homes and juvenile detention centers. He and some other boys escaped from one center in 1951, stole a car and headed to California, holding up more than a dozen gas stations along the way. He married a waitress in 1955, but continued a life of hold ups, stolen cars and credit-card fraud and she left him.

He landed back in prison, which for him, was a place of comfort. He used the time to immerse himself in the teachings of Dale Carnegie, Buddhism, Scientology and a group that worshiped both Christ and Satan called the Process. Along the way he learned how to control people and get them to bond to each other and, more importantly, to him. From Alvin Karpis, the last living member of the Ma Barker Gang, he learned how to play the guitar. Ironically, the latter may have most contributed to his ultimate undoing.

Released in 1967, despite his professed desire to remain in prison, Manson found his way to the Haight-Ashbury district of San Francisco, then the nation's hippie capital. He found a world of flower children, free love and LSD. He had found a home in the human potential movement and he set out to build a new kind of family.

Having been abandoned in the past by both wife and mother, Manson concentrated on recruiting women, particularly those lacking close paternal ties. Travelling in an old school bus, his growing family established communes at several locations, including the Spahn ranch in Chatsworth, where Wallace Beery, Tom Mix and Mack Sennett once made movies. By pimping out 19-year-old Lynn (Squeaky) Fromme to the then 81-year old George Spahn, the family got free rent. And when he met the Beach Boys after Dennis Wilson picked up two hitchhiking Manson girls, Manson thought he had gained entry into the music business. Wilson gave Manson some of the Beach Boys' gold records, one of which he traded for use of the Barker Ranch on the edge of Death Valley.

At the two ranches, Manson began programming his followers to bond and love each other through controlled environments and role-playing games called Magical Mystery Tours after his favorite group, the Beatles.

When the family ate, they surrounded Manson, who dined alone atop a high rock. Children were raised communally so parents couldn't pass on to them their hang-ups. Old ties to school, church and society were systematically eradicated, forging the family into what Manson called a "strong white race." He urged the denunciation of parents, the surrender of ego and past identity. To emphasize rebirth, typical of thought reform programs, Manson gave his followers new names. Susan Atkins became Sadie Mae Glutz and Charles Watson surrendered his old first name in favor of "Tex."

To weaken inhibitions and break ties to the past, Manson used LSD and sex orgies, arranging the couplings and even the positions himself. The goal was a simultaneous mass orgasm. Manson initiated a 13-year-old by sodomizing her in front of the group. The first time he had sex with Susan Atkins he told her to pretend he was her father.

While professing to be teaching independence, he made his family members more and more dependent—on him. Each was to find his own love, he said, but I am your love. And for that love, they should be willing to do anything—even kill. There was no death, only change. Death was not to be feared; it was beautiful. Only the ego died, not the spirit, and that was good.

Also typical of malignant cult leaders, Manson grew more paranoid and security conscious and his role-playing games took on a more violent edge. In the desert, the Manson family played war games in stolen Dune Buggies. Charlie gave each girl a buck knife and taught them how to slit throats. To prepare for home invasions, they practiced "creepy crawling," like soldiers under enemy fire.

Manson's murderous delusions peaked with the 1968 release of the Beatles' White Album, which he claimed contained coded messages meant only for him. According to Manson's teachings, a race war was on the horizon, but the family would be safe inside a "big bottomless pit." While "Blackie" would win, they were "too stupid" to lead and would come to the pit to ask for Manson's help. He said messages in the Beatles' songs foretold of this war—"You were only waiting for this moment to arise," a line from "Blackbird," was a call for the Manson family to arise. In "Revolution," "Piggies," "Sexy Sadie," and "Happiness is a Warm Gun," he found confirmation of his plan from the Fab Four. "Helter Skelter," named after a slide at a British amusement park, warned that "she's coming down fast."

But Helter Skelter wasn't coming down fast enough for Manson, so he sought to ignite it by making it appear that blacks were attacking whites. On August 9, 1969, Manson sent my ex-wig-selling partner Tex Watson, Linda Kassabian, Patricia Krenwinkel and Susan Atkins to 10050 Cielo Drive in Benedict Canyon–a house that had been occupied by such stars as Henry Fonda, George Chakiris, Samantha Eggar, Olivia Hussey, Cary Grant and Dyan Cannon. Manson thought record producer Terry Melcher, son of famed actress/singer Doris Day, might be living there, but he had moved into his mother's Malibu beach house with actress Candice Bergen and had rented the Cielo Drive house to film director Roman Polanski.

Polanski, who had just earned fame with a film about the devil called *Rosemary's Baby*, was away on location that night, but his pregnant wife, actress Sharon Tate, was home with friends: celebrity hair stylist Jay Sebring, actor Vytek Frykowski and his girlfriend, Abigail Folger, whose family founded Folger's Coffee.

Steve Parent, 18, was leaving the guest house when Watson shot him four times. The Manson death squad then entered the main house and tied up the occupants in the living room. Watson shot Sebring and Frykowski and stabbed them, plus Tate and Folger more than nine dozen times, saying "I am the devil and I am here to do the devil's business." When he ordered Susan Atkins to finish off Frykowski, the actor fought back, scuffling with Watson like a scene from a bad karate movie. Atkins managed to stab the actor in the leg and Watson clubbed him with his gun butt. The injured Folger also attempted to fight back, while the pregnant Tate pleaded for her baby's life.

Frykowski got the worst of it, suffering 51 stab wounds and 13 blows to the head with a blunt instrument. He was also shot twice. Tate was stabbed 16 times, Sebring seven times, Folger 28 times. When the killing frenzy was done, Atkins dipped a towel in Tate's blood and wrote the word "pig" on the wall.

Manson wasn't pleased; there had been too much struggling. Calm the victims with assurances that everything would be all right, he instructed. When they were quiet, he said, then kill them. To drive home his point, Manson took the same four plus Leslie Van Houten and Steve Grogan to the Los Feliz home of Leno LaBianca, president of the Gateway Supermarket chain, the following night. After Manson and Watson stole inside and tied up LaBianca and his wife, Rosemary, putting pillow covers over their heads, Manson disappeared and sent in Patrica Krenwinkel and Van Houten with orders to kill. Watson went to the living room and thrust a chrome-plated bayonet into Leno LaBianca's throat.

In the bedroom, Rosemary LaBianca managed some freedom and was swinging a lamp wildly to keep the Manson women at bay. Watson entered and stabbed her with the bayonet, then returned to the living room to resume his attack on her husband.

Leno LaBianca received 12 knife and 14 fork wounds, while his wife was stabbed 41 times. Watson carved the word "war" on Leno's stomach and "Death to Pigs" and "Helter Skelter" were smeared on the walls in blood. Because Manson wanted everyone to participate, Watson ordered Van Houten to stab Mrs. LaBianca, even though she was probably already dead. Van Houten stabbed her 16 times. Evidence at the trial showed that 41 of Mrs. LaBianca's stab wounds had been inflicted post-mortem.

Manson's race war never materialized. Just eight days after the Cielo Drive murders, police arrested several family members at the Spahn Ranch on auto theft charges. Believing ranch hand Donald Shea had snitched, Manson ordered family members to kill him. His remains weren't found until 1977 and one of those implicated in his death was Tex Watson.

Watson fled to Texas in October of 1969 and was arrested there almost two months later for the Tate-LaBianca murders. Hometown acquaintances, who couldn't believe the Watson they knew could be guilty of such monstrous crimes, hired a lawyer and fought extradition for nine months. Once back in California, it was reported Watson began regressing to a childlike state. He stopped talking and eating, dropping 55 pounds. He was admitted to Atascadero State Hospital for observation and remained there until he was deemed capable of standing trial the following February.

Ultimately, 12 murders were linked to the family and Manson bragged of 35. A horrified nation cringed as a remorseless Susan Atkins spoke of her deeds with pride. "You have to have a real love in your heart to do this for people," she said.

While Manson and his family were being tried for their crimes, followers gathered outside the courtroom and called for Charlie's release. To illustrate the level of control he still maintained over his flock, Manson carved an X on his forehead one day; his followers— including his co-defendants and those outside protesting—followed suit.

What could have prompted such insanity, such senseless blood-letting? I have no doubt as to the events that triggered Manson's murderous spree. He dreamed of being accepted by a society that repeatedly rejected him. When the Beach Boys urged record producers to sign him, he thought his dream had finally come true. He was about to become a rich and famous rock star. But the producers all passed and a devastated Manson was consumed by rage. It was time for revenge.

So he started preaching Helter Skelter, the typical cult leader's phony pitch to followers: All the forces of a corrupt world were aligned against them and they had to strike a blow for what was right.

In truth, Manson's deluded motives were much more self-serving: "You people have done everything in the world to me," he said of society during a parole hearing years later. "Doesn't that give me equal rights? I can do it to you people because that's what you have done to me."

Melcher, who was probably the intended victim of the first night's killings, had been one of the music producers who rejected him. Manson had been to the Cielo Drive home to meet with Melcher. The LaBiancas were the victims of a tragic mistake. Manson had once been to a party next door. On the fateful night, he simply got the wrong house.

But what about his followers? Were they not equally culpable, as prosecutor Vincent Bugliosi contended, insisting the family all "had murder in their hearts." Why didn't they leave the family, as others had?

The fact that some may have successfully resisted conversion doesn't change the strong likelihood that many could not. They were victims of a powerful brainwashing program administered by a charismatic cult leader, similar in many ways to the post-Korean War programs U.S. prisoners were subjected to.

By then, the memory of those events had faded; the horrors of Synanon and Jonestown were yet to come. It was much easier to accept the Manson family as an aberration, a unique blend of sociopaths uniting in the desert, so Bugliosi's view prevailed.

He was partially correct. Believing in Manson's Helter Skelter delusion didn't absolve his followers of guilt, even if they were convinced they were doing it for the good of mankind. Except for a few, like Lynette "Squeaky" Fromme, who tried to assassinate President Gerald Ford in 1975, there is scant evidence of psychotic tendencies in the pre-cult lives of the Manson family. The majority came from law-abiding, middle-class families—Van Houten had been a high-school princess—and had no history of violence.

Bugliosi pointed to their social alienation, but doesn't that describe many young people? Many of the rebellious, anti-establishment youths of that era turned into credit-card carrying, suburban yuppies.

The trail of blood here leads back to one twisted mind and his list of victims include the murderers as well as the murdered. In time, evidence surfaced confirming that Manson family members were victims of a ruthless thought-reform regime. In jail, away from his influence, all ultimately recanted their allegiance and expressed remorse. Some former family members have lived normal lives. In a book about his experiences, former family member Paul Watkins wrote that had he not been deprogrammed by a neighboring miner while Manson was away visiting the Beach Boys, he, as the second-in-command, would have led the Tate-LaBianca murder spree instead of Tex Watson. Watkins later became mayor and head of the Chamber of Commerce of a nearby Death Valley town.

Leslie Van Houten, however, has remained in prison for more than 40 years, having been turned down for parole on June 5, 2013, for the 20th time despite being an exemplary prisoner. I argued for her release as early as 1978 and tried, unsuccessfully, to convince Bugliosi she was a brainwashing victim. Perhaps because of his close ties to the victims' families, Bugliosi hasn't to my knowledge supported parole for any Manson family member, even though he acknowledges that Manson murdered through control and power over his followers.

Bugliosi has argued against comparing cult leaders such as Jim Jones and David Koresh to Manson's powers, contending that inducing mass suicides is a lesser act than getting people to commit murder for you. Actually, it is more difficult to convince people to take their own lives than to kill others. And Bugliosi apparently forgets that Jones also induced followers to commit murders earlier that day, before the suicides, and that his acolytes gunned down those who wouldn't take the poisoned Kool-Aid and tried to flee. Osama bin Laden has also convinced followers to both kill and die to advance his cause.

I also tried to convince Van Houten's attorney earlier this decade to let me help argue for her release, but was turned down. She won't be eligible for parole again until 2018. If I'm still around, I hope I'll be asked to help.

*   *   *   *   *   *

As for my long-ago friend Charles Watson—not Tex—he was sentenced to death on October 21, 1971, but was saved when the California Supreme Court invalidated all death sentences imposed in the state prior to 1972 as unconstitutional. The statute has since been amended and the death penalty reinstated, but it doesn't apply to those convicted before the revised law was enacted.

Watson became an ordained minister in 1979. He married Kristin Joan Svege, who visited him in prison, and fathered four children. However, after conjugal visits were cut off in 2003, thanks in part to the lobbying of victims' family members, she met another man and divorced Watson.

Watson, who blames his participation in the deadly spree largely on his abuse of amphetamines, has been denied parole 14 times and remains incarcerated in Mule Creek State Prison in Ione, Calif. His last denial was in November of 2011.

*   *   *   *   *   *

Watson's torturous journey was unknown to me for nearly 20 years. I didn't recognize the guy on the TV news with glaring eyes and bearded face framed by long and shaggy hair. And I didn't know anyone named Tex. He certainly bore no resemblance to the clean-cut, easy-going kid I knew.

But in 1988, I purchased Tex Watson's book, *Will You Die for Me?* at a Charles Manson memorabilia booth at the monthly Rose Bowl Flea Market. I opened the book that night and read the first chapter, about his arrival in Southern California in 1968 and his first job in Los Angeles as a wig salesman at Contessa Creations. The loud sound of the book thudding against the ceiling around midnight awoke my then-wife, who saw me pacing frantically at the foot of our bed crying out, over and over, "He was my friend. He was my friend." I was in shock, and my efforts to explain this to her came out as incoherent babbling.

For some reason, I never publicly disclosed this odd connection to the Manson family until recently. Partly, it was just too difficult for me to comprehend this bizarre confluence of two lives colliding like atoms in a supercollider and careening away in such opposite, but eerily related ways. Also, acknowledging any kind of connection to Charles Manson was a bit scary. Who wants Freddy Krueger in his dreams?

*   *   *   *   *   *

Epilogue:

In 1998, I was fixed up with a woman who lived in Benedict Canyon. After our second date, she gave me her home address and permission to pick her up there. The address was on Cielo Drive, which sounded vaguely familiar, although I couldn't pin down why. Maybe my uncle, who had lived in Benedict Canyon, had owned a house there? Or maybe it was the street of a movie producer I met while working on a film about surf rockers Jan and Dean, based on an article I wrote for Rolling Stone.

When you reach the street there is only a left turn; the street is narrow and the sign saying "Cielo Dr." slants downward helter-skeltered. One would expect to see a large black crow on top of it. When my headlights illuminated the sign, I finally remembered why it had seemed so eerily familiar. Worse, my date's home was next door to the fateful property—long ago razed—where Tex Watson and the Manson family slaughtered Sharon Tate and her friends.

To me, the street was a metaphor for the violence of cults and my near date with death as a result of commands given by another cult leader whose violent legacy would lead to Manson comparisons.

I liked the girl; she was very nice, but I never spoke to her again. I had escaped—at least metaphorically—Cielo Drive and all it stood for long ago, and I had no desire to return.

Chapter 4: Escape from Nichiren Shoshu and the 13th Century

It began with Nichiren Daishonin, a 13th century Buddhist philosopher. It ended, at least for me, with Linda Hager, a raven-haired beauty I met in Playa del Rey in 1972.

It was an episode that provided a fleeting glimpse of where my life was headed, even though I wouldn't get there for five years.

I had just graduated law school and was preparing for the bar exam; I was determined to pass it on the first try so my life wouldn't be further delayed. During the week, I holed up in my tiny studio apartment on the beach in Playa del Rey, studying from morning to bedtime. I only went out two evenings a week, and that was to a bar exam review course. On the weekends, I played volleyball. That was my life: no parties, no women, no interruptions. Here's how dedicated I was: When an exotic dancer I knew invited me to spend the weekend in a private room at a Playboy Mansion party, I actually said no, fearful that my recovery time would cut too far into my study time.

I finally took the exam later that year and returned home, free at last. As I pulled off my tie, a vision appeared outside my kitchen window: Linda Hager, with her little girl and her sister, Bette. Linda had long dark hair and shimmering olive skin and if it was true that God put Tina Turner on earth to teach women how to walk in high heels, then surely He put Linda Hager here to teach them how to walk in cutoff blue jeans. I quickly changed into beach attire, picked up her foot prints in the sand and hurriedly tracked them down to the beach— and confessed as much when I found her sitting on a beach towel.

We chatted, observing the usual courting rituals. She had been married to one of the Hager twins who sang on *Hee-Haw*. I said I knew Barbi Benton who also sang on the show. Suddenly, I noticed her four-year-old daughter playing on some dangerous rocks that jutted out into the water and warned Linda. According to her daughter's astrology sign, she responded, it was necessary that she be allowed to venture and take care of herself. I rounded up the little daredevil anyway.

That should have tipped me off that something was amiss, but love —or at least lust—is blind.

Even though I didn't believe in astrology, I asked her out anyway and was overjoyed when she accepted. When I called, she explained that her regular Nichiren Shoshu meeting was that night. I offered to pick her up afterwards, but she thought it would be nice if I went to the meeting with her. I was so smitten, I agreed without giving it a thought.

So I stepped off the metaphorical cliff.

*   *   *   *   *   *

Nichiren Daishonin, born in 1222 in the Japanese village of Kominato during a time of social unrest and natural disasters, was a Buddhist monk who sought explanations for the suffering and chaos that surrounded him. He concluded, like an early Abraham Maslow, that the answers lie within all of us. Everyone, he believed, had the power to surmount all of life's challenges; anyone could draw out the enlightened wisdom and energy of Buddhahood in his lifetime.

This philosophy was controversial, since most Buddhist philosophers of the era believed that only the chosen few could aspire to Buddhahood. His beliefs led to two separate exiles by the time he was 50 years old, during which he wrote extensively and created the first gohonzon, a figurine that symbolizes the ultimate law of life and the universe and to which Nichirens chant to this day.

Nichirin Shoshu, one of many branches of Buddhism that grew out of his teachings, gained a foothold in the U.S., not surprisingly, during the 1960s, when so many were seeking nontraditional paths to spirituality. Like Maslow, this Buddhist sect believed that all people were essentially good and we should strive to release our inner selves.

To do so required twice daily chanting—including the now familiar Nam-Myoho-Renge-Kyo—to achieve a state of tranquility and enlightenment. Then good fortune would come your way, as well as a job, good health and a loving spouse.

Nichirens believe in karma, the idea that good thoughts produce positive effects and bad thoughts negative ones. And by sharing their faith with others, they are taught, they promote a whole bunch of karma leading to world betterment. So U.S. branches sent out members to aggressively recruit others, sending men to recruit women and vice versa. I had thought I found a hot babe. She thought she found a recruit.

*   *   *   *   *   *

The meeting I attended looked like a variation on an AA meeting. Everyone was friendly and shook my hand. I listened as various members took turns telling their stories about how bad life was before they chanted and how much better it is now. Chanting made them better employees, which led to raises. A well-known actor participated, along with the son of a local sportscaster.

I didn't doubt their sincerity, or their successes. I just considered it the result of a giant placebo effect. I knew nothing of brainwashing or cults then, so I saw no potential for harm in a little chanting and positive thinking.

After the confessionals, the group went to another room to chant in front of a gohonzon doll located inside a cabinet, all the while rubbing beads in their hands. But I only had eyes for Linda, who looked gorgeous in jeans and a bikini top, a flower in her hair and legs folded firmly under her knees when she chanted.

Finally, the lay priest for the day took me aside to suggest I try it. Linda, he said, told him I had just taken the bar exam and chanting could insure my success. "Just chant and what you need happens," he said.

Talk about a hanging curve; I couldn't resist. "What if I want to rob a bank?" I asked.

"Then," he said, "you will realize what you really want and do it. Or you will be caught, rehabilitated and come out of jail a better person. Or you will get away with it and live in riches."

I was impressed. He had it covered from all angles. It brought to mind little Natalie Wood as the girl who wanted a house with a picket fence in *Miracle on 34th Street*. "I believe, I believe, it's silly but I believe," she chanted.

Her chant worked, but this was real life. I couldn't do it, even for the delectable Linda Hager. When she realized that some time later, our dating came to an abrupt halt, disappointing me and my law school mates, who eagerly dropped to their knees and chanted whenever she appeared at a party.

Then, on a Sunday, her sister Bette called. Linda was coming to her house, which was nearby, for brunch. Would I care to join? Would I! I said I would be right over. My best friend, Steve Brandt, was coming over for volleyball, so I left a note on my sliding glass door to come get me at Bette's.

The brunch was great and afterwards, the two sisters snuggled up to me on the couch. They wanted me to know how much I meant to them, how much they wanted me to pass the bar exam. If only I would chant, they promised, their soulful eyes gazing pleadingly at me, I would pass.

Surrounded by soft, beautiful flesh filled with possibility, my resolve—and common sense—weakened. They looked so caring and they had just made me this great brunch. What was the harm in trying?

Before I knew what was happening, I was on my knees in front of Bette's gohonzon, rubbing beads and chanting. Later, I thought, I will tell Linda that I was thinking of her, not the bar exam, while chanting. After all, she had assured me chanting would get me whatever I truly wanted.

And then I was seized by the hand of God. Well, actually, it was my friend Steve, who lifted me by my shirt collar and dragged me out of the room. It was my first exposure to deprogramming. I never saw Linda again.

With or without the chanting, I passed the bar and got a job as a public defender. Soon thereafter, I asked out a pretty court reporter, but she canceled our first date, explaining she wasn't allowed to date so soon after breaking up with her boyfriend. This edict was passed down by the sect she belonged to—Nichiren Shoshu. I couldn't talk her out of this and was alarmed by the control the group had over her.

Some see Nichiren Shoshu as a harmful cult, teaching that their beliefs are the only path to happiness; others see it as just another meditation process. I see it as a group that has some totalist tendencies but one that isn't particularly dangerous. Still, I wouldn't recommend it to anybody.

I'm not particularly religious, but I do often wonder whether it was all just a coincidence, or if Linda Hager, cutoffs and all, was meant to give me a glimpse at my future. Who knows? You decide.

Chapter 5: Escape from Golden State Manor

(Photo by Los Angeles Times Staff Photographer. Copyright © 1977. Los Angeles Times. Reprinted with Permission)

"Dr. Livingstone, I presume?"

—Journalist Henry Stanley, upon finding missing explorer Dr. David

Livingstone in Africa in 1871

In 1971, my last year in law school, I saw *Brian's Song*, a tearjerker of a movie about the tragic death of Chicago Bears running back Brian Piccolo. But the story wasn't really about his death, it was about the way he lived. "If I died tomorrow," I told a friend as the film ended, "they would have nothing to say about how I lived."

I spent the next three years adrift, wavering between a career as a lawyer and my first love, writing. But in 1974, while living in a $90-a-month Culver City apartment so sparsely furnished I wouldn't bring dates home, things started to pick up. I got some legal work from my brother Lewis and other attorneys on his floor and *Rolling Stone* magazine published my story on Jan and Dean. Still, I was 29 and had very little beyond a 1969 VW Bug, two Border Collie dogs named Tommy and Devon, and a sofa and rocking chair salvaged from neighbors' discards.

Then, my life turned in a direction I never would have suspected.

It started when my brother's high-school friend Myron Rosenauer, a Skid Row liquor store owner, called with a problem. T.B. Renfroe, a 57-year-old alcoholic he had befriended, told him via phone that he was being held prisoner at Golden State Manor, a nursing home for mental patients in Burbank. Rosenauer frequently cashed Social Security checks for Skid Row inhabitants and watched their things; in return, he got the bulk of their business.

I didn't take it seriously. Maybe the court sent him there on probation and he didn't understand that it was voluntary and he could walk out, opting for sentencing. I decided to ignore it.

But the next morning, the *Los Angeles Times* reported the arrest of a pharmacist who allegedly hired a hit man to kill the administrator of Rancho Los Amigos Hospital. Apparently, the administrator was going to testify that the pharmacist tried to bribe him to refer long-term patients to certain nursing homes.

That got my attention. If that could happen, if old or injured people were being shanghaied for their value as revenue sources, perhaps I should look further into T.B. Renfroe's story.

So I called Mary Williams, the caring young nurse who had allowed Renfroe to make that initial call, despite the home's restrictions on outside contact. She was afraid to talk on the nursing home phones, so I called her later at home. She told me Skid Row alcoholics who didn't appear to need nursing-home care were arriving there suspiciously. She said that at Division 80 of the county courts, Chuck Weldon, who allegedly counseled elderly alcoholics arrested for public drunkenness, was using his position to divert patients to Golden State. They were falsely told, she said, that they were serving jail sentences. Despite rumors that the facility's owners were connected to the Philippine Mafia, Ms. Williams agreed to stay on at Golden State Manor and help gather evidence and I agreed to help T.B. Renfroe.

She brought me Renfroe's original admission sheet, which stated that the referring agent was Louise Jones, the facility's administrator. Somehow, I doubted that Ms. Jones was hanging out on Skid Row seeking referrals. She also gave me a copy of a visiting psychiatrist's notes, which stated he found no medical reason for Renfroe to be in the nursing home. She further provided a list of nine other apparent victims who arrived at Golden State after being released from Division 80.

I gave Ms. Williams a retainer agreement to smuggle in for Renfroe's signature and instructed her to tell him to keep quiet and be patient and one day I would come for him.

Ms. Williams also referred me to a former Golden State bookkeeper who, for her own protection, had kept copies of checks issued by Golden State Manor to pay for these snatched patients, all signed by Ms. Jones.

Meanwhile, I interviewed deputy sheriffs and legitimate counselors at Division 80, aka the drunk court, including a representative of Alcoholics Anonymous. I even approached Weldon one day and asked for his card, claiming I had heard of his good work and my family needed help for an alcoholic uncle. Weldon said he belonged to the Senior Citizens Council, but his card had no address. It didn't take long to confirm that the organization didn't exist except for an answering machine.

In a month, I pieced together a case. Generally, when police scooped up a Skid Row resident for public drunkenness, the court gave him two days to sober up. But unbeknownst to the judge, who negligently told defendants that Weldon counseled the elderly without checking his credentials, the Golden State shill told them they faced long jail sentences unless they agreed to serve their time in a nursing home. When they were released after the two-day dry-out period, Weldon picked them up, again falsely told them they had more time to serve and delivered them to Golden State and a few other homes for $125 a head. The homes kept their new revenue sources as long as they could, with the help, if necessary, of whopping doses of Thorazine, all the while billing the state for their care.

A picture emerged of an industry that paid low wages to employees, hired parolees as orderlies and was awash in kickbacks and payoffs to get patients. Doctors, pharmacists and X-ray technicians billed the state for their services while providing little or no actual treatment to the victims. They would then kick back a portion of their gains to the homes. One doctor, Stanley Soho, billed the state for patient rounds at the homes that some alleged he never made.

My investigation concluded, I was now ready to fulfill my promise to come get Renfroe out. But it had to be carefully orchestrated. If I barged into Golden State Manor and demanded Renfroe's release, the facility would then quickly release all the detainees and shred any evidence of their presence. To prevent that, I laid out a plan to the County Department of Health and invited their investigators to join me. They agreed; while I fetched Renfroe, they would seize the files of others being illegally detained before they could be destroyed.

As I drove up the 405 Freeway towards Golden State Manor, I was exultant. I had thought about T.B. Renfroe and his plight every day since taking the case and now I was getting him out. I thrust my clenched fist out the window, reveling in the surprise Ms. Jones was about to receive, and sang the *Mighty Mouse* theme: "Here I come to save the day..." Fortunately, it was about 6 a.m. so there weren't many on the freeway to witness my lunacy.

I met the health investigators outside the home and we entered together. It was my first view of Golden State Manor; it was a real pit, with mental patients howling from behind bars. Since the orderlies in these homes often had criminal records, theft was rampant; cleanliness was not. What a place to be falsely imprisoned.

Ms. Jones, a heavy-set blond who inspired visions of the evil Nurse Ratched from *One Flew Over the Cuckoo's Nest,* looked nervous and asked three times for my business card. Ignoring these memory lapses, I dutifully provided one with each request. The county inspectors, meanwhile, informed her they were there to copy files.

"What about Mr. Renfroe?" she asked me.

"Why is he being held here against his will?" I responded.

She stated he wasn't and was free to leave.

"Good," I said. "Then he leaves today with me. Go get him."

Minutes later a short, thin, balding man in old clothes, with a smoker's cough and a walking cane, entered the room. I offered him my hand.

"T.B. Renfroe, I presume?"

If anyone, including Mr. Renfroe, got the reference to Stanley's famous quote, no one showed it. But I found the excitement of the rescue hard to ignore. It was an adrenaline rush I have never forgotten. I was now hooked by this case.

*   *   *   *   *   *

We left together and I drove him back to his seedy Los Angeles Street hotel. Over the next year I located other victims in the Los Angeles County jail population. Seven—the magnificent seven—asked to join the lawsuit. These victims had been sent to nursing homes all around Southern California. Each nursing home was owned by a different corporation but when you examined the corporate officers and directors you found the same people involved, something the Health Department inspectors didn't know until I showed them the corporate records.

I also learned how nursing homes operated. They needed a certain number of patients to cover costs; every patient thereafter was profit. The owners often funneled out the assets, leaving the corporations bankrupt. Then they would set up a new corporation to operate another home. At times, the same group of investors would use a different corporate entity to reacquire the same homes.

I convinced a judge to bypass doctor-patient privilege and allow me to inspect the files of all the suspected victims. If there was evidence of crimes in the records, I argued, it wouldn't be protected by the physician-patient privilege, especially since those involved were kidnap victims, not patients. The judge agreed and I eventually was able to present the court documents I believed proved the conspiracy. There were many smoking guns. Patient charts frequently contained notes from nurses and orderlies about patients requesting permission to leave and administrators telling their captives that they were there under court orders and couldn't leave. The charts also documented the frequent use of Thorazine to thwart attempted escapes. The judge ruled these pages admissible and not subject to doctor/patient privilege.

As I got deeper into the case, some attorney friends tried to talk me out of it. They warned of political blowback and vindictive insurance companies who would try to make an example of me in order to discourage others from trying to make them pay for the criminal acts of their customers. Besides, they argued, the case was a financial loser. How could I prevail against the armada of big defense firms the defendants would trot out? And what jury would award significant sums of money to Skid Row alcoholics who might use the funds to drink themselves to death?

But I thought of my heroes—Serpico and Davy Crockett and the prosecutor from Z. I knew what they would do. What other criteria should I consider? Besides, I liked the challenge of convincing a jury that these people deserved the same consideration as anyone else. I found them to be caring people, with their own kind of social structure, but reeling from some kind of horrible experience that prevented them from going home. They were frequently mistreated and mugged, but they rarely hurt others. And when they had money they shared it and looked after each other. I found that many were more content than people I knew living in homes.

They were victimized because the bad guys never believed they could fight back. Who would care about 72-year-old James Blackburn, who was shot full of Thorazine as he attempted to scale a fence to escape? And even if someone cared, what could they do about it? I was determined to show the bad guys that the public would care, that the legal system would care. I was 29; I could spare a few years to make those nursing home operators pay for what they had done.

It wasn't easy. Sometimes my clients disappeared and I had to go find them in county jail. So my cheap, semi-vacant apartment now became a useful asset. I used it during depositions to house my clients, prepare their testimony and keep them close by and off the sauce. They certainly weren't bothered by the trashy furniture. Once I went looking for T.B. Renfroe and found him in a hospital, suffering the DT's because he wanted to stay sober for the trial. He wanted to do it as much for me, the kid who had come to rescue him, as for himself.

So I pursued my case, just like my heroes would have. So what if Crockett and the Greek prosecutor died for their ideals and Serpico got shot. And I did receive some death threats, as did my brother. Telling me I was going to die was like honey to a bee and only stiffened my resolve. It hadn't dawned on me yet that someone might actually go through with it.

I not only went after the conspirators, I sued those whose negligence contributed to my clients' abuse. It turned out Weldon was himself a former nursing home operator who got connected with Ms. Jones, the Golden State administrator, by a pharmacist and a portable x-ray technician, who each got the whole chain's business in exchange. Key witnesses against the x-ray technician included his former wife and mistress, who bonded over their mutual distaste for the man who two-timed them. I also sued the Division 80 judge who failed to check Weldon's credentials and the Los Angeles County Sheriffs who turned the victims over to him and anyone else who profited from the scheme or did nothing to stop it, including the psychiatrist whose notes indicated that Renfroe didn't need hospitalization.

The defense argued that my clients weren't really damaged because they were better off in the nursing homes than on the streets. To support that theory, they produced Dr. Keith Ditman, who had once tried to cure alcoholics with LSD before eventually becoming a critic of the hallucinogenic drug. In fact, he had testified that the drug made Leslie Van Houten vulnerable to Manson's manipulations. We of course made sure the jury knew of Dr. Ditman's link to Manson, the all-time boogeyman.

To counter this benign portrayal, Dr. Lee Coleman, a psychiatrist referred to me by an organization that fought medical abuses, testified that the doses of Thorazine given were so excessive they could only be for purposes of control and certainly not for any legitimate medical reason. Dr. Coleman had never been an expert witness before, but was outraged at the actions of his colleagues at the nursing homes. His testimony was compelling.

Ironically, I would be linked to both witnesses for years to come. One of Dr. Ditman's alcoholic LSD guinea pigs was none other than Synanon's Charles Dederich, who claimed that the insights he gained from the experience led him to the founding of Synanon. And the organization that referred me to Dr. Coleman, I later learned, was also a future nemesis—the Church of Scientology. I later found myself on the opposite side when Dr. Coleman served as an expert in the Center For Feeling Therapy case.

At her deposition, Louise Jones produced a photocopy of Renfroe's admission sheet with her name whited out. I couldn't help smiling as I asked her what she thought might be on the original, knowing I had a copy in my briefcase with her name on it. By law, even mistakes can't be whited out on medical documents, since they're part of the official record. Errors should be lined out, corrected, initialed and dated.

Dr. Soho—the doctor who billed for rounds while allegedly never leaving his condo—kindly offered to testify against the other defendants if I dismissed the charges filed against him. If I didn't, he promised to lie and testify the others were innocent. I told him no deals and if he lied I would go after him for perjury. He was dumb enough to send me a written note detailing his offer, but at his deposition he denied the note was his and testified that he witnessed no violations.

It wasn't my last brush with Dr. Soho. He later sued a client of mine for defamation after the woman claimed during a TV interview that Dr. Soho made medical mistakes. We promptly sued him for medical malpractice. After repeatedly failing oral exams to test his knowledge, Dr. Soho was barred from practicing medicine in California for three years; he regained the license in 1984. After a sex-change operation in 1986, Dr. Sandra Soho was arrested on two felony counts of illegally prescribing controlled substances and accused by the State Medical Board of deliberately addicting patients and then profiting from their addiction. Her license was permanently revoked in 1992.

As the case dragged on, I was in danger of joining my clients on Skid Row, as my bank account sank to about $500. As expected, the nursing homes' insurance companies hired seven of the best defense firms in town. Fortunately Sanford Gage and Steven Cooper, two veteran trial lawyers, came to my rescue, swapping their financial support and legal guidance for half of the contingency fees from the nursing home cases. Gage, one of the best tort trial lawyers in Los Angeles, filed a class action suit on behalf of the victims we hadn't yet found, helped me prepare for my trial and conducted the jury selection process.

Despite my inexperience, Gage insisted I should deliver the opening statement, since no one else would match my passion for the case. I felt like the prosecutor in *Z*, pointing accusingly at the defendants as I described their lack of humanity in profiteering on the misery of people they regarded as society's outcasts and thus, helpless to resist.

The case never got to the jury. The judge insisted on holding a hearing out of view of the jury to determine if there was sufficient proof of a conspiracy before allowing testimony against one defendant to also be used to implicate others. This meant that we had to lay our case out in advance and that our witnesses would have to testify twice. It should have given the defense a big edge.

But when we proved the conspiracy to the judge's satisfaction, the defendants lined up to settle for a total of $300,000, a lot of money back then. After cost deductions, I got around $25,000, a pretty good pay day, but hardly a bonanza. As a Public Defender I got $17,500 a year. When you considered all the time I spent on the case, I probably made about 50 cents an hour.

The nursing home scandal garnered extensive news coverage, including a series of articles by Narda Zacchino of the *Los Angeles Times*. It was the start of a long professional relationship that would eventually leave us both in fear for our lives. The news coverage prompted the Los Angeles County Board of Supervisors, led by ex-TV news anchor Baxter Ward, to launch a massive investigation into the nursing home industry. I was propelled into the spotlight, called upon by the board to explain the intricacies of the case for TV cameras while the politicians posed and pledged to turn the nursing home industry upside down. I also consulted with the L.A. County District Attorney, who was forming a nursing home task force and sought guidance on the types of crimes to pursue.

I had promised T.B. Renfroe that I would bring him his money at our next meeting. So, when the settlement checks arrived, I hurried to his Skid Row hotel so he could endorse his. He had become family both to me and to nurse Mary Williams, who convinced her husband to take Arky, as the Arkansas native was known, into their home and care for him for life. I told her I would help.

But I never saw him again. When I returned with his money, he had been missing for several days. I checked the jails and the hospitals. Finally, I found him in the morgue. Narda memorialized him in a front-page story, with a large photo of him sitting on a cooler in Rosenaur's liquor store. He was described as the Skid Row alcoholic who launched the largest investigation into the nursing home industry in its history. The framed photo still hangs on my office wall.

A son I didn't know he had showed up to accept Arky's settlement money.

I took on a few more nursing home-related cases, but eventually decided they were too depressing to pursue full time. Often, my clients were too infirm to testify. But the adrenaline rush I got from the case tilted my career axis towards the law. I felt I could have more of an impact on lives as a lawyer than I could as a writer. But no more causes, I swore. They were too draining and restricted my personal life. While working out at the gym one day, I was approached by a man seeking donations for Skid Row missions. I shook my head no. "I give at the office," I said.

*   *   *   *   *   *

Epilogue:

I took a job with a small litigation firm in Beverly Hills, the Law Offices of Donald H. Cohen. With my proceeds from the case, I bought my first home in Pacific Palisades, a small, 1,100-square-foot place with a nice backyard for the dogs. I made new friends. I met a woman I thought I would marry. CBS was planning a Jan and Dean movie, based on my Rolling Stone article and screenplay draft.

Life was good, if still a bit unformed. Then, a former Culver City neighbor referred another alleged kidnapping case to me. It involved a man whose wife was sequestered in a drug rehabilitation community that was refusing to let him see or talk to her. The program had been hailed as a breakthrough in drug addiction treatment by Life Magazine and saluted in Congress. There had even been a movie made about it. But somewhere along the line, something had gone terribly wrong there and now, it was at my doorstep.

Its name was Synanon.

Chapter 6: Escape from the SLA and Tania

Mizmoons and Wolfe and SLA wheels,
The dizzy dancing way you feel
As every fairy tale comes real.
I've looked at life that way.
But now it's just another show,
You leave 'em laughing when you go.
And if you care, don't let them know.
Don't give yourself away.

I've looked at Patty from both sides now,
From up and down, and still somehow,
It's Tania's illusions I recall,
I really don't know Patty, at all.

—with apologies to Joni Mitchell

It was not the best of times.

Gasoline lines snaked around the block, truckers were on strike, the Vietnam War raged on, the dark cloud of the Kent State shootings still hovered and the daily news was all Watergate. It was the '70s, but for many, the protest era of the '60s lingered, particularly at the University of California at Berkeley, where the Students for a Democratic Society (SDS) had built a youth revolution.

Having just moved to a shabby, four-unit Culver City apartment building in 1974, I was barely staying afloat with a handful of legal projects and some free-lance writing. But my life was in the midst of change. The publication of my Jan and Dean article gave me some national visibility as a writer, even though it got shoved off the *Rolling Stone* cover by Richard Nixon's resignation. And just when I thought I was out of the legal profession, the kidnappings of Skid Row alcoholics by nursing homes pulled me back in.

I was still blissfully ignorant about brainwashing and cults, even as a black, Charles Manson wannabe, some hippies left over from the '60s and a confused, 19-year-old publishing heiress with Daddy and Mommy issues splashed those touchy topics all over the nation's media outlets, like a bucket of cold water in America's face.

*   *   *   *   *   *

The Hearst publishing empire was built by William Randolph Hearst, the inspiration for Orson Welles' 1941 film classic, *Citizen Kane*, and passed on to son Randolph. They were two peas from the same pod: wealthy, entitled and rigidly conservative. Patty Hearst, the third of Randolph's five daughters, rejected both the legacy and the family values.

She supported the liberal George McGovern for president and regularly slipped out of the family estate in Hillsborough—the wealthiest community in America—to attend rock concerts at San Francisco's Fillmore Auditorium. In Catholic school, she balked at scrubbing toilets for what she deemed "petty" rules violations, lied to the nuns about her mother having cancer to avoid taking an exam, experimented sexually at an early age, smoked dope and dropped acid. Her continual defiance finally forced her father to break family tradition and transfer her to a nonsectarian school. When she was 16, she became involved with her 23-year-old tutor, Steven Weed. She moved in with him when she turned 18, quitting school for a $2.25-an-hour department store job. After four months Dad gave in and agreed to pay her rent if she would return to school.

Of course, she chose UC Berkeley.

*   *   *   *   *   *

On February 4, 1974, just 15 days before Patty's 20th birthday and four months before a planned June wedding, Nancy Ling Perry knocked on Patty's door and asked if she could use the phone to report a car accident. As Patty opened the door she was tackled and tied up by Donald DeFreeze and Willie Wolfe, who also beat Weed unconscious with a wine bottle. A neighbor heard Patty pleading: "Please no, not me." They stuffed her in the trunk of their stolen Chevy convertible and sped off, having no idea how special their prize was.

Patty was now a prisoner in a very small, private war waged by a virtually unknown army—the Symbionese Liberation Army.

The SLA, with its logo of a seven-headed cobra, was an odd gang of would-be revolutionaries led by DeFreeze, who somehow sold the idea of black revolution against a white-controlled government to a bunch of white yuppies still living fever dreams of the '60s.

DeFreeze was the black flip side of Charles Manson. Like Manson, he spent most of his life behind bars, developing a hatred for society. He subjected followers to Manson-like group meetings, where their past lives were demeaned and they were sold a vision of a euphoric future, if only they confirmed their loyalty to the leader. Just as Manson had eventually said he had the right to pay society back for what was done to him, DeFreeze proclaimed himself "that nigger that is no longer hunted, robbed and murdered... the nigger that hunts you now." And he claimed, like his white doppelganger, that he was a prophet sent by God to foment revolution; that he heard hidden messages meant only for him in song lyrics and that political power grew from the barrel of a gun.

DeFreeze escaped from Soledad State Prison in 1973, renamed himself Cinque Mtume, after the leader of the mutiny aboard the slave ship Amistad, and founded the Symbionese Nation, using a variation of the word "symbiosis," defined as a body of dissimilar organisms living together in harmony.

He was ready to build his own, Manson-style family.

He recruited, as did Manson, middle-class whites from the well-stocked ranks of UC Berkeley radicals. Patricia Soltysik, his lover, was a pharmacist's daughter and self-avowed revolutionary and radical feminist. She also juggled a lesbian relationship with Camilla Hall, the daughter of a Lutheran missionary who became a social worker and peace activist. Soltysik inspired Hall to pen the love poem "Mizmoon."

Others included Wolfe, the son of a wealthy anesthesiologist, who dropped out of prep school to pursue the hippie lifestyle and eventually converted to Maoism; Bill Harris, an ex-Marine who returned from the Vietnam War a fervent antiwar activist; his wife Emily, a junior high school English teacher and former straight A student; and Perry, a former cheerleader, Sunday School teacher and Barry Goldwater campaign worker turned topless blackjack dealer and psychedelic drug enthusiast.

James Kilgore's economics degree wouldn't keep him out of Vietnam and that fear drove him into the arms of the SLA. Michael Bortin and Wendy Yoshimura joined later. Both were veterans of the Berkeley radical scene and both had been arrested for keeping a large cache of illegal weapons. Yoshimura, who was born in a World War II internment camp for Japanese-Americans, had also been linked to a failed plot by another radical group to blow up a UC Berkeley building. Angela Atwood, a theater major, met the Harrises at Indiana University and reunited with them after her marriage to political activist Gary Atwood failed.

*   *   *   *   *   *

The kidnapping of the Hearst heiress enthralled America. But the drama was only beginning. It kick-started a few days later when a tape recording of the kidnap victim was dropped off at a local radio station. "I'm with a combat unit that's armed with automatic weapons and there is no way that I will be released until they let me go," Patty said, stating the obvious.

DeFreeze, now calling himself General Field Marshall Cinque, demanded the release of Joseph Remiro and Russell Little, SLA members accused in the brutal murder of Oakland School superintendent Marcus Foster, who was shot with hollow-point bullets dipped in cyanide after Cinque branded him a "CIA fascist" for proposing the use of identification cards in Oakland schools.

Authorities rejected the demand. Fearful his daughter might get caught in a shootout between police and the SLA, Randolph Hearst decided to negotiate directly with the kidnappers. They demanded that he distribute $400 million worth of food to California's poor. Randolph donated $2 million, but the gesture turned into riots as volunteers tossed chickens from moving trucks into swirling crowds. Even though 100,000 grocery bags full of food were subsequently handed out, the SLA refused to release Patty, claiming the food was of poor quality. In a new tape, Cinque dismissed the gesture as "throwing a few crumbs to the people." He also rejected Hearst's $4 million cash ransom offer.

As the hostage crisis dragged on, Patty's taped words grew increasingly pro-SLA. Finally, on April 3, just two months after her kidnapping, a new tape was released. "I have been given the choice of being released in a safe area or join the forces of the Symbionese

Liberation Army and fight for my freedom and the freedom of all oppressed people," she said. "I have chosen to stay and fight."

This was a new Patty. She had shed her shoulder-length hair, 15 pounds and her fiance, who she cast aside for her new love, Cujo, the SLA name for Willie Wolfe. She was now Tania, after a fallen Che Guevara follower.

The media speculated wildly about this turn of events. Could this young girl, born into privilege, really have joined an underground guerrilla terrorist group? Had she been too sheltered as a child, or too rebellious? Had she been brainwashed? Was it all a hoax? Experts pointed to the Stockholm Syndrome, named after hostages in a Swedish bank robbery a year earlier who started assisting their captors when the bank was surrounded by police. Psychologists speculated that this was a subconscious survival trick concocted by minds under great stress.

I was hooked on the daily stories, but I wasn't buying Patty's new act. Surely, someone must be holding a gun to her head to force her to read some prepared script.

But the shockwaves kept rolling in. On April 15, the SLA robbed the Sunset District branch of the Hibernia Bank in San Francisco, shooting two people and getting away with $10,000. A bank surveillance camera picked up Patty, standing alone in the rear, barking orders and wielding an M1 rifle. She promised, according to a guard, to shoot the first SOB that moved.

Nine days later, another tape featured Patty assuring listeners that her gun was loaded at the bank, that her "comrades" weren't forcing her to participate at gunpoint and that the notion she was brainwashed was "ridiculous to the point of being beyond belief."

As the police closed in, the fugitive band moved south to Los Angeles, where, on May 16, Bill and Emily Harris botched an attempted robbery at Mel's Sporting Goods in Inglewood. But, as Bill Harris was being handcuffed, a hail of semi-automatic machine gun fire from a Volkswagen van shattered a store window. A ricochet grazed the owner's wife. In the ensuing chaos, the Harrises jumped in the van as it squealed away. Wielding the gun, in a black, curly wig and sunglasses, was Patty Hearst.

Imagine Tom Matthews' surprise later that day in nearby Lynwood, when the people test-driving the van he had put up for sale turned out to be Tania and her SLA cohorts. He knew because they told him so, right before driving to a hardware store to buy a hacksaw to remove Bill Harris' handcuffs; right before they treated him to a double feature at a nearby drive-in theater where they were to meet with fellow SLA members; right before Tania showed him how to use her automatic rifle; right before they assured him he wouldn't be harmed. "As long as I don't get shot, I don't care what happens," said the excited and curious high school senior, a baseball player who had a title game the next day.

The SLA members talked about robbing banks and Patty told Tom how proud she was to have fired on the sporting goods store and rescued her comrades, Matthews later reported. At sunrise, they hijacked another car and he drove his van home.

Ironically, Patty's shooting spree may have saved her life. Fearful that police might have tracked her from the sporting goods shootout, the other SLA members stayed away from the drive-in. Had the rendezvous taken place, Patty would have accompanied them to the Los Angeles hideout where a lethal confrontation with police soon began.

*   *   *   *   *   *

Parking tickets found in the van abandoned by the Harrises and Patty and an anonymous tip led police to the Los Angeles hideout. Unfortunately, that information also leaked to the local TV news outlets, which promptly aired it. Among the rapt viewers were DeFreeze and his followers, who naturally fled, only to be cornered in a bungalow a few blocks away.

A sleeping visitor there, 17-year-old Brenda Daniels, awoke about 2 a.m. to the sight of four women, three men and a batch of guns spread across the floor. DeFreeze politely handled introductions while hundreds of police, FBI, California Highway Patrol and Los Angeles Fire Department officers, along with a mass of TV cameras bringing it all live into the nation's homes, surrounded the bungalow.

Tear gas projectiles fired into the house drew heavy automatic gunfire in response. Two hours later, the house caught on fire. Patty's lover Wolfe, along with Soltysik and Atwood, burned to death in a crawl space under the house rather than give themselves up. Nancy Ling Perry and Camilla Hall were shot by police as they fled the building. DeFreeze, like so many cult leaders, got his martyr's wish, shooting himself in the head to escape the horror of immolation. It had never been a cause for Cinque. For him, it was about hate, notoriety and the fun of robbing banks. He knew the fun was over.

Most people assumed Patty was in the house. That didn't slow the law enforcement siege. Apparently, the possibility that she was psychologically damaged and worth saving wasn't a consideration. In all, more than 9,000 rounds were fired by both sides and most of them missed their intended targets.

I cried for Patty, still believing there had to be some justifiable reason for her actions. She was doing what she had to do to survive. Someone was holding a gun to her head or threatening to kill her sisters. In my youthful innocence, I couldn't imagine any other explanation.

Then the news surfaced. Patty wasn't part of the body count. The next day, the FBI charged her with 19 counts, including armed robbery. She was no longer a victim; she was now, officially, a fugitive from justice, her photo plastered on post office walls as one of the nation's most wanted.

*   *   *   *   *   *

In the weeks that followed, the three surviving SLA members lived life on the run. They bought a dented old car for $350 and drove until the battery died. They walked the streets, disguised as homeless people —not much of a stretch by then—and crawled under a house to sleep. A party broke out above them.

With their new, sky-high profile, they attracted some new members and sympathizers.

Kathy Soliah became the group's voice with the underground press and orchestrated protests against the Los Angeles shootings. Special help came from Jack Scott, a former athletic director at Oberlin College in Ohio, who wrote a book about racism and militarism in college sports after losing his job. Now an antiwar activist, he wanted to write a book about the SLA so he set out to make contact through the radical network in Berkeley. He found them hunkered down in an apartment filled with machine guns, grenades and mattresses blocking windows and doors. He later said he offered to take Patty anywhere she wanted to go, but she refused, wanting to remain with her comrades.

Scott and his wife, Micki, eventually helped the tattered remnants of the SLA move to an abandoned farmhouse on 87 acres of isolated farmland near South Canaan, Pennsylvania, where Patty could swing in a hammock while studying politics, SLA-style. They again aped the Manson clan, engaging in daily military drills. Like kids playing in the backyard, they crept under chairs, leaped on the dining-room table to dodge invisible gunfire and shot at targets with a BB gun found in the barn. Patty practiced her disguise as a pregnant teenager by painting freckles on her face and stuffing a pillow under her dress. According to Scott, they talked about political assassinations, scanning media pictures for potential targets. They never followed through, although Soliah did attempt to blow up some police cars. Her crude bombs failed to detonate.

Soon, they were drawn back to California, where Scott introduced them to a new friend: Bill Walton, a former all-American basketball player at UCLA. The imposing, 7-foot-tall Walton, a future all-pro and successful broadcaster, was then a youthful rebel looking for a cause. How deeply involved with the SLA Walton became isn't known and he has never spoken of it. But he allegedly met Patty and drove her around. He spent considerable time with the Scotts, and when questioned by law enforcement, publicly supported their refusal to give information about the SLA to a grand jury. He called his experience with the Scotts the most beautiful in his life.

On April 21, 1975, the reconstituted SLA robbed a bank near Sacramento and got away with more than $16,000. Patty drove the getaway car. Kathy Soliah allegedly kicked a pregnant woman, triggering a miscarriage. Another woman, Myrna Opsahl, was shot and later bled to death.

In September, acting on a tip from Jack Scott's brother, police found what was left of the SLA in a San Francisco apartment. They arrested the Harrises as they were jogging outside. Inside, the police found Wendy Yoshimura and Tania, aka Patty Hearst. When Patty arrived at the police station after her arrest, she gave a defiant, clenched-fist salute to the media and described her occupation on the booking report as "urban guerrilla." Released on $1.25 million bail, Patty reunited with her sisters and family.

It wasn't a pretty picture, but at least she was safe. Or so I thought.

*   *   *   *   *   *

What had happened to the sheltered little rich girl in those months after the kidnapping? Was she victim or predator? It was a critical question for the team of lawyers preparing her defense. In one survey, 68% believed Patty should be sent to prison; two-thirds thought she joined the SLA voluntarily and half thought the kidnapping was a fake.

Once removed from the SLA's influence for a sufficient period of time, here is the story Patty would tell:

After her kidnapping, she was imprisoned for 56 days, often blind-folded, in a hot, stuffy closet lit by a bare bulb and furnished with a portable cot. There, she claimed, she was raped and brutalized by Cinque and future lover Wolfe and constantly harangued about politics and her useless former life. Her old lifestyle was attacked as nothing more than potted plants and nail polish.

Her father was denounced as part of a ruling class sucking blood from the common people. His refusal to meet their ransom demands proved that he loved money more than her. "I felt my parents were debating how much I was worth," she said. "It was a terrible feeling that my parents could think of me in terms of dollars and cents."

As she grew more vulnerable, the group switched tactics. In classic brainwashing mode, they became more sympathetic, confiding to her that they all had once lived like her, but had come to see the exploitation of such an existence. They were ready now to fight and die for the people. Patty started participating in daily group discussions, confessing disillusionment with her parents and finally, sympathy for the SLA. As a reward for that, she was allowed to roam about the apartment.

Even Steven Weed, her lover of three years, now seemed lacking. Why had he not attempted to rescue her? His once-attractive radicalism paled in comparison with the passionate Maoism of her new love, Willie Wolfe. When Weed appeared on a TV talk show saying she had been brainwashed, Patty denounced him. "Frankly," she declared on a subsequent tape, "Steven is the one who sounds brainwashed."

This progression from captive to comrade didn't surprise experts. "She's frightened and inclined to believe these people are really monsters," explained Dr. Frederick Hacker, a psychiatrist who wrote a book about the Arab-Israeli hostage crisis at the 1972 Munich Olympics. "Then they treat her very nicely. She finds they are very much the kind of people she is—upper-middle-class, intelligent white kids. She finds a poetess, a sociologist. They tell her how they have found a new ideal and how lousy it was at home." This, he argued, would resonate with Patty, whose home life, at least in her mind, wasn't so hot either. "To convert someone, you don't clean the brain out," he said, "you put something in it."

This was textbook brainwashing according to the experts brought in to examine Patty after her capture—Dr. Hacker, Dr. Louis "Jolly" West, Margaret Singer, the nation's foremost expert on cults, and Dr. Robert J. Lifton, author of the bible on brainwashing, *Thought Reform, the Psychology of Totalism.*

Was she or wasn't she? That mystery still clings to Patty. Was she still brainwashed during a later jailhouse conversation with a friend, tape recorded just before her release on bail? It's unlikely that all the effects of brainwashing would have worn off so quickly. Confusion, certainly, would be commonplace, but Patty's responses raise questions: "I guess I'll just tell you, my politics are real different from way back when," she said. "Obviously, so this creates all kinds of problems for me in terms of a defense. When I was first arrested, I was still a real mess. I said a lot of crazy things."

*   *   *   *   *   *

Patty's return to the bosom of her family couldn't have been easy. She had never been close to her mother, Catherine, who was alternately accused of being either too strict or too lax by some close to the family. And while Patty was no longer spouting radical dogma, she was still making, in her mother's view, inappropriate choices. She quickly found a new man to lean on—Bernard Shaw, her bodyguard. The polar opposite of her previous beaus, he was a husky ex-cop and a conservative Republican. But to her mother's dismay, he was also married.

That was a sensitive subject for her, since her own marriage was collapsing from the stress of her daughter's ordeal and her husband's serial philandering. After Randolph upbraided her for a public comment he didn't like, telling her he didn't want to see her name in the newspapers again until her obituary, she developed a drinking problem, her marriage of nearly 40 years ended and the family estate in Hillsborough was sold.

*   *   *   *   *   *

Two years exactly from the day of her kidnapping, the trial of Patty Hearst began. Leading Patty's defense team was F. Lee Bailey, the famed barrister who defended the Boston Strangler and Dr. Sam Sheppard, the Ohio neurosurgeon convicted in 1954 of murdering his pregnant wife. Ironically, Dr. Sheppard claimed she was killed by cult-like attackers who knocked him out. Bailey eventually got the conviction tossed on appeal and then won the second trial.

By the time Patty's trial started, Tania, with her tough-girl sweaters, jeans and clenched-fist politics, was gone, replaced by a soft-spoken Patty, with dyed red hair and tastefully conservative clothing. Was this the real Patty or was it Memorex? Had she really self-deprogrammed or was this just another disguise, a Patty replica hastily assembled by her family and lawyers?

I thought she was real. And with all of the expert testimony about brainwashing and the natural tendency of the American public to sympathize with a 19-year-old, kidnapped student, I thought the jury would acquit her. Unfortunately for Patty, Bailey didn't fully understand or trust the brainwashing defense. He suggested at various times that his client did only what she had to do to stay alive. This contradicted all of her experts, who testified that brainwashing victims don't act out of fear, but out of an exhilarating sense of answering to some new calling.

Worse, Bailey instructed her to invoke Fifth Amendment protection against self-incrimination when asked about other crimes she committed while under the SLA's influence, fearing that those charges would become new indictments. But Patty needed to admit to those acts and convince the jury that she did them because she had been manipulated into believing it was for the good of mankind. Brainwashing is an all-or-nothing position. She couldn't claim to be under the group's control only part of the time.

U.S. District Judge Oliver J. Carter ruled that Patty had waived her fifth-amendment rights by claiming to be brainwashed. Ignoring the ruling, which was correct, Bailey continued to advise her to remain silent. She took the fifth 42 times and the judge ordered her testimony stricken from the record. It didn't help that Judge Carter rejected brainwashing as a defense and instructed jurors that to be acquitted, Patty had to be acting out of "immediate fear for her life."

Patty also didn't help herself with inconsistent and unflattering testimony. She testified that after two months in the closet, her mind was no longer her own. If that was true, why would the SLA have to script her recorded messages and force her to deliver them, as she also claimed. And she denounced Wolfe, who she had once claimed was the love of a lifetime. "He was just as bad as any of the rest of them and I think it's insulting to anyone who's ever been raped to suggest that that could turn into a seduction and love affair afterwards," she testified. But if she was, indeed, brainwashed, the jury knew, falling in love with one of her captors wouldn't be unusual. And how could she love him, jurors said after the trial, if he had really raped her? She further testified that for a period of time she thought she was "fooling" the SLA with her professions of loyalty. If that was true, why didn't she ever try to escape after gaining the group's trust?

Prosecution experts contended that Patty was radicalized before she ever heard of the SLA and would have clung to the first appealingly radical ideology that drifted by. They also made an issue of the fact that while Patty described almost every room in the apartment where she was held in exacting detail, she offered almost no detail about the closet where she was allegedly imprisoned for so long.

Both prosecution points are shaky. Blocking out details of the place where she was brutalized would be perfectly understandable. And should she be considered guilty because she had a past that made her susceptible to radical programming? While all, save the psychotic, are capable of being brainwashed, some are definitely more susceptible— the young, those without strong religious or family ties, those who are insecure or have suffered recent trauma. The important question is this: Was she victimized by forces she couldn't control? It didn't seem fair to argue that her psychological state might have made her an easier target.

After a two-month trial and only 12 hours of deliberation, Patty was convicted and sentenced to 35 years in prison, which was later commuted to 7 years to be served in nearby Pleasanton, a minimum security facility.

*   *   *   *   *   *

From her cell, Patty hired a new lawyer to pursue a new trial or a presidential pardon. But for that to happen, she told her father, they needed to change the public's view of brainwashing through a media blitz.

Coincidentally, this is where I came in. I was just another average Joe following the story with fascination, but in June, 1977, I became involved in my first Synanon case and used the media attention I got to inadvertently launch what Patty had prayed for—a concentrated effort to get the media to warn people about the dangers of brainwashing lurking in some of these political, psychological and spiritual movements and self-help groups. Just as Patty wished, brainwashing was now squarely in the public eye. The story got even bigger a year later when I barely survived a bite from a rattlesnake placed in my mail box by members of Synanon. They were branded a terrorist organization by the press, which pointed out the similarities to Charles Manson and revisited the troubling questions raised by Patty's case.

Leo Ryan, a California congressman, was gathering signatures on a petition for Patty's release when he flew to Guyana in November, 1978, to investigate tales of another brutal cult. He never returned. Jim Jones ordered members of his People's Temple to murder Ryan and his entourage before directing the mass suicide of 900 followers via poisoned Kool-Aid. His death, more than his petition, turned attention back to Patty's plight.

Brainwashing was now a white-hot topic. ABC had me on television six nights in a row to explain it and one example I used was the Patty Hearst case, contending that her continued imprisonment was unfair.

Patty was now being seen as a victim again. John Wayne, the Duke himself, summed up public sentiment: "It seems quite odd to me that the American people have immediately accepted the fact that one man can brainwash 900 human beings in a mass suicide but will not accept the fact that a ruthless group, the Symbionese Liberation Army, could brainwash a little girl by torture, degradation and confinement."

Just 22 months into her prison term—three months after Synanon placed that rattlesnake in my mailbox—Patty was released from prison by President Jimmy Carter. She was eventually pardoned by President Bill Clinton in 2001; it was the final act of his presidency.

*   *   *   *   *   *

After Patty's trial, the SLA faded from public view. Patty married Shaw and moved to Connecticult to live a sedate, conservative life filled with two daughters, fashion, charitable work and dog shows. She dabbled in acting, most notably an episode of *Veronica Mars* in which she portrayed a wealthy woman who faked her own kidnapping.

Bill and Emily Harris pleaded guilty to kidnapping in 1979 and served seven years each. They eventually divorced. Bill became a private investigator; Emily a computer consultant (hired by MGM).

Then, over 25 years later, both Kathy Soliah and James Kilgore were discovered through tips from the *America's Most Wanted* TV show. Soliah, aka Sara Jane Olsen, was arrested in 2001 after living for many years as a civic-minded soccer mom with two daughters. A year later, police found Kilgore living in Zimbabwe as Charles William Pape, a married college professor and father of two. Away from SLA influence, both had lived normal, productive lives.

Thanks to new forensic evidence, all four, plus Bortin, were linked to the Sacramento bank heist during which Myrna Opsahl was killed. The Harrises were jailed for another eight years. Soliah had six years added to the eight awaiting her for her earlier guilty plea in the attempted police-car bombings. Bortin and Kilgore got six years each.

Both Patty and Wendy Yoshimura, by then a watercolor painter in Oakland, agreed to testify against their former cohorts in exchange for immunity.

Only Joseph Remiro, sentenced to life for the Marcus Foster murder, remains in prison.

*   *   *   *   *   *

To this day, the Patty Hearst case haunts me. I had always disagreed with the jury's verdict. It seemed far more likely to me that she was a misguided rich girl coerced by an evil force than a hard-core terrorist just waiting for the opportunity to strut her radical stuff. When asked, I still say she was brainwashed.

And yet, there are troubling contradictions.

Years after her release, Patty told reporters she never tried to escape because she was deep in despair, feeling she had nothing left to go home to. But a successful thought reform program generally produces exhilarating peak experiences, since people feel they have been blessed with the true light of righteousness. While her conduct then suggested she felt just that way, she was now saying something else.

In her 1982 book about her experiences, *Every Secret Thing*, she denied participating willingly in the Hibernia bank robbery, which contradicted the known facts and suggested she wasn't brainwashed. If she had been, she would have been a zealous participant. Like the jurors, her accounts of rape and brutality also didn't ring true for me. In true brainwashing programs, victims are put under stress and verbally attacked, but not raped. Kindness, applied at the right moment, is much more effective than violence.

Cinque relished his Robin Hood image; he wanted to be revered by the radical underground and raping Patty wouldn't have helped him. And if you believe, as the jury did, that Patty and Wolfe were lovers, it seems unlikely that romance would have grown out of rape. Everything about Wolfe, including his desire to help prisoners, says he is not a rapist.

A film adaptation made the brainwashing argument more persuasively than Patty's book and seemed to convince many that the rape claims were real (Randolph Hearst said he wouldn't watch the movie).

For her part, Patty has said she was a victim of the times, that in today's world, she wouldn't even be charged, "because people don't charge kidnap victims for crimes they committed while in the company of their kidnappers."

Wouldn't they? Was her experience, in the end, that much different than John Walker Lindh's? While Patty didn't seek out Cinque, as Lindh did Osama bin Laden, both were subjected to oppressive thought reform processes.

*   *   *   *   *   *

Epilogue:

I always thought Patty and I were destined to meet, perhaps at some brainwashing awareness symposium where we could sit in a corner and compare experiences, both of us having been victims of the same phenomenon, albeit in vastly different ways. What questions might we have for each other? But the years passed and it never happened.

But I have often imagined what I might say to her:

"It is certainly unlikely you would have been robbing banks if you hadn't been kidnapped, but is that really the whole story? Brainwashing isn't the only reason people convert to radical causes. Some do it for the power, some for particular personal needs. I understand what you went through, the constant battering of your former life and your family. I can understand how it could influence you, as it has so many other impressionable young people exposed to destructive cults. I can also understand your anger at your father's financial bartering, Weed's comments and your mother's silence. I even understand how you could eventually bond with these people, who seemed like kindred spirits.

"A successfully brainwashed person isn't just a follower, but a zealot. That is how others described you. But you later denied that you were a zealot. If you weren't, you weren't brainwashed. You can't have it both ways.

"Still, I wonder if your post-SLA statements aren't just some form of denial, a reluctance on your part to accept your own gullibility, a common trait among victims of destructive cults in later phases?

"But whether you were coerced into believing the SLA's radical creed or not, that isn't an excuse for committing armed robbery and endangering people's lives. The SLA murdered people. It was a miracle more didn't die and you participated. For all that, a 22-month prison term isn't too high a price to pay.

"The truth is, Patty, nobody knows you. The title of your book, "Every Secret Thing," is more appropriate than anyone could guess. Your grandfather, through the magic of Hollywood, gave us the mystery of Rosebud; ironically, we may never discover your Rosebud."

SECTION II:

From Miracle
to Madness
to Mayhem

Chapter 7: Escape from Synanon
Part 1: Down the Rabbit Hole

It's a fancy building now, housing the Del Mar Hotel, Restaurant and Bar. Nothing about the Santa Monica structure hints of the rampant violence and abuse fomented there once upon a time when it was known as Synanon, the drug rehabilitation clinic that sought to reshape the world.

I had no clue what was going on at Synanon in 1977, when Ted Raines asked me to rescue his wife Terry, a depressed woman who sought treatment there and instead was subjected to a brutal brainwashing program. Certainly, I had no inkling of the sea change my life was about to undergo. All I knew was, something wasn't right.

So ended my dream of a normal life.

I had just started seeing a woman named Trudy that I met at a plant nursery with her two kids. She was a beautiful, tanned woman with reddish brown hair and when she smiled, I melted. I volunteered to tote her plants to her car and we chatted. I learned we had a mutual friend. I hurried home and called the friend, who had just gotten off the phone with Trudy, who wanted to make sure I knew she was single.

Before long, I was crazy in love, although a bit gun shy. Twice before I had contemplated marriage, but never got to pop the question. My first love talked me into going to law school, but left me to marry a lawyer before I started the first semester. I met the other in law school and decided eight years later to marry her. About 15 minutes after making that decision, she called to tell me she was marrying some guy she met on a ski lift two weeks before. Depressed, I left the office early and—for all you kismet fans out there—stopped at a plant nursery and met Trudy.

I started having visions of a life with this woman and her kids, a life unfettered by exhausting, soul-draining cause cases. Suddenly, I had no doubt: I loved Trudy and wanted to spend my life with her. The nursing home case, with its heavy-handed villains, sad victims and legal twists and turns, had carved a large, stressful chunk out of my life. Never again, I swore, when it was over.

Who was I kidding? The detritus of the law—fender benders, marital squabbles, business disputes—bored me silly. When the Synanon case was dropped in my lap, I felt relief. I had missed the adrenaline rush this kind of case gave me. It was a narcotic, that rush, and I was getting addicted. In the end, that addiction brought me a great deal of satisfaction; it also cost me dearly. I had brought something evil into the lives of the people I loved.

*   *   *   *   *   *

I engineered Ms. Raines release and about a month later, she called me from a Long Beach hospital and thanked me for saving her life. Why did she think that? I asked. Because without my intervention, she explained, "I would have become one of them."

Her statement startled me. How could someone be taken over so completely by someone else? I began searching for books about brainwashing and former Synanon residents who could explain how the group operated. Several were afraid to talk; those who did spoke sadly of a place that had once helped many people but had turned into a cesspool ruled by violence and one man's madness.

My education about cults and brainwashing—and my new life—had officially begun. And night after night I would share what I learned with Trudy.

I often debate whether I should feel grateful for Charles Dederich, the man who founded Synanon and led it on this dizzying ride from acclaimed drug rehab center to reviled cult. Thanks to him, and the cases that resulted from his actions, I was now steering confidently into a career in law, abandoning the journalistic career that I had always considered my destiny. And his frequent rants about me over "The Wire"—Synanon's Big Brother-like broadcast system, which reached all of its far-flung facilities—informed frightened residents who wanted to leave where they could go for help. It was the best advertising I ever got—and it was free.

Of course, I had no idea how much danger I was wading into. One Synanon "splitee," as those who left the group were derisively dubbed, warned me that Dederich was training a military hit squad—the Imperial Marines—and had already assaulted many people. "You will never believe the crazy story I just heard," I told my boss, Don Cohen, afterwards. "They must have some real nut cases in there."

*   *   *   *   *   *

The pain and loss that marked Charles Dederich's childhood in Ohio would haunt him for the rest of his days and inform every decision he ever made, good or bad. His father died in a car crash when Dederich was four and his youngest brother succumbed to influenza four years later. He would never again allow himself to get close to children—including his own. When he was 12, his mother married a wealthy man. Convinced he had lost his close relationship with her—and his role as the male head of the household—the unhappy and rebellious youngster spiraled into some dark and troubling times.

In 1942, he nearly died from a case of meningitis that plunged him into a coma, but was saved by a new miracle drug: penicillin. He awoke a changed man. His partially paralyzed face, a pronounced tic and a drooping right eye crushed his vanity and enhanced his conviction that people were staring at him. He also complained that he had developed a "black hole" in his memory, foreshadowing a time years later, when the black hole allegedly would return in the wake of multiple investigations of beatings and attempted murders relating to Synanon. He developed a morbid fear of death and dealt with it as his father and his father's father had—he drank—a compulsion that eventually cost him two marriages. His conviction that he had lost his Oedipal battle over his mother to his step-father led him to abandon his family and move to Santa Monica and become a beach bum.

After being found intoxicated and unconscious on the floor of his kitchen one day in 1956, he was taken to Alcoholics Anonymous. He took to AA like a true zealot, attending meetings daily and eventually quitting his job at Hughes Tool to counsel alcoholics full time. He lived on a $35-a-week unemployment check and some donations.

Dederich's obsession with finding more effective ways to treat alcoholism prompted him to volunteer for an experimental program developed by Dr. Keith Ditman, who had been an expert witness for the defense in the Golden State case. Dr. Ditman wanted to see if LSD could help in the treatment of alcoholism.

The acid trip triggered a catharsis that changed Dederich's worldview. To save his alcoholics, he needed to drive them to peak experiences like the ones he had on acid. Gripped by an inexplicable bout of paranoia on a business trip, Dederich confined himself to his hotel room and read Emerson's tome on self-reliance. The book eased his fears and he emerged from that room convinced that he was destined to cure the addicted. He began holding group sessions in his apartment after AA meetings, sessions which gradually grew more psychoanalytical and confrontational. For many, this was a welcome change from AA's "tea party talks," where everyone congratulated each other for being sober. In Dederich's room, alcoholics reprimanded each other for past and current destructive behavior. Meanwhile, he pored over books on Eastern philosophies and Western psychology, including the social engineering of Skinner and later, the self-actualization of Maslow.

The seeds of what would become the Synanon Game were being planted. They fully bloomed years later when he read about the brainwashing techniques of Mao.

When the alcoholics he counseled objected to drug addicts that dropped by, he kicked out the alcoholics, broke from AA and opened the Tender Loving Care Club in a seedy Venice storefront, where stale food was hustled from catering trucks and a hose through a window served as a shower. There he created Mao and Maslow-like encounter groups, where patients were encouraged to attack each others' past behavior. These sessions were alternately called symposiums or seminars. In 1958, one of his drug addicts slurred those words into something that sounded like "seminosium." After everyone stopped laughing, Dederich took a stick and scratched out variations in the beach sand, eventually coming up with Synanon, which reflected his AA roots. With net assets of $50, the fledgling Synanon Foundation Inc. was established. One day, Dederich predicted, the name would be bigger than Coca-Cola.

Initially, the attack therapy groups were called "synanons," later they became "the game" to reflect the concept of adult play time. In the game, you could say anything to another participant, whether true or not, to demean or praise. Only violence, or the threat of it, was banned, a rule instituted after a woman threw her high-heeled shoe at her husband. Dederich feared violence would restrict people's willingness to speak freely; he also feared it would attract the attention of law enforcement.

Newcomers were assigned to clean toilets; when they demonstrated compliant behavior, their jobs and living conditions improved. Negative behavior earned them a demotion or a verbal undressing, known as a "haircut," and sometimes demeaning signs to wear around their necks. All residents were summoned to witness haircuts so the verbal abuse could "carom" throughout the populace.

The essential elements of the Synanon program were now in place.

*   *   *   *   *   *

In 1959, donations from the Friars Club enabled Dederich to move his little operation to a vacated National Guard building in Santa Monica. But Synanon's new neighbors, fearful of the impact of addicts unleashed on their community, complained to authorities. Dederich was subsequently convicted of operating without a health license and out of zone. He got a 60-day sentence after refusing an offer of probation if he moved from the neighborhood. To the community's dismay, his apparent success at rehabilitating addicts earned him public sympathy; after his jailing, Gov. Edmund G. Brown, Sr., pushed through a bill exempting Synanon from licensing laws. Santa Monica agreed to hold off on enforcing the zoning issue when Dederich promised to move. He didn't and a weary Santa Monica abandoned efforts to enforce its zoning laws.

Now a public martyr, Dederich attracted the attention—and financial support—of the rich and famous. Actors Robert Wagner, Leonard Nimoy and Ben Gazzara, among other show business luminaries, came to Synanon to play the game with addicts and hookers. A 14-page spread in *Life* Magazine spread the word about the place that was dubbed the "Miracle on the Beach" in Congress; Columbia Pictures made a flattering movie starring Edmond O'Brien, Chuck Connors and Stella Stevens.

By early 1964, Synanon was attracting both addicts and non-addicts— dubbed "squares"—with its emphasis on living a self-examined life. But Dederich, whose program didn't include any follow-up monitoring or treatment for those who left, became frustrated by a high relapse rate among addicts. Considering the program a failure, he abolished the concept of "graduation" in 1967. Those who "split" the program would find "open manholes" awaiting them on the outside, he warned, and to prove his point, he posted bad news gathered about "splitees" on the wall. Members were urged to become permanent residents in the drug-free utopian world he now envisioned. As in any brainwashing regimen, he began to realize, compliance could only be achieved through constant reinforcement.

To support this new vision, he created a business empire selling promotional items, parlaying that income and donations into an extensive real estate portfolio that included gas stations and apartment buildings. Synanon would eventually own its own fleet of trucks, automobiles and motorcycles, a mini-armada of 21 boats, a squadron of ten airplanes and its own airstrip. It was hugely profitable, especially since the nonprofit organization didn't have to pay taxes—or its in-house employees.

Dederich also created the "Synanon Trip," an intense, weekend-long version of the Synanon Game for squares that brought in even more money. A precursor to programs such as est, the Synanon Trip attracted affluent professionals, who were "gamed" in a contained weekend environment until they broke and accepted Synanon as their only salvation, frequently surrendering their lives—and assets—to Dederich's growing social experiment.

"At the end of this rainbow," he promised the weekend trippers, "there will be a pot of gold. You will learn more about yourself, your fellow man, the world, the nature of reality, in one weekend than you would in four years. You may change your value system, notions about life and viewpoints about people. It will produce a new breed of human beings with greatly expanded potentials."

To house his expanding operations, in 1967 he purchased the Club Casa del Mar, a beachfront hotel in Santa Monica built in 1926 as a swank beach retreat for wealthy locals and temporarily converted to a center for military operations during World War II. The city claimed its lease of the adjacent beach to the previous owner included a "no-assignment" clause, which meant the sale voided the lease. But instead of pursuing its claim through the legal system, police and bulldozers were sent in to forcefully root out Dederich and his minions from the beach, destroying cabanas and racquet ball courts, and erecting a fence. The resulting protest led to the arrest of Synanon sympathizers and again whipped up community support and increased donations for the organization. Dederich declared that Santa Monica had fallen into the hands of "Mad Dogs" and vowed to ruin every government official involved. When the city backed down, Synanon became untouchable. It soon amassed the largest land holdings in Santa Monica.

*   *   *   *   *   *

Now, Synanon was asserting total control over its' residents' lives. They were pressured to turn over their assets to the organization. A policy of "containment" cut off contact with outsiders; with that, Dederich became the lone voice guiding their lives. Now well into what Dederich called Synanon II, the New Society, the group became an experimental, hermetically-sealed community that increasingly saw the outside world as a crab pot filled with enemies.

The group's new focus on lifestyle, rather than drug addiction, prompted the IRS to challenge its tax-free status in 1974, so Synanon declared itself a religion. Welcome to Synanon III. In a typed letter written by head attorney Dan Garrett outlining the benefits of becoming a religion, someone scrawled a question across the bottom: "Who will be God?"

Everyone knew the answer.

In this new order, Synanon expanded, building communities in Marin County, where Dederich and his wife, Betty, ruled like royalty —complete with robes and thrones. In 1975 he moved the group's so-called "Home Place"—defined as wherever he lived—to the Badger Mountains above Visalia, California, building a Roman-like culture with pools, spas, waterfalls, art works and newcomer slaves to do the work and serve the elite. In this relative splendor, the Old Man declared he no longer wanted to be surrounded by "dope fiends," who wanted Synanon to remain a rehabilitation center. Through games and shunning of resisters, he forced out those who wouldn't conform to his new vision. He called this a "squeeze," as in "squeezing rotten fruit from the trees."

Seeking even firmer control over his flock, he continued his campaign against children. Earlier, he had ordered that babies were to be raised in "the hatchery" by selected adults, who were instructed not to play with or tickle the infants, but to keep their distance and give them space to crawl. Contact with biological parents was discouraged; the children belonged to the community. Mothers who tried to visit too often were called "headsuckers."

Now, Dederich decided that Synanon didn't want to add any more children to its population because they sapped time and attention from the organization's more important goals and cost money to raise. Men who had been members five years or longer were forced to get vasectomies and pregnant women abortions, including one woman who was four months pregnant.

In a speech called "Childbirth Unmasked," Dederich dismissed childbirth as nothing more than "crapping a football" and declared that abortions, once considered evil, were now seen as "squeezing a boil, nothing more." He estimated that raising a child sapped up to $200,000 worth of energy from the community over 18 years. "Children are a very bad investment," he said. "We have not cashed in on any children born into Synanon… There is no profit to this community in raising our own children."

The game continued to evolve, as Dederich pushed for more intense emotional breakdowns. He instituted 72-hour games, then never-ending "perpetual stews," hoping that the long hours of activity with little sleep would produce a state of inebriation without alcohol or drugs and lead to the insight-producing peak experience he had on LSD. In the mass euphoria that would follow, participants would become more committed to the program, he correctly theorized.

In the early days of Synanon, heads were shaved for punishment. By 1975, everyone shaved their heads as a symbol of loyalty, even the women. Bib overalls became the organization's uniform of choice, since they increasingly saw themselves as doing the world's work.

*   *   *   *   *   *

When his wife, Betty, died in 1977, Dederich, now 63, chose a new, 31-year-old bride from the rank-and-file. The experience inspired him to order that all couples break up and take new partners every three years, to "avoid the otherwise inevitable pain and loss of death and divorce."

Some believe it was Betty's death that unleashed Dederich's fury and led to all the violence. Yet when Dederich created a paramilitary group within Synanon, it was officially named "Her Majesty's Imperial Marines." Betty attended their clandestine training camp and often spoke of a more militant Synanon.

Besides, Synanon's wave of violence began in 1974, three years before her death. It grew from the injection into the Synanon mainstream of new kinds of members, who weren't as malleable as Dederich's old dope fiends.

One example was the "Punk Squad," a forerunner of tough-love youth rehabilitation programs such as Scared Straight. Synanon convinced parents, judges and probation officers to send juvenile delinquents to Synanon to participate in the program so Synanon could further claim to the IRS it was still a charity. But unlike the addicts, the street-wise kids hadn't volunteered. All they wanted was to get back to the streets, so they resisted Synanon's brainwashing program. With behavioral change progressing at a snail's pace and the punks mouthing off at old-timers, an impatient Dederich saw beatings as a quicker path to obedience and respect. Hit them in the face, knock them down, and then game them over the experience, he said.

With that, Synanon began sliding down the slippery slope. The next step was public beatings of members caught stealing, one beating broadcast live on The Wire so everyone could hear the screams. After that, the organization turned on outsiders who, as Dederich said, "needed a good lesson in manners."

As Dederich grew more paranoid about enemies outside the compound, his soliloquies on The Wire grew more militant and attacks on Synanon's neighbors escalated. Publicly, he warned people not to "mess" with Synanon because he couldn't control his members. But on The Wire, he persistently urged members to be more aggressive when confronting troublesome outsiders, to deliver a "message" that it wasn't wise to cross the increasingly truculent group.

The organization had fallen down the rabbit hole into darkness and bloodshed.

Part 2: The Rise of Violence

It had been boiling for some time, an inner rage enveloping those who had devoted themselves to Charles Dederich and Synanon's changing way of life. Enemies were everywhere—from the "splitees" who rejected the Synanon lifestyle and left, to local residents who were getting nervous about their neighbors' growing hostility, to the pack of media and legal jackals hounding them.

Now, after 17 years of nonviolence, that inner rage was finally set free, with lethal consequences. As documented by internal memos, reports and recordings discovered by investigators and attorneys, plus police reports, here is a chronology of the major incidents of abuse and violence that marked this new era of Synanon's existence.

It is by no means complete.

March 3, 1975: Ronald Pearson and Michael Clancy had been flying their model airplane on hilltop property adjacent to Synanon's Marin facility, but their truck got stuck in the mud when they tried to leave. Soon, they were surrounded by Synanon members armed with clubs and ax handles who had been scouring the area for a pair of bounty hunters who were rumored to be after a Synanon resident. Pearson and Clancy were forced into a van and taken to Synanon, where they were pinned against a wall and searched while a gathering mob shouted for some leg-breaking while others videotaped the event. Before proceedings got out of hand, sheriff's deputies arrived and the two men were released. The police report on the incident called it a "possible kidnapping," but no arrests were ever made.

March 4, 1975: A purple truck forced Synanon resident Tom Quinn's truck off the nearby Marshall-Petaluma Road, prompting a widespread search by a fleet of Synanon vehicles. After reports of a sighting, jitneys ferried 30 Synanon residents to the quiet old west town of Tomales and surrounded a purple truck parked in front of Diekmann's General Store, prompting a tense, town-and-gown confrontation with local residents. Bitter words were exchanged, a punch or two got thrown and police finally broke it up before it turned in to an old Western brawl befitting a John Ford movie.

It was another near-miss, but clearly, tensions were rising, as was Synanon's appetite for aggression. In a letter to Mike Garrett, son of attorney Dan Garrett, Synanon's second-in-command, after the Tomales showdown, Dederich noted that "our neighbors are getting to the point where they are beginning to constitute an annoyance to decent people." Garrett wrote back that he advised the parties in the incident that in any "creep emergency we should be concerned with the lesson involved more than the legal technicalities."

June 9, 1975: Alvin Gambonini, a Marin rancher whose property bordered both Synanon's Home Place and its Walker Creek compound along a two-mile stretch, drove with his wife and three children to check on some property he had leased to a tenant who was out of the country. Gambonini had gotten along splendidly with Synanon residents at first. He once loaned them his cattle truck so they could haul cows to the Point Reyes Fair. He donated all the gravel Synanon wanted and gave plowing lessons by doing an entire Synanon orchard. That changed in 1974, when he attempted to stop Synanon from building a road through his property. They already had an easement on an existing road and when they also started widening that one, they threatened to sue him if he interfered.

The relationship further deteriorated with the arrival of the Punks in 1974. Punk Squad runaways came to his house in the early morning hours, some shaking, some crying, most with tales of horror and abuse. Gambonini reunited them with their parents, often paying for their bus tickets home.

Now, Gambonini was confronted by a group of Synanon residents who had just emerged from a chest-thumping game in which Dederich ranted about instilling fear of Synanon in outsiders. Was he the one who had been sawing off the Synanon sign near his property? Pumped-up resident Ron Eschenauer reached in the window and repeatedly punched the rancher, triggering another ugly mob scene. One man jumped on the hood of Gambonini's Impala while others kicked at the windshield, tried to break the rear window with a fence post and beat on the car with a flashlight. Still others hurled rocks and bottles, yelling at the Gamboninis to get out of the car. While his family screamed hysterically, the farmer sat stoically in his seat, his face and shirt covered in blood. One tooth was cracked, another chipped, a muscle in his arm was torn and his face bled from cuts that would become permanent scars. His wife threw herself over his body as a shield while a son crawled out the rear window, eluded Synanon pursuers and ran for help, returning with a cavalry of local sheriff's deputies.

While Eschenauer and two other Synanon residents were arrested, they were allowed to plead no contest to misdemeanor assault charges. Only Eschenauer spent any time—15 days—in jail; he was fined $250. The other two received $500 fines and probation. It was a small price to pay for Synanon sainthood. The day after the incident, they were summoned to Dederich's mansion office, the Red Room, and honored for their actions. Eschenauer became a member of Synanon's Inner Circle and received a place of honor at the Old Man's dining table plus new housing in one of Synanon's most luxurious buildings near the Red Room.

The confrontation pleased Dederich. In a letter to security chief Mike Garrett, he lauded the Synanites involved for the way they "dealt with our neighboring pig." Thus encouraged, his followers continued the beatings of outsiders in the ensuing months and delivered the same to splitees they tracked down. Some of the incidents were highlighted in Synanon's year-end report. A man caught siphoning gas was held prisoner for eight hours and told his legs would be broken if he tried to escape. And ex-musician Bill Crawford, a long-time resident, wrote that "we tracked down and caught two guys who were trying to run our kids off the road and they ended up with a lot less hair than they started out with."

With more weapons being introduced into Synanon, the report stated, it was becoming less reliant on external law enforcement agencies. "All public safety people and many other men and women in the community are learning the martial arts, baton handling, crowd control techniques and other self-defense measures," the report concluded.

February 20, 1977: For Synanon, this was a day filled with blood lust. It started early in Santa Monica, when a gang of Synanon residents surrounded a Volkswagen van parked near its building. Inside, Tyler Mulrooney, a 17-year-old surfer who had just gotten off his night-shift job, was taking a nap before hitting the beach. Acting on reports of a drunk who urinated on a nearby wall, the gathering mob slashed the van's tires and tried to jimmy open a locked door. A passing police unit rescued the terrified teenager, but unwisely left after a tow truck arrived. The Synanon mob quickly reemerged; this time, Mulrooney wasn't so lucky. After dragging him into a nearby parking structure, they punched and kicked him repeatedly. Cyril Lutzky, alone among her Synanon peers, attempted to stop the assault, pulling off attackers and screaming, "This is not the type of place Synanon is."

She was, unfortunately, wrong about that and for her trouble she was dragged before a group of fellow residents and warned never to take a position against Synanon again. When police returned, Ed Siegel, a Synanon resident and mortgage banking executive, told them that Mulrooney threatened the group and that 65 Synanon residents would back his story.

A few hours later, another gang of Synanites surrounded a car in that same garage and convinced four young African-Americans to exit. After stripping them of wallets and jewelry, they, too, were beaten. Synanon residents had been ripped off before and the police had done nothing about it, one resident yelled, so they had to take the law into their own hands. The four were told to leave, but the mob pursued them anyway; three escaped, but 21-year-old Anthony Gene Rivers was recaptured and beaten unconscious.

No charges were ever brought in the assault; a few Synanon residents were arrested for the earlier attack and pleaded no contest. They didn't serve any jail time.

In Visalia that same day, young Eddie Stevens and his friend Roger Walker were so engrossed in conversation, they missed a turn and plowed their car into a Synanon fence. Again, a crowd of Synanon residents appeared, several armed. Suggestions rang out from the crowd: "make them eat dirt"; "drag them out, beat them and say they were hurt in the wreck"; "kill them." Stevens offered to pay for the fence and before anything else happened, police arrived and took the young men home.

February 21, 1977: Hoping to retrieve their car, Stevens and Walker returned in two cars, bringing along some friends from nearby Dinuba for protection. After again promising to pay for the damages, they were directed to the car, which had been moved onto Synanon property. Once inside, they were again accosted by a mob armed with ax handles, blackjacks and baseball bats. Stevens, in one car, managed to escape, but the others were savagely beaten. The victims scattered, trying to escape, but were pursued and the beatings continued. One boy was dragged out of a pay phone booth where he was asking his father to send help. His father could hear the beating. Nearby residents eventually got the bloody and bruised boys to the hospital.

Synanon tried unsuccessfully to file trespassing charges against the young men, who would forevermore be known in Synanon lore as the "Dinuba Punks." Since the victims were unable to positively identify any of their similar-looking, bald, overall-clad assailants, assault charges were dropped.

In his rants on The Wire, Dederich preached a "Don't-Tread-on-Me" mantra that infected the populace. A so-called Goon Squad formed to take action against outsiders, which became known as "Hey Rube" incidents; nearby residents were put under surveillance with infrared equipment; Synanon started patrolling the roads surrounding its facilities, trolling for trouble; and a growing number of Synanon residents carried guns and practiced shooting at dummies dressed in fatigues.

"We are our own worst enemy," wrote Art Warfield, a Synanon resident and reserve Marin County sheriff's deputy in a letter to Synanon officials after the Feb. 20 incidents. "Our own lives were in jeopardy by our own people by the flagrant use of firearms and our attacks upon enemies so violent as to endanger lives." The beatings of the Dinuba Punks, he continued, "went far beyond the pale." He also worried about weapons handed out "indiscriminately" to untrained people. "A loaded gun was pointed into a resident's face to demonstrate how a safety works," he wrote. "A loaded .45 automatic was aimed at a person's hand and the trigger pulled."

Warfield suggested training a National Guard-like unit of 28 men who would be held in reserve in case of emergencies. But Dederich already had his own, far more aggressive, plan—a select group of men trained in weapons and attack procedures that would provide security and engage in covert operations. Initially, the unit was called the "mini-Marines," but eventually became the "Imperial Marines."

One of the most eager applicants was Dr. Doug Robson, a resident for five years and past director of Synanon Health Services. Among his qualifications, Dr. Robson listed his participation in several Hey Rube confrontations, including the Tomales standoff. He boasted of having fired thousands of rounds of ammunition since he was five years old, of having gotten a vasectomy—sure to please Dederich. In his application, he said the urgently needed training sounded "fantastically fun," a return to the camaraderie of his high school football days.

March 9, 1977: At the first of his newly created "Think Tables," where a microphone was placed over his dining seat, Dederich pontificated over The Wire while he dined about his philosophies and the future direction of Synanon. As he spoke casually of beating up thieves beyond recognition, taking pictures to show others, and if necessary maybe killing a couple of them, tapes were made for replaying on The Wire and scribes took detailed notes, documenting the philosophy that Dederich thought would win him the Nobel Peace Prize.

March 20, 1977: The first 16 members of the elite military force were selected. Dr. Robson made the cut, along with the youngest member, 18-year-old Lance Kenton—the son of famed band leader Stan Kenton—and Joseph Musico—an addict known for violent tendencies—both of whom would eventually play a significant role in my life.

April 9, 1977: Kenton and Musico caught a 4-1/2 foot rattlesnake at Depot Flats, the remote training area near the Badger Mountain facility. Rattlesnake hunting was a popular pastime for the trainees. At one time, the group kept a dozen rattlers in a three-foot-deep pit. From this, they learned that the snakes would remain content in a confined space until someone reached in. Attracted to body heat, they would then strike. They also learned how to remove the snake's rattles for souvenirs.

May 19, 1977: Dr. Robson delivered a lecture on rattlesnake venom to the trainees. He described the variables involved in determining the toxicity of the venom (age and size of snake and how long since its last discharge) and what it did to the human body (pain, swelling, weakness, nausea and shock). Whether the victim survived, he said, depended upon his size, how quickly the venom was absorbed into the bloodstream and how soon anti-venom was injected.

July 2, 1977: Reacting to a series of random threats, Synanon imposed a Red Alert lockdown on all facilities and intensified security around Dederich. Patrols searched unsuccessfully for a man who drove by the Santa Monica building threatening to "get" Dederich if he didn't leave the state and another who threatened to "blow up the building" after absorbing a beating from a Synanon mob.

July 19, 1977: A band of Imperial Marines on motorcycles descended on the San Rafael Civic Center after a resident reported hearing Charles

Morin threaten to "burn Synanon down." The Marines dragged Morin into the bushes for a beating. Synanon security logs noted that the group had a "man-to-man talk with our friend at the Civic Center and taught him a lesson." When Imperial Marine field leader Carl Anderson described the event on The Wire, Dederich, realizing that the private radio signal could be picked up outside Synanon, told him he must be talking about a dream he had last night. After that, all beatings reported on The Wire started with: "I had a dream…"

July 21, 1977: The Marines continued to drill, playing war games and staging mock raids to test security. They also kept clamoring for guns, particularly magnums. Citing a recent Red Alert at Walker Creek in a letter to Anderson, Marine Allen Hubbard wrote that without guns, a "hostile and armed perpetrator" would slaughter security forces. Every property should have a gun locker, he advised.

July 26, 1977: The minutes of a Synanon board meeting illustrated the growing siege mentality permeating the organization: "We are going through a period of religious persecution and escalating violence. We must protect ourselves. And if necessary, take the law into our own hands."

August 2, 1977: Doug Robson was named head of Synanon's security forces after Dederich read a letter in which he boasted of "happily" supervising Red Alerts for 36 hours straight, of participating in hunts for people believed to have threatened Dederich's life and of three smaller confrontations with drunks "who we dealt with for abusing our home." He replaced Anderson, who fell into disfavor after his indiscretion on The Wire and the discovery that he had exaggerated his military experience. Synanon now had a security chief whose enthusiasm for aggressive action perfectly suited the tenor of the times.

September 5, 1977: At Think Table, Dederich defined Synanon's new religious posture: "To physically respond to all aggressors, to crack bones and deliver the message that if you mess with Synanon, you can be killed dead. Physically dead."

In that same speech, he also identified Synanon's biggest enemy. It wasn't "dingbats like the Dinuba Punks," but lawyers who wanted to take the group's money—the most evil, unscrupulous and greedy of which was, of course, me.

September 7, 1977: Upon hearing of an unauthorized mission into the Watts neighborhood in Los Angeles, Dr. Robson reprimanded the residents involved for not getting clearance from his department before acting. "Sending groups of Synanon people off property on missions which are physically dangerous and of questionable legality is extremely expensive and must be done when indicated using our very best equipment, thinking and personnel," he wrote. "We are very new in exercising our present aggressive posture. Many mistakes will be made in these activities, and some people are certain to get hurt. There is no excuse for making these mistakes or suffering any casualties with anything less than our best effort."

September 14, 1977: Robson was chastised for calling the police about an incident on the property. "I now understand," Robson wrote to Dederich, "gut level, that we are willing to handle essentially any incidents on our property, including ones calling for us to use premeditated deadly force, without calling the police."

November 1, 1977: Mike Garrett had finally had enough. Synanon had become "murderous" and his own father had become a "dangerous man," he said. So he left and went into hiding to avoid Synanon fanatics who hunted down and assaulted "splitees."

November 11, 1977: It started with a near accident, which likely resulted from a misunderstanding between two drivers. But then a Synanon resident cursed a local trucker, sparking a brief chase and a tense confrontation that ended without violence. A second road incident a day later bruised feelings on both sides and heightened tensions, but again resulted in no real damage. Once the initial anger had subsided, most people would have forgotten all about it and gone about their business. But to hyper-sensitive Synanon, the confrontations with Ron Eidson, a burly trucker and self-avowed redneck, were seen as another example of the harassment heaped on the organization by outsiders. Dederich was especially upset about the refusal of four Synanon residents to get out of the car when Eidson offered to fight all of them at once.

The two sides were on a collision course. Synanon started searching for Eidson, entering other properties with rifles drawn. A Synanon patrol, recognizing the car involved in the previous incidents, chased Doris Eidson home one day. Now, they knew where the Eidsons lived. Eidson called Synanon's Doug Robson, seeking to work things out, but the conversation deteriorated into shouting and threats.

"We intend to have these roads absolutely safe," Robson said. "We are a bunch of religious fanatics and we'll do whatever we have to do."

The next day, Dr. Robson called again, saying the situation could be resolved if Eidson would publicly apologize. When Eidson refused, Robson said he had his warning and then hung up. It was nearly midnight when Doris awakened a sleeping Eidson. Two vehicles were outside the house, their headlights shining inside. They could see four men, all with shaved heads, wearing bib overalls. "We're here to get our apology," one man shouted. Two more men emerged from behind the shed with sawed-off shotguns. Eidson and his 15-year-old son, Jeff, went outside with rifles and when Doris followed with a camera, a scuffle ensued. After one of the men got Jeff's rifle and pointed it at him, Eidson realized they were outnumbered and his family was in jeopardy. He surrendered, turned over his rifle and told Jeff to give up. "We're going to kill you," one man screamed. "And we're going to shoot every son-of-a-bitch in Badger." Another, more practical, man realized that the sheriff might arrive soon. "We don't have time to kill you but we're going to work you over good," he said. "We will be back to finish you and your family off if we have any more problems with you."

As Doris and his three children watched from inside the house, Eidson was brutally beaten and kicked and finally knocked unconscious by a gun butt to the head. Jeff could see the attack in larger-than-life, silhouetted shadows dancing on the trailer across from the house and could hear the sickening sounds of the blows landing on his father. When the assailants finally left, Eidson was taken to the Exeter Hospital, where he stayed for two days.

Eidson subsequently identified three of his attackers from photos, but the prosecution didn't go well. Synanon lawyers filed a barrage of motions to prolong the case and deplete the resources of the District Attorney's office. They sent look-alikes to make definitive identification of the suspects difficult. Eventually, charges were dropped against all but Dave Gilmour and the charge against him was reduced to misdemeanor assault. When Synanon lawyers won a change of venue motion, the case was dropped altogether.

The experience steeled Synanon's belief that it could get away with anything and so the harassment of Eidson and other local residents continued. They spied on ranchers with binoculars and occupied the Badger Inn, scaring off customers and forcing its closure. On any given night, the Eidsons could hear people on their property imitating chickens and coyotes, and see flashlights blinking in the distance. Once, he fired in the direction of some chicken sounds, which promptly stopped. "I've never shot at a bald-headed chicken before," he told Jeff.

December 9, 1977: Dr. Robson filed his security report for November, calling it the "Month of the Hunt," when eight people who had "stolen from Synanon" or "insulted or harassed Synanon people" had been tracked down across the country. Further, he reported, he was establishing a network of ex-residents in San Francisco, Tulare, Los Angeles, Detroit and New York to provide information against Synanon enemies. The word was getting out, he wrote, that "when you leave Synanon, where your life was saved, and you were supported beyond your means, you leave in debt. The debt can be paid back by various sorts of favors. People who do not acknowledge the debt or remain neutral when we are in need become our enemies and when we are annoyed it is not good to be our enemy."

December 26, 1977: After *Time* Magazine ran a negative article on Dederich's Changing Partners directive, calling the once respected drug rehab just another "kooky cult," Dederich was enraged. He had welcomed *Time*'s reporters and given them broad access to Synanon's facilities and people. He had fantasized about being named *Time*'s Man of the Year and that had now evaporated, along with his dream of winning the Nobel Peace Prize. On The Wire, he delivered an angry, paranoid rant, which became known as the "Time for a Battle Cry" speech. Synanon's livelihood was being threatened by "these filthy bastards," he said, including the "dirty, rotten, stinking punks from *Time* who came in here and enjoyed our hospitality. Synanon has within it—and this is not messianic nonsense—the plans to save the goddamn world. But almost every religion or movement or philosophy which has any chance of making any improvement at all in the human condition is smashed at the outset."

He vowed to destroy the people at *Time* and the ex-Synanon residents who were interviewed for the article. Now it was the time of the Holy War.

December 28, 1977: Dr. Robson submitted a belated Christmas wish list to his own personal Santa, Charles Dederich. He wanted Colt .45s, 12-gauge Remington police pump shotguns, .23-caliber Ruger mini-14 carbines with twenty-shot clips, Winchester rifles with long-range scopes and a year's supply of ammunition. The estimated cost: more than $50,000, which would later swell to more than $70,000. On New Year's Eve, Santa delivered his approval. But even that, apparently, wasn't enough, as the buying spree continued. It made for some unusual dinner chatter. One night, Trudy asked me what was new. "Nothing much," I replied. "The attorney general says Synanon's weapons purchase totaled $307,000, including armor-piercing bullets." (It was believed to be the then-largest purchase of weapons in California history.) What do you say after that, "and how was your day, dear?"

January 13, 1978: Just days after suing *Time* Magazine, the Synanon weapons stockpile started to arrive from a variety of gun dealers. Alarmed, the Bureau of Alcohol, Tobacco and Firearms declared that ex-felons weren't allowed to possess guns. Synanon replied that California had given it permits to use firearms in training a private police force, which was needed, in part, because of the frenzy whipped up by the *Time* article. During a subsequent interview with Connie Chung of CBS, Dederich denied any connection between the article and the arms escalation, although he mused that if the magazine was to send people to do Synanon harm, "we would do them harm first."

January 17, 1978: At the age of 17, Kim Meyers was sent to Synanon's Tomales Bay facility by his father, who was tired of dealing with his son's use of LSD and marijuana. Three years later, he escaped after fellow residents threatened to shave his head as punishment for refusing medical treatment for a dog bite. After three difficult years outside the group, he returned to a changed Synanon, steeped in paranoia and militarism. On this day, he sought a meeting with Dederich to air his observations about the group's changing direction. Instead, he was confronted by several of the founder's underlings, attempted to escape again and was seized for questioning. Unhappy with his answers, the interrogation turned into a brutal beating—multiple punches, kicks, ear-twisting and the breaking of his fingers, one-by-one. Afterwards, he was handcuffed to a chair for several hours while his captors conferred with Synanon attorneys David Benjamin and Phil Bourdette, who ordered him transported to San Francisco for further questioning. At the Golden Gate Bridge toll booth, Meyers flung the car door open and made a desperate dash for freedom. Afraid of drawing attention, his captors let him go. Sheriff's deputies questioned him and referred him to the San Francisco Police Department. Forced to take a bus there, he arrived, only to find Bourdette chatting amiably with police about the "misunderstanding." Despite Meyers' ravaged face, police didn't believe that anyone at Synanon, a group that "helped people," would commit such a brutal assault. They escorted him back to Tomales Bay the next day to retrieve his truck, but no charges were ever filed.

February 6, 1978: After two months at Synanon's Badger facility for treatment of a barbiturates problem, 30-year-old Michael Lee Franklin wanted out. So he started walking down Highway 245 towards Petaluma, his home. He was soon overtaken by a man and woman in a Synanon vehicle, whose persistent offers of a ride he resisted. They left, but returned in five minutes and demanded that he let them search his bags for items allegedly stolen from Synanon. "You shouldn't have anything, you shouldn't even have the shoes on your feet," the man said. "You are going to be lucky to get out of here with anything at all."

The confrontation soon turned violent. The man knocked Franklin down and kicked him repeatedly with his steel-toed boots: he punched him about a dozen times in the face. Only when Franklin jumped into a nearby creek did the pair stop and drive away—with most of his belongings.

At a nearby house, Franklin got assistance from rancher Tom Oberg, who drove him to a nearby bar, where they found five deputies. The deputies documented his injuries: numerous lacerations, abrasions and contusions about his face, head and hands, plus large abrasions on his legs and cuts on his hands; a large swelling above his right eye and blood on his face. His coat was torn and his clothes were coated with dirt and mud. The next day, he passed a polygraph test about the assault and deputies surveying the crime scene found evidence supporting his claims.

Afterwards, Det. Rick Logan tape recorded an interview with Franklin, during which he provided a detailed description of Synanon, its operations and its abusive and violent behavior. But Marin County Dep. Dist. Atty. Jay Powell refused to file charges against the Synanon pair who attacked Franklin, saying it appeared to him to have been an incident between "relatively equal matched individuals in mutual combat." He didn't investigate any of Franklin's claims that violence was now a Synanon philosophy trickling down the chain of command. He paid no attention to Franklin's tale of the training of the Imperial Marines and the weapons buildup. Det. Logan's tape was tucked away in a closed file, where it would remain even as the Marin County Grand Jury raised concerns about some of these same issues a month later.

March 14: 1978: In an interview with NBC, Dederich noted that "bombs could be thrown into odd places, into the homes of some of the clowns who occupy high places in the *Time* organization." He insisted he wouldn't instigate any such action, but couldn't prevent it, either. When reporter Jess Marlow commented that some at *Time* might consider the statement a "thinly veiled threat," Dederich said that was their problem. "I think it's kind of decent of me to warn them to be careful," he added.

March 20, 1978: Tom Cardineau, a Coram, N.Y., factory worker on his honeymoon, wanted to show his new bride Donna the Walker Creek facility, where he had kicked his heroin addiction. He had lived there for four years, amidst continual warnings that he would relapse if he left. But he eventually risked it when he saw Synanon drifting away from its original mission. While he knew Synanon didn't welcome splitees back, he didn't think there was any harm in driving by and pointing out the place.

But the Synanon he would soon encounter was engulfed in what it perceived as a "Holy War." Speakers on The Wire bombarded residents with a steady drumbeat about the organization's enemies, like a scene from George Orwell's *1984*. In this atmosphere, there was no such thing as a casual visit to Synanon.

As Cardineau drove past the property, a green Dodge jitney pulled behind his rented car with its horn blowing. When he stopped, a man Cardineau recognized as Phil Black ordered him to leave. "Wait a minute, didn't you used to live here?" Black asked as he got closer. Cardineau nodded. "You fucking splitee scum bag," Black snarled.

When Cardineau attempted to leave, the jitney pursued and was soon joined by others. They blocked his way and forced him to pull over. He was thrown to the ground and, after a half-hour of curses and threats that they would unleash an attack dog on him, he was handcuffed and taken to Synanon's Trade Center for interrogation. Which former Synanon members had he been in touch with in New York? Who knew he was coming to California? Who sent him to spy on Synanon? Was he employed by *Time* Magazine? Was he here to assassinate Chuck Dederich?

When he professed his innocence, he was called a liar and beaten, his chair finally toppling over backward from the barrage of blows. He was then taken to the Pole Barn, near the compound's entrance, tied to a pole and attacked again. Conscious, but bloodied and dazed, he was carried out, put in his car and told to warn everyone in New York to stay away. His wife instead drove straight to the police.

Felony charges of false imprisonment and battery against four participants in the Cardineau beating were eventually reduced to misdemeanors by Municipal Court Judge Gary W. Thomas, who ruled that Cardineau wasn't detained with violence and his subsequent medical treatment wasn't ongoing. The judge apparently didn't consider being thrown to the ground, handcuffed, tied to a pole, menaced by an attack dog and worked over by four men sufficient cause for a felony finding. After pleading guilty, the defendants were sentenced to probation and community service. To Synanon residents, the message was again clear: You could do a "caper," be a Synanon hero and receive little punishment. Two burly Synanon goons visited Cardineau in New York and warned him about the consequences of filing suit himself. He never did and refused to cooperate with any legal actions against Synanon.

September 4, 1978: During a game involving members of the board, Dederich groused about his followers' failure to take care of the "creeps" menacing Synanon. Specifically, he said he wanted attorney Paul Morantz and splitee Phil Ritter, who was trying to get his child out of Synanon, "taken care of."

September 21, 1978: A tired Phil Ritter arrived at his Berkeley home at about 5:30 p.m., thinking of nothing more than an evening of relaxation. The 34-year-old Greenpeace and anti-nuclear activist had lived for eight years at Synanon, serving as director of transportation. But 18 months earlier, he left, dismayed about the mass vasectomies mandated by Dederich, and urged police to investigate the group. If that wasn't enough to get him on Synanon's enemies list, he had just won custody of his three-year-old son from his ex-wife, who had remained at Synanon but had recently disappeared with the child. On The Wire, Dederich had recently stated that anyone who tried to take a child away from the Synanon school and a Synanon mother should be taught a lesson. Specifically, he said, someone should "break the knees" of one of these "assholes." These were odd words from someone who had previously separated most of Synanon's children from their mothers and paid no attention to his own when they were minors.

As Ritter headed towards his front door, he heard footsteps behind him. He briefly saw a man raising his arm, holding something. He remembers being struck repeatedly in the head and shouting for help before losing consciousness. Neighbors ran outside and chased the assailants away. One neighbor jumped in his car and pursued the red Toyota that sped away from the scene with two men inside, but eventually lost it. The license plate number he jotted down proved to be nonexistent.

At the hospital, Ritter could barely talk. The right side of his face was completely blackened; he developed meningitis and spiraled into a semi-comatose state. His family was told he might die. By the next day, he had rallied, but remained on the critical list. No one was ever prosecuted. Years later, former Synanon members named Imperial Marines Joe Musico and Allan Hubbard as the assailants. Ritter eventually recovered.

The Ritter attack shook me from my complacency. I already knew I was in danger, but this was different, this was an escalation. Had neighbors not chased the assailants away, Ritter would be dead. He almost died as it was. And I knew Synanon wanted me even more than they wanted him. After all, I had started Synanon's problems with the Raines case. I had become the principal protector of splitees. I had gotten children out, won a large judgment and instigated an inspection by the Department of Health. I had lobbied against a proposed state bill at the request of Barbara Boxer and Diane Feinstein, then on the Marin County Board of Supervisors, that would have shielded Synanon from any licensing requirements (it was defeated by a single vote). Most of all, I knew about Synanon's plans to attack its enemies using a specially trained team. Worse, they knew that I knew.

I told Bud Stone, the Berkeley homicide detective in charge of the Ritter investigation, there was no doubt Synanon was responsible for the assault and detailed other beatings. I told him of my conversation with former Synanon attorney Harold Benjamin, who heard through sources that Dederich had gone on The Wire to call for an attack on me and had broadcast my address. I asked Hal Marston, my attorney, to call Stanley Fleischman, a famed constitutional lawyer who had represented Synanon and tell him about my conversation with Benjamin. Fleischman, whose daughter was a Synanon member, supported the group but was no fanatic and would oppose violence. If he inquired about it, I calculated, Synanon's leaders would know that word of its plan was out and would hopefully drop it. But Dan Garrett responded to Fleischman with a "Fuck you." I also asked Dave Mitchell of the *Point Reyes Light*, who would eventually win a Pulitzer Prize for his coverage of Synanon, to investigate forever if anything happened to me that looked like an accident. He reported the threat against me to the Marin District Attorney, who, as usual, did nothing.

I bought a shotgun and told a reporter so Synanon would know I was armed. Whenever I left my home, my head was on a swivel, like Linda Blair in *The Exorcist*. I searched under my car each time before starting it, was careful crossing streets and thought of hiding my border collies, Tommy and Devon, but eventually decided against it, since their barking was my best early-warning system. The most difficult thing I had to do was prepare my mother for the worst. I told her that no matter what happened, I wouldn't have done it any other way.

Even Trudy, the woman I wanted to marry, didn't take the threat seriously. We had recently broken up—primarily over my obsession with the Synanon case. But we were still friendly and she called to tell me her son was going to do a report in school on the $300,000 judgment

I had won for the Raines family in September. I strongly advised against it and told her they shouldn't even talk about me. She thought I was exaggerating the threat, trying to whip up sympathy in an effort to win her back.

That hurt most of all. I couldn't get through to her and I knew they were coming. All I could do was wait.

Part 3: A Venomous Special Delivery

The Old Man took his seat at the center of the main table. A microphone dropped from the ceiling hung over his plate, just as it did at every meal. It was 6 a.m., time for Morning Court. As his deep and resonating bullfrog voice boomed out over The Wire to all the organization's facilities, permeating every room and hallway, his every word was preserved on tape for future replays. Calmly and deliberately, as if talking of minor building repairs or spring planting, he spoke of Synanon's enemies and how it should respond to aggression. Everyone must be prepared to go to jail, as he once had for them. The greatest threat, he said, were lawyers. But Synanon wouldn't play by their silly rules; they would play by Synanon's rules. It would be like a fighter "stepping into the ring expecting to follow the Marquis de Queensbury rules and then winds up with a bottle in his face or a chair leg shoved down his throat," he explained. "I'm quite willing to break some lawyer's legs and then tell him the next time I break your wife's legs; then I'm going to cut your kid's arm off; and try me, because this is only a sample... you son of a bitch. Like that. And that's the end of your lawyer. That's the end. And all of his friends. You see... It's a very satisfactory, humane way of transmitting information."

*   *   *   *   *   *

Terry Raines was about to fall into a giant Venus fly trap.

When Raines, a Santa Monica housewife suffering from depression and paranoia, was referred to Synanon by a nearby family planning clinic in 1977, she vaguely recalls someone warning her that if she went inside, she wouldn't come out. In her confused and fragile state, she went anyway.

She didn't know that the group was in the final stages of a startling transformation from drug-rehabilitation center to Big Brother-dominated cult, complete with budding Synanon cities and its own private military force—a transformation that paralleled its leader's descent into megalomania and madness. Charles Dederich had even named the group's evolutionary stages: Synanon I represented its drug rehab origins; Synanon II, its alternative-lifestyle commune stage and finally, Synanon III, its emergence as a self-proclaimed new religious order in 1974.

Inside, Raines was asked if she wanted help, if she would obey all rules without question. She was advised to always answer questions with yes sir and no ma'am. When she agreed, she was seized. Her waist-length hair was chopped off under protest. Her mumbled requests to notify her husband and arrange to have him picked up from work were ignored. She was dragged across the street to a Synanon-owned apartment building and locked up. The next morning, she was put to work chopping vegetables. By the third day, she was transported by bus to the group's Tomales Bay facility in Marin County and put up in a tent.

When she again asked to contact her husband, she was told he knew where she was and didn't want her. As the days passed and he didn't come to Marin County to get her, she came to believe that was true and that Synanon was now her home. She was never told her husband had showed up in Santa Monica, demanding her release.

*   *   *   *   *   *

Eleven-year-old Ben Mohagen, home from school, had a quick snack about 2 p.m. before going outside to ride his bicycle. He wondered why a green Plymouth driving down his street was going slower than he was. Then, it passed my house and sped up. As he played, the car circled the block five or six more times, lingering by my house each time. Alarmed, he ran inside to his mother. "Oh," his Mom said, "That's probably just the police checking Paul's house. He's been worried since winning some big court case." Reassured, Ben resumed his ride and didn't see the car again.

*   *   *   *   *   *

Ted Raines was informed by phone that his wife had joined Synanon and he should come pick up her keys. His attempts to speak to her, to have her examined by a doctor, were rebuffed. Terry had decided to "do something with her life," he was told. When he showed up with a friend, demanding her release, a group of Synanon residents forced them to leave.

He concluded correctly that his psychologically fragile wife was being brainwashed and desperately sought help to free her. But few people wanted to tangle with Synanon, which had a reputation for aggressive litigiousness and lately, for outright violence. The police told him his wife was an adult and had entered the facility voluntarily. His letters to the media and elected officials, all the way up to the President, didn't help, either. One day, he met a man who had once lived next door to me. "I know a lawyer that got a lot of Skid Row alcoholics out of nursing homes that were holding them against their will," he said. "He ought to be able to get your wife out of Synanon."

When he called, my mind dredged up a single memory, of my high school graduation party on a Santa Monica Beach. Quite drunk, I wandered close to an old National Guard building, but stopped when I heard loud screaming inside. "That's Synanon," a friend explained. "They cure drug addicts." *Good for them*, I thought. Still, the place scared me and I hustled away.

At first, I thought there might be an easy solution to Ted Raines' problem. Surely, Synanon must be licensed and I just needed to get the Health Department to investigate. But inexplicably, it wasn't and worse, wouldn't allow the department's inspectors on its property. The man at the agency spoke in hushed tones about the organization, as if fearing he would be overheard.

I convinced Synanon to at least let the couple talk on the phone, during which I repeatedly urged Ted to ask his wife if she wanted to come home. She was disoriented, but finally said yes. At that point, I grabbed the phone and demanded that she be brought back to Santa Monica and released. The Synanon woman I spoke with reluctantly agreed, if we would sign a form waiving legal liability for any injuries.

The next day, I got my first glimpse inside Synanon. It looked like an oversized thrift shop, filled with second-hand rugs, fixtures and chairs occupied by bald and bearded men wearing overalls. When Terry was finally produced, after a 2-1/2-hour wait, she had the blank stare of a zombie. She obviously had suffered some kind of psychotic break. As we had planned, Ted and a large friend we brought along for support, quickly ushered her out the door while I vamped, writing out a vague and meaningless waiver form. I kept glancing outside and when I got the signal that they were in the car, I flipped the Synanon woman the bird and hustled out. Yes, it was childish, but I was young and caught up in the moment. This appealed to all my white-knight-rescuing-the-fair-damsel fantasies.

I sued Synanon on the Raines' behalf for the kidnapping, false imprisonment and attempted brainwashing of Terry. The waiver form I penned meant nothing; it was coerced and we couldn't sign away Terry's rights, anyway. Besides, it didn't include any language releasing Synanon from liability for seizing her and holding her against her will. It only released them from liability for letting her go. The group was vulnerable and its legal department was furious. More important, Charles Dederich was furious. On The Wire, he bellowed: "Who is this guy Morantz...Why didn't someone break his legs?"

The legal challenges of the Raines case were daunting. As the police had noted, she was an adult and had entered Synanon voluntarily. A former Synanon member warned me Synanon's battalion of volunteer in-house lawyers could bury me in motions. Few attorneys had the resources to pursue a case that would take so much time away from other, more profitable litigation. Fortunately, the case was filed in Santa Monica Superior Court, which designated a single courtroom to hear all motions for all cases on Fridays—so Synanon couldn't clog up more than one day a week. I ordered my secretary to block out Friday mornings for the next three years.

"Is that so you can be available to respond to Synanon's motions?" the ex-Synanite asked.

"No," I replied, "that is so Synanon can be in court every Friday to respond to my motions."

And so the war began.

*   *   *   *   *   *

Edie Ditmars looked out her window, wondering who the dogs were barking at. She saw the 1972 green Plymouth parked in my driveway and the slender young blond man, dressed in sport coat and tie, striding purposefully towards my porch.

She remembered what I had told her about my concerns, about reporting anything unusual. She ran to her living room window for a better look, but lost sight of the man. She heard a plunking sound, like a mailbox lid closing. The young man returned to the car. She managed to jot down a few numbers from the license plate, but felt no urgency to report it. After all, the man looked clean-cut and respectable and people frequently dropped things off at my house when I was out.

From her perspective on the sidewalk, Meredith Bass saw the man put something in my mailbox. Meredith, who had recently celebrated her ninth birthday, went on playing.

*   *   *   *   *   *

Thomas Weather's daughter Jo Anne entered Synanon on April 24, 1977, when she was 19 years old. While she smoked marijuana and took valium prescribed by a doctor, she wasn't an addict by any legal definition. She just wanted to get away for a few days after a depressing breakup with her boyfriend. So she called the local "drug hotline" and asked for a rehab center, stressing that she didn't want a cult. The volunteer recommended Synanon. To insure her admittance to the facility, she lied and said she had a heroin problem, even though she had no needle marks. Nobody checked. She donated $29.85 and surrendered her driver's license.

When her parents were denied contact with their daughter, they negotiated a phone call through an attorney. But Synanon legal counsel Dan Garrett canceled it, determined to discourage anyone who had read about the Terry Raines case and dared to think they could get their relatives back, too. When Jay Grissum, Jo Anne's boyfriend, tried to see her, he was forced out by several men with guns. Come back in a year, he was told.

About the same time, Bob Manchester hired me to retrieve his nine-year-old daughter from Synanon. Beverly Manchester had taken their three kids into Synanon after winning custody following a divorce. Bob, whose drinking had contributed heavily to the divorce, was now sober, employed and remarried. His other two daughters were already out. Julie, 17, had been so rebellious and sassy, Synanon had consigned her to the Punk Squad, where she was struck and made to clean up pig feces with a carrot stick, among other punishments. It didn't change her attitude, so after several failed escape attempts, she was released. The last thing Synanon needed was an unruly malcontent riling up others. The other daughter, Karen, escaped after a visit by hiding under a blanket in Bob's car. Linda, age 9, remained in Synanon with her mother, who had married a fellow resident, a former *L.A. Times* reporter who was now Synanon's publicist.

Julie Manchester signed a declaration that would eventually trigger state investigations. Synanon's idea of education, she stated, was limited to sermons about the evils of the outside world. If she left, she was told, she would be raped by a drug abuser; her only salvation was Synanon and she should never leave. Within Synanon, she stated, parents and children were separated. Julie said she rarely saw her mother, who wouldn't acknowledge her when they passed in the compound.

Julie also told of seeing three boys beaten for trying to escape. When, at age 13, she tried to escape with two other girls, she was returned by police and subjected to days of punishment. She had to eat standing up and was allowed to sleep only three hours a night. Other children were summoned to see her punched in the stomach and slammed against a wall, an example for others who might yearn for freedom. After another failed escape, she stated she was repeatedly punched in the face.

$$* \quad * \quad * \quad * \quad * \quad *$$

I was in a rush. The first game of the World Series between the Dodgers and Yankees was about to begin and I was eager to forget my troubles and relax in front of the TV with the shotgun by my side. That little accessory was purchased a few weeks earlier in my first visit to a gun shop. I didn't really know what I wanted, so I told the proprietor what I needed: "Something that could stop three to five guys if they crashed through my door."

I entered my small house about 5:30 p.m., petting my border collies, Tommy and Devon. As was their habit, they jumped up at me before dashing out the door to play. As I put my Synanon evidence books on the kitchen counter, I saw something dark and elongated through the grill of my mail chute. It seemed to fill the space, but I really couldn't see that well because the inside of the box was dark. Compounding the problem, I stubbornly refused to wear my ill-fitting contact lenses and the glasses I had finally ordered after overcoming years of vanity hadn't arrived yet.

I thought maybe someone had found a scarf nearby and stuffed it into the nearest mail chute. Or maybe it was an odd-shaped package. I've always been amazed that I never considered the possibility of a bomb.

As I headed back towards my room I lifted the grill with my right hand and nonchalantly grabbed the mystery object with my left.

It wasn't a scarf.

*   *   *   *   *   *

Like Terry Raines, Jo Anne Weathers had voluntarily committed herself to Synanon. Unlike Terry, she didn't suffer from mental disabilities. That meant winning her release would be even more difficult. I briefly considered seeking a conservatorship with the father as her guardian. But in Katz vs. Superior Court, a court-ordered conservatorship that removed adult Moonies from the Unification Church to free them from brainwashing was overturned by the appellate court, which ruled that conservatorships were only appropriate for people who couldn't care for themselves or presented a danger to themselves or others.

Bob Manchester's problem was more complex because of the divorce and custody issues, but at least it involved a minor, subject to the court's determination of the child's best interest. Combining them, I thought, might strengthen Weathers' case. But I feared that Synanon would program Jo Anne and Linda to denounce their parents in court and demand to stay. And if Synanon's legal department represented Beverly Manchester, her ex-husband didn't have the funds for a prolonged custody battle.

So I convinced the family law commissioner in Santa Monica, who didn't like Synanon, to issue warrants ordering the organization to produce both in court to verify their safety, which meant the authorities would take custody of them and bring them to court. Hopefully, away from Synanon, I could provide them with enough evidence of Synanon's violent nature and their parents' continuing love to convince them to request release. Once home, they could be deprogrammed if necessary.

But Synanon officials ignored the warrants, sneaking the two out the back door when sheriffs came to gather them. They promised to deliver them to the court, but I knew that meant my chance to break the group's influence over them was gone. Indeed, when they appeared, they had been carefully prepared by Synanon's attorneys. They were surrounded and comforted by fellow Synanon residents and made to believe that their ordeal made them special. Jo Anne was told that the purpose of the court proceeding was to put her in jail.

When Synanon refused to stipulate to the family law commissioner's authority, the cases had to be transferred to Judge Robert Feinstein, who quickly dismissed them. Jo Anne, he ruled, was an adult and appeared in court unharmed and expressing a desire to stay in Synanon. I asked to cross-examine her; if I could prove that Synanon had lied to her in just one instance, I thought the programming would unravel and she would request a release. Judge Feinstein said no. As to Linda, the court ruled she was unharmed and the issue of custody should be heard by the court that heard the divorce case.

*   *   *   *   *   *

It lashed out, too quickly for me to react. I could see its mouth open, its fangs sink deeply into my wrist. I screamed, let go and watched in horror as more than four feet of snake dropped to the floor and recoiled, poised to strike again. I saw the v-shaped head and knew it was a rattlesnake. I quickly glanced at my wrist, leery of taking my eyes off my foe, but somehow hoping beyond hope that what I had felt wasn't real. I saw the marks. Those bastards, I thought. They had really done it.

I felt like the gin rummy player who discards the wrong card and wants a do-over. I wanted another chance to be more careful. It's not as if I didn't know something like this was possible. I had received plenty of warnings. That's why I bought the shotgun. That's why I always checked underneath my car before cranking the ignition. My dogs had left scratch marks on the grill; why didn't I heed the warning? Why wasn't I wearing my contacts? How could I be this stupid?

In the midst of my self-reproach, I realized my scream had brought the dogs running—straight at the snake coiled between me and the open door. If I didn't act quickly, the border collies, who were like my children, would be bitten. I had to risk it. Inching slowly around the snake, I pushed the door shut just before Tommy and Devon reached it.

*   *   *   *   *   *

At first it seemed my efforts had only made things worse. But sometimes things work out in unexpected ways.

As a reward for her loyalty, Jo Anne Weathers was given a position in the president's office in Santa Monica. In her new post, she saw another side to the organization. She heard attorney David Benjamin report on The Wire that they would get rid of attorneys seeking to harm Synanon and I was to be the first. He described me as a hunched-over old man who resembled a rat. When a man asked to leave, she witnessed a gang of residents jump him and, in her words, "beat him to a pulp." At a general meeting, 16 people were selected randomly and beaten because some money was missing. Over The Wire, she could hear Dederich's cries to "break their legs."

She was also disturbed by the pain she saw on her mother's face that day in court and upset that Synanon never told her that her mother had called. She started questioning Synanon doctrine. Who said no one could make it in the outside world? Why were all males required to get vasectomies? Finally, late at night on October 1, 1977, while in the Marin facility, she sneaked out a window, crept through bushes to the highway, hitchhiked to Point Reyes and called home. She became a compelling witness for me.

*　　*　　*　　*　　*　　*

I knew I had to remain calm, to slow the spread of the venom through my bloodstream. Ice would help, I remembered from my childhood study of reptiles. But first, I had to insure that nobody would wander in before I could get someone out to capture the snake. I unlocked the sliding door in the living room so someone could get in and slipped out the kitchen door, locking it and the front door so no kids could enter. That's when I lost it. "Call the police, an ambulance," I shouted as I ran in the general direction of Edie Ditmar's house. I don't remember it, but I'm told I rammed her door with my shoulder hard enough to knock it off its hinges. "I have been bitten by a rattlesnake," I wailed. "Synanon got me."

Fortunately for me, Irv Moskowitz, an electronics supervisor in Caltech's chemistry department, was late for Yom Kippur services. Irv, who had just completed the snakebite portion of a CPR course, was tying his shoes when his mother said someone was yelling for his life. When he spotted the bite marks on my wrist, he feared I would suffer brain damage or worse if the venom reached my brain. With one hand—and in spite of my delirious resistance—he dragged me towards Edie's driveway, while ripping his shirt for a tourniquet.

Buckets of ice were carried from neighboring homes and emptied on my body. Moskowitz cut my wrist with a knife and a jacket was thrown over me.

*   *   *   *   *   *

When Dederich ordered that Beverly Manchester and her Synanon mate split up and take new partners, he agreed; she didn't. Instead, she took Linda and left. As usual, the brainwashing wore off in about 90 days and Beverly eventually went on TV and spoke out against Synanon, with her daughter in hand.

But I was still playing defense; I wanted to play offense, to let Synanon know they couldn't intimidate me, as they had other attorneys. I also wanted a forum for the horrific tales of violence, brainwashing and child abuse I was gathering, stories that might change the apple-pie image generated by Synanon's publicity machine. I believed the public needed to know what was going on before they turned over relatives or cash. I called Narda Zacchino, who had covered the nursing home case and told her that this, potentially, was bigger. She read the declarations I filed in support of the two motions in the court file and wrote a story about Synanon's violence and abuse. It was picked up by the *Associated Press* and sped across the country as if carried by Paul Revere.

*   *   *   *   *   *

Lying on the ground, another frightening thought struck me. Could this be the day, as in The Godfather, when Synanon takes care of all its enemies? "Call Narda Zacchino," I said. "Warn her. She could be next."

I could hear the sirens. The nearest fire station was less than two miles away, yet another piece of good fortune. I asked the paramedics, Dale Schulz and Gary Smith, if I was going to die. I contemplated seeing my father and my childhood dogs in heaven. But they assured me I would make it. The shock must have been wearing off, because I was starting to feel pain. If I concentrated hard, I thought, maybe it would go away. It didn't. So I concentrated hard on an image of Olivia Newton-John, my big celebrity crush, who I had finally met the prior Thursday. It had been going well—she liked the Jan and Dean movie—until my client, who had invited me, told her I had wanted to meet her for nearly three years. I could see the "stalker" flash in her eyes and retreated. My arm still throbbed. I pleaded with the paramedics to keep talking to me, to distract me from my pain and my fears. That worked the best. "Where was the snake?" Schulz asked. He looked shocked when I told him. "It was attempted murder," I said. "Synanon did it."

*   *   *   *   *   *

The Synanon story was now out. The California Department of Health and a Marin County grand jury launched inquiries. I was invited to testify before the grand jury and I brought along former members. The panel issued a scathing report about Synanon's violence, its hoarding of weapons, its operation of an unlicensed medical clinic and the dangerously aggressive and defiant state of mind that seemed to permeate the organization. It recommended action by local and state agencies.

But the report didn't spark much action by the powers-that-be in Marin, especially Sheriff Louis Montanos, who was close friends with Dederich and Garrett. Synanon supported Montanos' election campaign and he had reciprocated by issuing both permits to carry concealed weapons. He employed two Synanon goons as part-time deputy sheriffs. He denounced the report and refused to follow its recommendations.

The refusal prompted Dave Mitchell, the young publisher of the tiny *Point Reyes Light* weekly newspaper, to launch his investigation into Synanon. Suddenly, I didn't feel so alone. I subscribed to the paper.

*   *   *   *   *   *

At the emergency room, my pain was peaking and I begged for pain and anti-venom medication. By now, my hand was grotesquely swollen and blistered and the muscles in my arm trembled. It felt like my hand was in a vise, with some sadist cranking it tighter, relaxing, and then happily squeezing it again.

But doctors were cautious. Before I could get the needed medications, they had to test for allergies, they had to be sure it was a rattlesnake that bit me. Was I sure? I combed through my memory. I saw the head, the recoil. It was a rattlesnake. But I suddenly felt some doubt. No rattle. Why didn't I hear a rattle? I later learned that the men who delivered the snake turned it into a silent assassin by removing its rattles.

*   *   *   *   *   *

In May of 1978 I received a phone call from the bravest woman I have ever known. Ernestine White was a tough-as-nails black grandmother who, in the middle of a Detroit ghetto, built White Records, a music store cited in the Congressional Record as a shining example of female entrepreneurship.

But her daughter, Rita, had entered Synanon in 1972 to be with her drug addict husband, Otis Butler. She died of cancer there a year later. Her husband eventually left, abandoning their three children because he didn't feel capable of raising them. Ms. White spent hundreds of thousands of dollars on legal fees fighting Synanon for custody and visitation rights. She finally won the latter and regularly flew in from Detroit to spend time with her grandchildren. But as the organization started to change, she was told she could no longer take the children off Synanon grounds, no matter what the court ordered. They would consider in-house visits, she was told.

I agreed with her fear for her grandchildren's future. Jay, then 17, was eligible for the Imperial Marines. At 16, Neidra could be mated with a stranger. Joey was 15 and reportedly wanted out.

But I was pessimistic about our chances. I knew that each of the children was old enough to be emancipated—declared adults—and thus allowed to make their own decisions. I assumed from past experience that if Ms. White tried to get custody, Synanon would program the children to testify that they hated her. I believed I could show that the children were living in a dangerous environment by pointing out the pile of money Dederich reportedly had spent to provide his followers with more weapons than local law enforcement. Perhaps they were only trying to scare people, but it sure looked like Synanon was preparing for war. Why else would they be playing war games and staging mock invasions on various facilities? Why else would they be patrolling the roads near their facilities and assaulting anyone who got too close?

But I also knew they would counter with tales of vandals and attacks that required some form of protection; I feared it might be enough to convince the court to ignore what was becoming a frightening reality.

Fortunately, we got a big break. Barbara Podesta, Ms. White's other daughter, decided to peek in Joey's backpack while on a visit with her mother. While Ms. White was out with the kids, she copied the startling school essay she found there. In it, Joey called Charles Dederich a great man who everyone had to obey. He wrote that Synanon was a new religion and that everyone would have to learn Syndo—Synanon's own brand of martial arts—to prepare for a holy war against its enemies. He also described how Synanon members were ordered to switch mates by Dederich and how Ben Parks, who ironically had worked at White Records as a teenager, and his long-time mate Dottie, were dumped into a ditch at gunpoint when they refused.

Joey's grade was an A-plus.

There wasn't a judge alive, I was convinced, who wouldn't put the kids on the first plane heading east after reading Joey's essay.

*   *   *   *   *   *

That night, I was transferred to USC-County General, some 25 miles away, which was known for its expertise with snake bites. Dr. Josephine Bufalino, trying to lighten the mood, laughed as she asked how this could have happened to a grown man. She stopped laughing after I told her and she spotted the police guard forming around my room. A nurse explained that the anti-venom I was receiving—11 vials worth—was made by injecting a horse with snake venom, then harvesting its antibodies. "That explains," I said drowsily, "my sudden craving for hay," prompting a friend to smile and say that proved I was okay.

I asked the police to contact Trudy and prayed she would come. Our breakup was still an open wound for me. By now, it was hard to refute her contention that I was too obsessed with Synanon. At least she now knew I wasn't crying wolf about Synanon's intentions towards me. When she arrived, she lifted the bed sheet and saw the giant blood bubble perched on my arm. "I didn't believe you," she said, apologetically. The doctors chased everyone out, but she refused to leave. "He's so alone," she said, planting herself in a chair next to my bed. I closed my eyes.

I awoke to a different world. She was still in the chair and the fear I had been living with for so long was gone. It had finally happened and I had survived.

*   *   *   *   *   *

We knew it would strengthen our case if we could convince Otis Butler to assign custody to Ms. White. Would he do the right thing? Again, Synanon helped us out, dispatching two Imperial Marines, Lance Kenton and Allan Hubbard, to deliver a heavy-handed demand for more money from Butler for the care of his children. Butler, a religious man, felt physically intimidated and prayed for the

Lord to give him a sign. Our custody papers arrived at the right time and he agreed.

Still, if we served Synanon with the custody papers, I was sure they would hustle the teens out the back door and seek emancipation. I called Lt. Art Disterheft, the undersheriff of the Marin County Sheriff's Department, who I knew was a straight shooter who had risked his job by secretly supplying information to the *Point Reyes Light*. He said if we came to Marin County for help, his boss, Sheriff Montanos, would tip off Dederich.

So I hatched a plan. Ms. White would ask very nicely if she could see her grandchildren at Synanon's San Francisco facility if she promised she wouldn't take them out of the building. Synanon agreed. Lt. Disterheft had told me the block-long urban building, donated by the state, could be more easily surrounded than the sprawling, rural Marin compound.

So on a Friday morning in June of 1978, Ms. White arrived in San Francisco. I had been preparing the police, detailing Synanon's history of violence and the group's supply of weapons, which might surpass their own. We put another attorney's name on the custody order, to avoid any emotional reaction by a Synanon representative upon realizing my involvement. The police instructed Ms. White to present the order and demand custody of the children. The police would only act if they said no—which they did. After she retreated outside, police officers poured out of 11 cars and trained their guns and rifles on the surrounded building. Another cadre of officers stormed inside. Synanon handed over Jay and Neidra to Ms. White and agreed to put Joey on an airplane to Detroit after officers threatened to send a force to Visalia to retrieve him. When news arrived that he had boarded the plane, we broke out the champagne.

But Synanon didn't give up. Members contacted the children while Ms. White was at work, promising them legal aid to file for emancipation and instructing them to harass Ms. White by calling Australia and leaving her telephone off the hook.

Ms. White countered by bringing in Ted Patrick, who kidnapped and deprogrammed more than 1,000 cult victims in his career, sparking the creation of a cottage industry of cult rescuers. Many lives may have been saved by Patrick and others, but kidnapping is still illegal and the sometimes brutal techniques used by deprogrammers could be as wrong-headed as those used by cults. Patrick was arrested many times for kidnapping, but juries sympathized and usually set him free, reasoning that he was preventing a greater crime. Beset by some guilty verdicts and multiple suits filed by cults, Patrick eventually quit the business and now lives quietly in retirement. I was never comfortable with kidnappers and never used their services, but many despairing parents felt there weren't any other options.

*   *   *   *   *   *

The attack on me was Synanon's Pearl Harbor. It finally awakened the sleeping giant Dederich feared most—the Los Angeles County District Attorney. The State Attorney General and U.S. Department of Justice would also later wade into the battle. Synanon was doomed. Still, the legal war would rage on for another decade.

Thanks to information from splitees, police quickly identified two young Imperial Marines as suspects in the snake attack—Lance Kenton and Joseph Musico. Kenton, son of famed band leader Stan Kenton, was an expert in rattlesnakes, often catching them near the Badger facility. Musico was a former Vietnam veteran who had bragged of wearing a necklace made of severed ears. He had come to Synanon as an alternative to prison for a drug conviction. In Synanon he was able to live a virtuous life until Dederich, knowing of his violent history, tapped him for his Marines.

Kenton and Musico pleaded no contest to charges of assault and conspiracy to commit murder. They were sentenced to one year in prison and ordered to sever ties with Synanon. I had recommended the relatively light sentence because I couldn't shake the feeling that people whose release I engineered—and who later became friends— might otherwise have drawn the fateful assignment. I fervently believed that most of the people at Synanon were victims of brainwashing and not inherently evil. Kenton had been dropped there at age 11 and at 18 made the youngest member of the Imperial Marines; Musico had become addicted to drugs during the Vietnam War. They were ripe targets for Dederich's version of coercive persuasion.

Since his release, Kenton has lived a relatively normal life, or as normal as could be expected for someone who works for Charlie Sheen. Musico, however, returned to his drug dealing ways and died in 2000 after being hurled off a building by a rival dealer.

In the summer of 1978, a warrant was issued for Dederich's arrest in Washington, D.C., for striking a photographer. Dederich had purchased a building there in hopes of setting up an embassy to the White House. But he didn't stay long, fleeing to Europe, where his 22 years of sobriety ended. Witnesses said that's when he gave the orders for the hits on Ritter and me. He eventually returned to Lake Havasu, Ariz., where police found him in a drunken stupor and arrested him for plotting to have me killed. Police found Think Table summaries there detailing the use of the Imperial Marines to attack enemies.

Dederich eventually pleaded no contest to the charge of conspiracy to murder and got probation by agreeing to step down as chairman of Synanon and cease any efforts to participate in its operations. Court-appointed doctors said he was too ill to survive in jail. The district attorney, and also my friend, asked for my approval of the sentence. I couldn't bring myself to push for what amounted to a death sentence, so I did. Dederich lived a secluded life, with only his selected wife for company, until his death in 1997.

In the months that followed the attack, Trudy and I reunited, which in my mind made it all worthwhile. But it didn't last. One day, we were sitting at home watching TV, like any normal family with three deputy sheriffs standing guard, when a local news show played excerpts from a seized Synanon tape. There was Dederich, ranting about killing lawyers then going after their wives and children. I looked at the frozen expression on her face and knew it was over. Trudy wanted love and companionship and to enjoy life with her family. She couldn't handle the constant stress, the threats and my obsession with these long-running cases. She feared for her kids. I understood. It would be many years before I felt relatively safe again. How could I ask her to share my life? Why should she?

When she later married someone else, it felt like I cried forever. But I knew it was the right decision for her. Hell, even the lawyers I worked with didn't want to share my life. They told me I had to drop these kinds of cases or quit.

So I quit. I set up an office in my home and did what I do best: got back to work. Before long, a string of cult cases queued up at my door, begging for my attention.

*   *   *   *   *   *

Epilogue:

Hearing I was ill, Trudy contacted me several years ago. While happily married and living the life she wanted, she still thought of me and could not forget the ordeal we shared. It still haunted her.

The call stirred feelings I thought I had put to rest long ago. But any lingering doubts I might have harbored about the wisdom of her decision to distance herself from me and my life vanished some time later when I read about Tsutsumi Sakamoto and his family.

Sakamoto was my Japanese doppelganger, considered the leading anti-cult lawyer in his country after successfully suing the Unification Church. In 1989, he and his family disappeared while he was in the midst of battling Aum Shinrikyo, a cult obsessed with visions of the apocalypse.

For six years, the fate of the Sakamoto family remained a mystery. Then, in the wake of Aum Shinrikyo's deadly sarin nerve gas attack on a Tokyo subway, which killed 12 and injured thousands, members of the cult rounded up by police confessed to murdering the family and led police to the bodies.

The details of the deaths were grisly. During a home invasion, Tsutsumi was bludgeoned with a hammer; his wife was beaten. The entire family, including their infant son, were injected with potassium chloride. When the injection failed to kill Tsutsumi, he was strangled. Their teeth were smashed to frustrate identification, bed sheets were burned and the tools used in the murder were tossed into the ocean. The bodies were placed in metal drums and hidden in three separate rural areas, hoping to fool police into thinking the murders weren't linked.

The cult's leader, Shoko Asahara, was convicted of ordering the subway attack in 2004 and, as of this writing, still awaits execution.

The brutal and senseless murder of the Sakamoto family stirred up many dark memories for me. In the years following the rattlesnake attack, I had naively believed that I was safe from cult threats. Who would be foolish enough to take a run at me now and reap the media whirlwind that was sure to follow? It was a rational conclusion. But you can't expect rational acts from sociopaths; the brutal deaths of the Sakamoto family served as vivid testaments to that chilling fact.

I realized now Trudy and I would never have escaped completely from that paralyzing cloud of fear. After all these years of remorse, I was grateful that she and her kids were out of harm's way and finally resigned myself to their loss. If one of her kids had reached for the mail that day, I don't think I would have ever recovered from the guilt.

Over the years, I had shrouded myself in the delusion of safety. But deep down, I don't think that fear ever went away. It was like a dormant virus, laying in wait for something to awaken it.

It didn't take much.

A full ten years after the rattlesnake bite, I spotted a car parked in front of my house. Four men wearing tuxedoes were opening music cases and pulling out what I swore were automatic weapons. The old panic seized me instantly. I had run scenarios like this a thousand times in my head. My plan had always been to vault over my back fence, then the neighbors' fence and so on until safe.

But that was a plan built on youth and vigor. My fence-vaulting days were well behind me. Instead, I decided to rush down the slope of my front yard, catch them by surprise, somehow capture a weapon and defend myself.

Bad plan; I know.

Anyway, I was halfway down the lawn in my Charge-of-the-Light-Brigade moment when I recognized that the music cases were just that and the weapons were guitars and violins. It was a mariachi band scheduled to play at a Cinco de Mayo party down the block.

So much for heroics.

Part 4: A Date with the Devil

"Please, Mr. Dederich. Please answer the question. This is a deposition. The law requires that you answer... you've been convicted already... you have no Fifth Amendment protection."

But he just sat there smugly, arms folded, acting as if the rules didn't apply to him. He was glaring at me, as were the shaved-head zealots in white t-shirts and blue overalls that surrounded him. I broke into a nervous sweat. "If you don't answer," I said quietly, almost whispering, "I will have no choice but to ask the court to hold you in contempt." The perceived threat activated the zealots like some zombie horde. They left his side, crossed the room and formed a circle around me, edging closer and closer, until I could barely see Dederich. I was shrinking; I had to get away...

My eyes flipped open, my foggy brain trying to process the incessant sound intruding on my fitful sleep. Finally comprehending, I picked up the phone and blearily acknowledged the Holiday Inn operator's wake-up call.

It was only a nightmare, but the realization didn't provide any solace. After all, in a couple of hours, I would be facing the real thing.

It was Nov. 10, 1981, and I was at the Holiday Inn in Visalia, Calif., about to face my bête noir, Charles Dederich. The Old Man. Big Daddy. The ruler of the sprawling Synanon kingdom. The man who sent two men and a snake to kill me.

How many victims of attempted murder ever get to interrogate the person who ordered their death? I was filled with a witch's brew of feelings: apprehension, excitement, curiosity and dread. For four years he had been tramping through my brain like some raging Nazi storm trooper. I listened to so many of his recorded rants, I knew how he thought. Sometimes, while stuck in Los Angeles traffic, I could hear his deep, rumbling voice telling me what to do. Had I, too, been stuck in his mind all these years? When the preliminary hearing in the murder conspiracy case began in 1979, he watched me testify for days on end, but who could tell what he was thinking, sitting stonily in his wheelchair, hidden behind dark glasses? He had heard my story; now I was here to get his.

To be sure, the war between us was now, finally, over. It ended in 1980, when Dederich and two of his Imperial Marines pleaded no contest to charges of attempted murder. With the intense public scrutiny the rattlesnake attack had brought on cults, it would be sheer madness for anyone to take a run at me now. After living in fear for years, I no longer needed to keep a shotgun by my side; I no longer needed police protection.

There were small, but revealing gestures of this new detente. At a court hearing, Miriam, who had been paired with Synanon attorney Phil Bourdette as part of Dederich's mate-swapping initiative, gave me $10 for parking when I discovered my wallet was empty. At Dederich's sentencing, I made it a point to sit between his wife and daughter, my way of announcing a ceasefire. Afterwards, I volunteered to lead the press in one direction, so they could escape in another. I know what you're thinking. The man wanted me dead. Why did I feel compelled to help him? It's hard to explain. Even though we had never formally met, a powerful, if creepy, bond now linked us inextricably, whether I liked it or not. For some twisted reason, I now saw the world through the prism of Dederich's madness. It wasn't a pretty sight and for a long time, it didn't make me the most convivial cocktail party guest.

The prospect of now being face-to-face with him was unnerving. I felt like Clarice Starling, the young FBI agent in *The Silence of the Lambs*, facing Hannibal Lecter for the first time. What if his entourage was packing? I knew Synanon routinely armed its security force. I had been offered a gun for this meeting, but declined. I wasn't looking for trouble. If they were armed, I would demand they remove the guns, like some sheriff in an old western facing down a gang of desperados. If they refused, I would adjourn the deposition and seek a court order compelling them to do so.

I showered and dressed, then followed the industrial-grade carpeting down the hallway to the motel's utilitarian conference room, walking slowly as if to put off the inevitable. I hadn't slept much, but that was offset by the adrenaline surging through me. The court reporter was setting up at a plain table more suited for a poker game with friends than an august legal proceeding. I handed her two legal documents identifying the formal reason for this gathering—the last two civil cases I had against Synanon.

One involved Dan and Marion Ross, who had surrendered most of their life's savings to live at Synanon forever. But when they resisted increasing their payments and refused to split up and take new partners, defying Dederich's edict, they were literally thrown out on the street. They asked for their money back; Synanon called the payment a donation and refused.

The other case involved Ron Eidson, the rancher who was savagely beaten in front of his wife and four children by a gang of armed men with shaved heads and overalls after refusing a demand by Synanon official Doug Robson that he apologize for a series of tense road confrontations with some of its members.

The local prosecutor, fearing Synanon reprisals, dawdled in making a criminal case in the assault and eventually let it drop. Because there wasn't a single attorney in the area with the guts to file a civil case against the well-armed and angry organization, the one-year statute of limitations for personal injury cases expired in November of 1978. Two years later, Eidson was still trying to find some way to sue Synanon. He called a Los Angeles attorney, who in turn called me. It was just after the criminal case was over; I was recuperating, but I needed this case, if, for nothing else, to prove to Synanon the snake hadn't intimidated me. And this case needed to be heard, both for the Eidsons and for the region. Both had been terrorized long enough.

I bounced up to Visalia for a crucial hearing in a tiny, eight-seat commuter jet, popping seasickness pills all the way. Synanon had filed a motion to dismiss, citing the statute of limitations. My clients, I contended, were the victims not only of Synanon's acts of terrorism, but of the cowardice of law enforcement and the legal bar in Tulare County. Having intimidated local prosecutors and attorneys into inaction, I argued, Synanon couldn't now hide behind the statute of limitations. "There's a new sheriff in town and I am here to finally bring justice to the Eidson family," I proclaimed, in a show of bravado. The judge smiled; I don't know if he bought my legal argument, my chutzpah, or was just glad someone had finally shown up to fight the good fight, but he denied Synanon's motion to dismiss.

And so I bought a big bottle of seasickness pills and for the next year flew often in that eight-seat bounce house for hearings and meetings, always staying at this Holiday Inn—a local hot spot because it had a music lounge, which says it all about Visalia. I made some friends there—even a girlfriend for a time—and they threw parties for me whenever I came up.

All those trips, the years of litigation and fear, the months of recuperation, the hearings and all the time spent poring over a mountain of Synanon documents had led me to this moment.

I sat down, pulled out a yellow legal pad and a pen—lawyers' tools before the invention of laptops—spread out outlines and key documents so they were readily available and stacked four evidence books on my right. I was as ready as I could be. I pondered my strategy. What did I hope to accomplish here? Much of what I needed to win my cases had already been revealed in depositions from related cases or in the documents discovered at Synanon.

But I wanted so much more than that. After all this time, I wanted to make sense of it all. I wanted to take the measure of this man who had been my obsession for so long, who had cost me the love of my life and nearly, my life. I wanted to understand what had happened at Synanon, a beautiful dream that had spiraled into chaos and brought hurt to so many. Why? How had it come to this?

*   *   *   *   *   *

A door opened far to my left. Charles Dederich hobbled in, leaning on a cane. He looked so frail, not at all like the man on those recordings with the booming, authoritative voice. At least he's out of the wheelchair and sober, I thought. He was accompanied by Bourdette and Gary Gibeaut of Shields and Smith, a defense firm hired by Farmers, Synanon's general liability carrier. But there was no entourage, no bald zealots, and thankfully, no guns. It shocked me at first, then I realized the Old Man wouldn't want his disciples to see him forced to answer my questions.

So we began, in an eerily quiet room thick with tension. As I explained the ground rules of the deposition, Dederich interrupted. "I might state for the record," he said, "that the series of massive strokes a couple of years ago left my memory completely unreliable. Some things I can remember with great clarity, some I can't."

It might have been a ploy to avoid answering uncomfortable questions. Certainly, as we proceeded, Bourdette frequently objected, shutting off avenues of inquiry. But I felt I knew the man. He had always been shockingly candid with the press. He was proud of all he'd done, no matter how the rest of the world viewed it. I believed that he wanted to answer my questions.

Eventually, he couldn't help himself, revealing much of what I needed to know. He acknowledged, for instance, that, as the founder of Synanon and creator of its methodology, "part of my job… was to pressure people, to make them do things they did not want to do. That's a pretty good description of my job."

Did he pressure people into getting vasectomies, abortions, changing partners? Did he pressure people into committing acts of violence? Bourdette repeatedly instructed him not to answer questions about specific policies—known internally as "notions"—that Dederich imposed on his followers. To get those answers, I would have to lodge a complaint with the court, which would, hopefully, order him to return and answer. (The court did so and even sanctioned Synanon for Dederich's refusal to answer questions about specific policies. But Synanon eventually settled the cases and I never faced Dederich again.)

He did concede that, in general, when he "yelled about a notion" in a Game, on The Wire, or at one of his periodic Think Tables, he had the ability to "sell the notion" to the community. He was an excellent salesman, he said, smiling proudly.

I asked whether these life-altering "notions" of his grew out of the pain he felt when his wife, Betty, died. "I would be able to say that it grew out of my life experience from the cradle up to that point," he said.

That explained so much about why he created and how he ran Synanon. Dederich's negative view of life and humankind stemmed largely from his tortured childhood—the sudden death of his father in a car accident when he was four years old, the death of his brother four years later and his mother's remarriage when he was 12, which made him feel that he had lost his special role with her. It had all left him adrift, feeling abandoned by those that he loved and unwilling to feel that pain again. With Synanon, he had created his own gigantic family and sought to control their every breath. Now with a cast of worshippers and the power to kick anyone out whenever he got the itch, Dederich cared less about people leaving. But he enjoyed making them believe they would be stupid to do so.

"I don't recall ever making any representations that we would produce a cure and that a person could then go out somewhere else and live another kind of a life," he explained. "I was content with the one notion: if you want to live a life free from drugs and crime and the attendant nuisances, stick around at Synanon, it's a pretty good life." He said people were stupid to think that in leaving Synanon they could start over.

So he developed methods that would forge bonds his followers couldn't break, methods that paralleled those used by Mao against American prisoners during the Korean War.

"Have you heard the term 'coercive persuasion?'" I asked.

"I don't recall whether I did or not," he said. "My only experience with it has been like buying an automobile. If you want coercive persuasion, just go out to a used car lot, you'll get all you want."

"Have you ever heard coercive persuasion referred to as 'brainwashing?'"

"I was in the business of washing brains," he explained with obvious sarcasm. "People with dirty brains came to me and said, 'Oh, Great One, wash my brain so I don't shoot no dope no more,' and I did it to them and they thanked me and then went off and didn't shoot no dope no more. Brainwashing is another silly thing. I've never seen a brain washed."

But later, he displayed a fairly sophisticated knowledge of one crucial brainwashing technique, admitting that "if you kept people awake long enough you could make them believe anything."

I switched gears, asking if part of his treatment process was to cut off communications between newcomers to Synanon and their friends and relatives outside the organization, another important element to most brainwashing regimens.

That was essential to the treatment, he agreed.

"And inside the Synanon environment, you control the information?"

Again, he agreed.

To aid rehabilitation and strengthen your hold over followers, I continued, did you attempt to convince them that they needed to protect themselves from enemies outside of Synanon?

"I probably did," he conceded. "It's a device that as a father and a grandfather I've used—the boogeyman will get you if you don't watch out—you tell that to infants so that they don't run out in front of an automobile after dark and get their head smashed or something like that. It sounds reasonable that I would do that."

I asked whether this led to the "Don't Tread on Me" posture that resulted in a string of violent confrontations with outsiders.

"Well, one defends oneself against aggression coming in from the outside in various ways," he said. "You're making a large thing about the 'Don't Tread on Me' posture. We play with words in Synanon, we have a good time. You have to be a good spoofer to stay in this ridiculous business."

I asked about his aggressive attempts to recruit "squares" such as the Rosses—non-addicts also known as lifestylers—in order to transform Synanon from a drug rehabilitation center to an alternative-lifestyle commune. That notion, which became known as Synanon II— attracted professionals with money. As the organization became larger, he explained, there was a greater need for smarter people with higher education levels. "Attempting to run the whole thing with a lot of people who managed to get as far as the sixth grade and then quit was getting a little bit hairy," he said.

Was part of his pitch to the squares the idea that giving to Synanon was investing in their home? Did you tell them that they would become a "proprietor" or an "owner" of the organization?

Dederich acknowledged that he had. Since the Rosses claimed that representation prompted them to sell their home and turn over the proceeds to Synanon, this was a key admission for me. Later, the couple was thrown out of Synanon when they refused to change partners and resisted efforts to increase their payment to the group. They weren't alone; Dederich attempted to force out many lifestylers who resisted his notions. It became known as "the squeeze."

Dederich added, however, that because Synanon was an experimental society in which everyone knew that things could change, no one had the right to ask for their money back. He said he frequently "gamed" lifestylers to increase their payments, comparing it to the actions of a chief executive officer of a charitable foundation. "I probably did it almost every time I had an opportunity," he said, proudly.

"Synanon games are a good platform for that; I remember taking $10,000 from Marty Levitt… a nice piece of change. I heckled him into it. I'm pretty good."

"Do you recall," I asked, "making statements to the effect that the 'squeeze' is like 'squeezing the rotten fruit off a tree' and that 'when people leave we will grow stronger?'"

"I might have," he answered. "I don't recall. I probably thought that. That's kind of a reasonably intelligent way of assessing any kind of group; you get rid of the bums, the organization prospers. Everybody knows that."

He admitted he could accomplish these squeezes by yelling at people, firing or demoting them, or putting them through a game. Poor job performance could trigger an attack, he said. So could long hair or leaving the property to go to a movie. And the verbal assaults were often delivered in front of others, so the message would "carom" through the organization. "There's hundreds of ways," he said, "to make it a less-desirable place for less-desirable people."

I wanted to press harder on the violence that seemed to envelop Synanon in the mid-1970s. I asked him if he thought good and evil existed, or whether morality depended upon circumstances.

"People commit acts that some people think are crimes and some people think are evidence of patriotism or religious fervor," he said. "I can't come to terms with that; I don't know when violence is good or bad—like I don't think anybody else does."

He said he couldn't remember if he approved of the use of violence to protect Synanon, but added, "I could not rule it out." Yet, he insisted that after 23 years "our record of nonviolence is probably the greatest of any group that's run something like 20,000 through its doors."

If there was violence—and he insisted there wasn't much—he blamed it on the aggression of outsiders. After about 20 years without such problems, he said, "somehow the word got out that you could have a lot of fun by going to a Synanon house and beat people up or destroy property or something like that and so we adopted a 'Don't Tread on Me' posture and it worked well." He estimated there may have been about five incidents of violence, "nothing serious at all."

I asked how a policy such as "Don't Tread on Me" would be implemented. He acknowledged that, as chief executive officer, "decisions of that magnitude would of course be made, or at least confirmed, by me." He called it an effort to put up a threatening—albeit false—face to "scare the nuts away."

But by any rational measure, Synanon's threatening face wasn't so false. "Mr. Dederich, if somebody got hit several times in the face and had bruises and contusions about their face and had to be hospitalized, would you consider that to be violence?"

"Do we have 50 or 30 people that were hit in the face and got head bruises and contusions and were hospitalized?" he asked.

"Well, I would say that you have quite a few, yes."

"I know that people get bruises and contusions in football games and those are not considered acts of violence. I don't know what you're really talking about."

"What about hitting a person over the head with a gun, would you consider that to be an act of violence?"

"It depends on how hard, what kind of gun, what the situations were, was it an accident? I can't answer questions like that."

"Mr. Dederich, as I understand it, the 'Don't Tread On Me' posture was a message that people were to leave Synanon alone because various members of the community had been attacking Synanon members in your opinion; is that correct? "

"Yes, that's kind of short form, but that's right. We had a string of annoyances. We were subject to media violence in the very early days of Synanon down in Santa Monica and later on other kinds of violence, let's say, were directed at Synanon. And then the big media violence came out. That is beginning to abate and now we're subject to legal violence. These things are no surprise to me. I went into kind of an unusual business and attracted the attention of a lot of nuts in the country and nuts keep coming up all the time. We're in the midst of it right now. This will abate. I don't take it seriously."

His all-inclusive concept of violence included governmental actions against Synanon, such as "mad dog Saturday," when the city of

Santa Monica sent police to take adjacent beach property away when Synanon moved into the swank Del Mar Club. He acknowledged that Synanon had run into many zoning violation cases and that was part of it, too. He defined media violence as vicious attacks by print or broadcast outlets and legal violence as foolish and unjust lawsuits. "Violence is violence whether it is legal violence, media violence, physical violence, robbing and stealing, destruction of property, it's all the same thing," he said.

Ron Eidson had committed violent acts against Synanon, in Dederich's view, by "scaring the life out of a bunch of our girls on at least one occasion." He added that "some measures were taken so that he wouldn't do it again. The dramatic effect of beating him up and beating him with the gun butt in front of his, quotes, 'wife and child,' unquotes, is one way of saying it. Another way of saying it is a couple of guys made it clear in the only possible way to a bumpkin like that, don't mess around with our girls and frighten them to death. We don't want them frightened in your bumpkin way. You have behaved that way to make them think that they were in danger of serious bodily harm, like rape or other violations to their persons and so on. If that person had been allowed to continue and we hadn't done something about it, I suppose we would've had to move out of that area. Now we can't sell 1,800 acres of land in one place and 360 in another place just because a bumpkin gets out of hand from reading idiotic stuff in the media and watching it on television. We can't do that, you see."

Whatever he did against those that he felt transgressed against Synanon stopped the violence, he concluded. He just couldn't remember what it was.

I asked whether he declared a "Holy War" against outsiders. "It doesn't hurt to remember that there are 17,000 or more disgruntled ex-residents all roaming around ticking like time bombs... all ready to bite the hand that feeds them," he said. And it was his responsibility to protect his flock. His position, he boasted, was "an awesome responsibility, counselor, but I accepted gratefully."

When I asked if the Holy War speech had been broadcast to Synanon facilities 30 times—which it had—would he expect his followers to take it seriously? He was instructed not to answer. But he had previously acknowledged that people "took him seriously when he spoke." He got the same instruction when I asked him to verify a written order to security forces that, as part of the new, militant posture, "we might have to sacrifice someone."

As we neared the end of the deposition, I attempted to sum up the major points. Dederich admitted he used his skills as a salesman in forums such as games, general meetings and think tables to convince people not to use dope. And he used those same skills and forums to convince people to quit smoking or to lose weight, along with his more radical notions—mass vasectomies, abortions and changing partners. He acknowledged that he could "patch" into any game to influence its outcome.

And so there it was. He had admitted the tools he used to get Synanon members to follow his notions and do things they didn't necessarily want to do. He said he didn't know "where I was going with this," but having admitted to using these tools, he couldn't escape responsibility for using them to promote the violent acts that were clearly outlined in the organization's own recordings and memos.

I knew the deposition had been a success. What had happened at Synanon was told in Dederich's own words. If anyone ever wanted to know the hows and whys of Synanon, it was all here, all put down by a court reporter in two half-day sessions in a Visalia Holiday Inn.

Dederich began to complain of exhaustion and wanted the proceeding to end. As we wrapped it up, he asked me a question, off the record, about my statement that there were 30 incidents of Synanon violence (there were actually 88 I know of, but I wanted to work up to that number).

"Was there that many, Paul?"

It was the first time he said my name.

"Yes," I answered.

He looked down in silence. He never responded, but there was really no need. And so the deposition ended. I never saw or heard from Charles Dederich again.

I heard that he spoke highly of me after returning to Synanon and predicted that one day I would join. When told this I laughed, and said to a reporter: "Truth is I had joined long ago."

*   *   *   *   *   *

Epilogue:

When Dederich died in 1997, Phil Bourdette asked if I would attend the funeral. He thought it would show the media that I had enough compassion and understanding to pay my respects and acknowledge he had done some good things. I thanked him for the invitation and said I would, but later decided against it. I thought I would be accused of public grandstanding and worried that my presence might anger Synanon loyalists.

I considered visiting the gravesite some day, but I never did.

Part 5: An Act of Betrayal

A man on a walking tour of Europe comes across a remote monastery, where he hears a howling that the brothers say they do not hear. Following the sound, he comes upon a cell with a man locked inside. The man says he is being held captive by a crazy monk. The visitor confronts the monk, who contends that the man is the Devil and is imprisoned by the staff of truth. Unconvinced, the visitor removes the staff and releases the man, who proceeds to transform into the Devil and disappear in a cloud of smoke and fire. Shortly thereafter, World War II breaks out.

—"The Howling Man," an episode of the Twilight Zone (11-4-60)

In 1982, I learned the true meaning of betrayal. It devastated me and slanted my view of the world forevermore.

Synanon's libel suit against *ABC News* had just gone to trial. The suit was laughable and I wasn't the only one who thought so. Everyone associated with the case expected a quick victory followed by a malicious prosecution filing by ABC against Synanon. Even Synanon, in blissful denial on most legal issues, seemed to know it was a lost cause, offering to drop its case and pay $70,000 to ABC employees it had allegedly harassed in exchange for a promise not to pursue the malicious prosecution case.

ABC rejected the offer, seemingly determined to punish Synanon for its brutish behavior. My own brush with death was still fresh in my mind when an *ABC News* employee came home and found a lizard impaled on her front door. At an ABC shareholders meeting, Synanon members, having purchased stock so they could attend, menacingly asked board members if they had protection for their wives. ABC had told its lawyers to get them and to forget about the cost. That made ABC an instant hero in my eyes. My admiration grew when they ordered a two-night miniseries about my fight with Synanon.

As the case proceeded, nothing happened that changed our optimism. After each day of the trial, I chatted with ABC's lawyers, Bob Fremlin and Chris Brown of Lillick, McHose and Charles, to review that day's events and plot strategy for the next Synanon witnesses. They introduced a pile of incriminating documents during the cross-examination of Synanon's witnesses and I could sense their growing confidence. Eventually, they decided they didn't even need to put on a defense.

Even Synanon's efforts to prolong the case to inflate ABC's legal bills were failing: the judge finally had enough and issued an order limiting the time they had to make their case.

It was all falling into place.

But in June of 1982, attorneys from ABC's corporate headquarters in New York swooped into town and went into chambers with the judge and Synanon's lawyers. When they emerged, they announced a settlement. Terms weren't publicly disclosed, but I learned that ABC, incredibly, had decided to pay Synanon $1.25 million to drop its case, the money divided between Synanon and Dederich. As one reporter put it, Synanon got paid $1.25 million for terrorism.

*   *   *   *   *   *

Soon after ABC's betrayal of the public trust, I decided to hold a Synanon theme party in an attempt to lift splitee spirits. In Synanon, you attained full membership on your fifth anniversary; June, 1982, marked the five-year anniversary of my involvement with the group, so I invited ex-members to my house to celebrate. I sent out invitations mandating that everyone come with shaved heads, bib overalls and ax handles. At midnight, we would all change partners. Door prizes included a Gambonini Tractor, a vasectomy reversal and Charles Dederich tape recordings. In one room I put chairs in a circle with a sign over the entrance saying:

"Synanon Game Room: Abandon All Hope Ye Who Enter."

Donning my custom-made "Splitee" t-shirt, I told my guests that now that I had become a member, I was about to become a splitee.

I thanked them all for their bravery and told them what ABC had done. The network had shown it didn't care about them or its responsibility to the general public. The New York lawyer that negotiated the settlement had told Brown and Fremlin that the world had forgotten about Vietnam and they will forget about this, too.

The party was great fun. "The Network of Friends," as the ex-members became known, had been like a support group to me, even showing up once to move the contents of my house when it was threatened by a Malibu fire. We shared common experiences and spoke a common language. For a long time, they were the only people who had an inkling of what I was going through and the only ones with whom I didn't feel the need to explain myself.

But the party didn't help my sagging spirits. As the realization sunk in that ABC paid off the organization that tried to kill me and had attacked so many others, I became deeply depressed and was bedridden for three days. I had spent years fighting cults and now I wondered whether I had been wasting my time. While I tilted at windmills, sacrificing any semblance of a personal life, this publicly-held corporation, which operated under one of only three lucrative national broadcasting licenses handed out by the government, was blithely disregarding public safety for financial expedience.

Like the man in the *Twilight Zone* episode, ABC had set the Devil loose on an unsuspecting world. With this settlement, Synanon once again felt empowered and sued *Reader's Digest* and Dave Mitchell of the *Point Reyes Light*, alleging that it was libeled by an article in the magazine recounting how Mitchell won the Pulitzer Prize for his courageous coverage of Synanon. *Reader's Digest*, unlike ABC, refused to back down and won on summary judgment.

I also feared the settlement would embolden Synanon to resume its reign of terror. Was anybody who fought them going to be safe again? The man in the TV show could at least claim ignorance as an excuse for his tragic blunder. ABC knew precisely who the howling man was.

*   *   *   *   *   *

So why would a supposedly sane group of corporate executives reject what looked like a slam dunk victory in court and instead shell out a sizeable jackpot to the opposition?

It all started with Synanon's massive purchase of weapons in March, 1978. KGO, ABC's San Francisco affiliate, aired the story and illustrated it by superimposing the Synanon logo over the photo of a man with a rifle, unaware that the man pictured was Lee Harvey Oswald. Synanon sued, claiming the graphic defamed its reputation.

Synanon enjoyed suing journalists; over the years, it sought more than $400 million in libel actions against ABC, *Time*, *Reader's Digest* and syndicated columnist Jack Anderson.

Personally, I thought if anyone had been defamed it was the long-dead Oswald.

In the ABC case, Synanon repeatedly refused to produce requested documents, despite a series of court orders. But Synanon's lawyers would make a tragic mistake. To appease the court, they agreed to let the network's lawyers comb through the San Francisco warehouse, which was filled to the brim with boxes of documents.

Synanon's legal brain trust thought ABC's lawyers would waste countless hours going through the boxes without finding anything incriminating. After all, Synanon attorney Howard Garfield had already ordered Dr. Robson to scour the foundation's facilities and send him any documents mentioning violent encounters. They would then claim they were protected by the attorney-client privilege.

Unfortunately, Robson's team had badly botched the job. The warehouse yielded a treasure trove of memos, letters, reports and recordings laying out in exquisite detail the organization's descent into violence. Eventually, jurors saw these documents; they heard tapes recorded in 1977 in which Synanon's founder called for a "new religious posture" that advocated violence against people who interfered with Synanon.

The case was in the bag. But it all came crashing down because of insurance. Under ABC's liability policy, the carrier claimed, the cost of its legal defense was deducted from any liability payout. So, when the cost hit the company's $1 million maximum liability coverage— shockingly low for a major network constantly exposed to potential lawsuits—the policy was terminated and the carrier, Lloyd's of London, had no further obligation. ABC was now on the hook for its own defense while Lloyd's sought repayment of the sizeable defense costs it had already advanced in excess of the policy's limits.

Fearful of ruinous exposure to litigation without insurance coverage, ABC sought to get the policy reinstated and its debt to Lloyd's wiped out. To determine the premium, they needed to agree on the financial exposure of all pending litigation—which, of course, included the Synanon case. Synanon, aware of ABC's limited liability coverage and Lloyd's suit, filed a second lawsuit, but hadn't yet served it. The implication was clear: Synanon would move forward with the second action if ABC didn't settle and after Synanon lost the first case. They knew they couldn't win, but the object was still to inflate ABC's costs as much as possible. ABC and the carrier decided to liquidate the problem by settling. That would give them a fixed expense they could use to estimate the cost of the new policy. And the insurance carrier agreed to foot the bill for the settlement.

Needless to say, ABC no longer seemed so heroic.

Like any journalistic entity, ABC had a responsibility to fight for the truth. But money trumped all. I even offered to finish the trial for ABC free of charge. The network never responded. And, as if to add insult to injury, the network cancelled the miniseries about my fight with Synanon. The screenplay—by Scott Swanton—had already been completed and paid for.

Maybe I was being too simplistic, but I couldn't reconcile the company's actions with my beliefs. There was no room in my world for such selfish thinking. At least Synanon had an excuse for its transgressions—its behavior was a predictable outcome in a contained, totalistic environment controlled by a disturbed genius. What was ABC's excuse? I was 37 years old and I had just discovered that Santa Claus didn't exist.

Not surprisingly, ABC got Synanon to agree to keep the settlement secret.

*   *   *   *   *   *

Angered by the cover-up, I leaked the story to the *Los Angeles Times*. KGO, the ABC affiliate, defying its parent company, aired the news as well. An ABC spokesman, Dick Connelly, said that the network couldn't comment other than to say redundantly that the case had been settled by "mutual agreement of both sides." Connelly also said ABC and KGO-TV stood by their original broadcasts, although the network's actions sent a clear message that it didn't. A Synanon lawyer and former member, Sharon Green, refused to discuss the settlement.

I continued with my cases against cults and added abusive psychotherapists to my caseload, but it wasn't the same. Before, I pursued these cases because I believed that I should. Now, I pursued them just because I could. For years, members of the jury in the case held an annual picnic to honor Brown and Fremlin and signal their dissatisfaction with the settlement. Brown shrugged off the settlement, saying it was just a job. Fremlin took it very hard and died young, due to heart failure. His daughter went on to law school and heard lectures which contended that ABC settled because its lawyers spent too much money defending the case. Some estimated the costs at $7 million over four years, which seems high to me. But the case did require the taking of tons of depositions and many billable hours searching through more than 200,000 documents.

Before the settlement, I had decided that Synanon was toothless and no danger to anyone anymore. Now I wasn't so sure. I started getting late-night calls from someone who wanted to discuss a possible cult case. I kept telling him to call during office hours, but the calls continued. Once, he described the notebooks I could create about the cult; they sounded eerily like my Synanon notebooks. Another time, he talked about how I played beach volleyball. I knew it was Synanon. On his final call, he said, simply: "Paul, another snake is coming."

$$*\quad*\quad*\quad*\quad*\quad*$$

The seeds of Synanon's destruction actually dated back to 1979, when the organization's highest priority was to keep Dederich out of jail for orchestrating the attempt on my life. Synanon's lawyers argued desperately that tapes, Wire logs and Think Table summaries seized by the LAPD in which Dederich described violent attacks and advocated the murder of lawyers—the worst of whom, naturally, was me—were merely hyperbole, fantasy, an extension of Synanon game playing. In other words, it was not to be taken seriously. But I presented evidence that linked Dederich's recorded statements to actual deeds of violence.

I then demanded that the court require Synanon to produce other tapes and documents that mentioned me or the group's policies regarding violence. Only a few were produced, many with long, silent gaps. Meanwhile, we tracked down more members willing to testify, including one who was present at some of the attacks and a former Imperial Marine.

The pre-trial period for both the criminal prosecution and my civil suit against Synanon for the rattlesnake attack lasted more than 18 months. It was a particularly trying time, as I was immersed in building a case while simultaneously fighting off Dederich's legal team, which spent considerable effort trying to discredit and intimidate me. The barrage included parking a Synanon truck opposite my home, sending members inside my office to serve documents and making calls to my home. Doug Robson's wife left her card with my mother's neighbor to let me know they knew where she lived. At a press conference, Synanon officials told the media they should consider the possibility that I staged the rattlesnake attack to besmirch Synanon and publicize my vendetta against cults. Using my old high school and college yearbooks, they tracked down old friends and ex-girlfriends in a campaign to uncover some dirt on me. I frantically called everyone I could think of who knew Trudy, urging them not to mention her if approached by Synanon representatives. We were no longer together, but I had to make sure she was safe.

Their efforts were wasted. A trial date was finally set in the summer of 1980 and Dederich, Kenton and Musico decided to plead no contest to the charge of attempted murder.

I thought that would end this lengthy war, but I was wrong. A Pulitzer Prize for his coverage of Synanon didn't protect Dave Mitchell from being sued for libel by a Synanon reinvigorated by ABC's copout. I was still angry when the United States Department of Justice called in 1982. "Where in the fuck have you guys been?" I barked. But when I calmed down, I realized this might be my best chance to get the Devil back in his cell.

DOJ lawyers Frank Hertz and Tom Lawler thought they had a simple misuse of charitable contributions case. They didn't even know about Synanon's history of terrorist acts. They had called simply because someone gave them my name. But they were eager to hear my story and I eventually signed on as a consultant. Their primary goal was to defend the IRS against a Synanon lawsuit attempting to overturn the revocation of its tax-exempt status and the issuance of liens for $55 million in back taxes and penalties. With my guidance, they shifted their approach, arguing that Synanon was a terrorist organization and thus didn't qualify for tax-exempt status, regardless of any charitable work or its designation as a religion.

By then, both the courts of law and public opinion were turning against Synanon. In a 1983 Washington, D.C., case, Synanon attempted to reverse the purchase of some local property and get its down payment refunded. The property owner, Stuart Bernstein, filed a cross-complaint, stating that Synanon concealed its true identity as a terrorist organization. He sought damages from Synanon for harassing and intimidating tenants in order to force them to move out, and argued that the group and its legal team had been destroying evidence of terrorism—primarily tapes that had been partially or totally erased or destroyed in order to prevent them from being used as evidence to prove that Dederich had conspired to murder me. Much of Bernstein's evidence came from me; the DOJ provided him with witnesses it had uncovered. After a 10-day pretrial hearing involving 11 witnesses and a horde of Synanon documents, Judge Leonard Braman ruled that officials of the organization had erased, altered or destroyed more than 100 tapes, thus perpetrating a fraud on the court of "the most grave and serious proportion." With that, he dismissed Synanon's case.

The DOJ team asked the United States District Court hearing the tax dispute to take judicial notice of Judge Braman's findings, since the issue of violence was a key element in the case. When Judge Charles Richey read Judge Braman's lengthy ruling about erased, altered and destroyed tapes, he must have experienced strong feelings of déjà vu, considering his involvement a decade earlier in the Watergate scandal. Judge Richey did adopt the findings in the Bernstein case, dismissing Synanon's lawsuit against the IRS because of the destruction of evidence. Thus, he didn't need to rule on Synanon's violence, although he did note that there had been sufficient evidence to rule on that issue as well.

With Synanon now on the hook for all the back taxes and penalties, its only hope for survival was to earn sufficient money to pay off the liens. But in 1986, that hope was dashed after a critical article appeared in *Forbes* magazine about ADGAP, Synanon's merchandising arm and its main source of income. ADGAP sold promotional items to a host of Fortune 500 corporations with the sales slogan "buy from Synanon and save a life." It was projecting revenues of $30 million for the year. But *Forbes* claimed that ADGAP's success was due primarily to the ignorance of its corporate clientele about Synanon's violent past, the murder attempt against me, the $55 million tax lien and a new criminal case against Synanon officials for obstruction of justice arising out of the evidence destruction. The article quoted representatives of IBM and Westinghouse, who, having learned the awful truth, said it was "doubtful" they would be doing any more business with ADGAP. After the article, that pool of money dried up while interest on the unpaid tax liens continued to grow.

By 1991, Synanon had exhausted all appeals. Unable to pay its swelling tax burden, the one-time "miracle on the beach" was forced to close its doors. The Tomales Bay property became a park and the Marconi Conference Center was turned into a nonprofit meeting center and museum; the Badger property was converted into a housing development. The old "hatchery" building in Tulare, where babies had been taken to be raised, still stands—albeit in dilapidated condition—as a reminder of times gone by. Once a year it springs to life as a contemporary art exhibit named "The Hatchery: East of Fresno."

In the end, Synanon went the way of Al Capone, a violent crime organization brought down by the tax code.

*　　*　　*　　*　　*　　*

Epilogue:

I never expected a Paul Morantz Day with a parade and a street named after me to commemorate my decade-plus battle with Synanon. But after all I had been through, I'd be lying if I said I wouldn't have appreciated some form of acknowledgement. I certainly got my 15 minutes of fame after the rattlesnake attack, but that was more morbid curiosity than heartfelt thanks. Would it have been different if ABC hadn't buckled and had gone ahead with the planned Synanon movie? I'll never know.

But there were two touching incidents that I still recall with fondness.

The first was a party I attended in Santa Monica in the late 1990s. Most of the guests were AA members, but alcohol was supplied for the other attendees. When the supply ran low, I volunteered to get more. At a small liquor store on Main Street, I picked out some beer and wine and handed my credit card to the proprietor. "Your money is no good here, Paul," he said. "You can come back any time you want for anything the store has, but we will never take your money."

I had no idea how this man knew me and why he would do such a generous thing until I looked across the street at the familiar, red brick building, now a hotel, that once housed a drug rehab center gone mad. "It was so terrible back then," he said. "They marched down those streets like Nazis intimidating everyone. You drove them off. You come back here any time you want; just don't bring your money."

I was crying as I left, but I could never bring myself to take advantage of his offer.

The other incident was a retirement party for Mike Carroll of the Los Angeles County District Attorney's office in 2000. I was one of the few civilians invited to honor him. As the master of ceremonies, former district attorney and California attorney general John Van de Kamp mentioned the prosecution of Synanon and Charles Dederich as one of Carroll's biggest accomplishments.

"And Paul Morantz is here with us today," he said, pointing at my table. Suddenly, everyone in the room—a veritable who's who of Los Angeles law enforcement—rose from their seats to give me an ovation. Then, Mike Carroll came to the microphone. "The thing I will remember most in the office," he said," was the courage of Paul Morantz." After the speeches, the current attorney general and a host of others came over to introduce themselves and shake my hand.

It may have been Mike Carroll's night, but it was my day.

Finally, on my birthday in 2013, I received a very nice gift in the mail. It was an official Commendation signed by Pam O'Connor, Mayor of the city of Santa Monica, on behalf of the City Council, which had lots of "whereases"—one of which heralded my fight against Synanon and another recognized my lifelong efforts—"which earned the respect and affection of many." It was a long time coming, but it proved the old saying: better late than never. I consider it one of my most prized possessions.

At 17 in Army basic as part of the Reserves at Ft. Ord.

20 years old, at USC. Staff photo for the *Daily Trojan*.

With my father at my USC Law School graduation.

Age 32. On the set of "Deadman's Curve" with Jan Berry and Richard Hatch, who played Jan in the movie.

Trudy with my dogs, Tommy and Devon, in her backyard. This was prior to the snake attack.

My secretary wrapping my hand to reduce swelling as I recovered from the snake bite.
(Photo courtesy of the Associated Press)

1978 Christmas card with my dog Tommy, following the snake attack. The caption read, "Your gift is in the mail!"

Me at 45, with my son Chaz at age 5, and my dog, Olivia.

In my mid-50s, just before I became ill.

Survelliance images taken of Field Marshal Cinque (Donald DeFreeze) and Tania (Patty Hearst) during the Hibernia Bank robbery, in 1974.

Mugshot of Charles "Tex" Watson, following the Tate-LaBianca murders.

Synanon.

the people business.

Advertisement for Synanon.

Some Synanon people used to shoot dope. Now they don't. They traded dope for a life free from fear and drugs and violence—a life where an honest day's work gets you a day's pay.

Some Synanon people never shot dope. They didn't have a "problem." They moved into Synanon because in it they saw an alternative lifestyle where, in exchange for hard work, energy and money they are rewarded with citizenship in a drug-free, crime-free, violence-free community.

Together, nearly 2000 ex-dope fiends and "squares," the people who live in Synanon, are working to change a part of the world by demonstrating what it means to be old-fashioned good neighbors.

The size of our world is getting a little larger each day. Drop by and get to know us.

Synanon Foundation, Inc., 1215 Clay Street, Oakland, California 94612. Telephone (415) 444-3624.

Other Synanon communities in San Francisco, Santa Monica, Tomales Bay and Badger, California, and in Detroit and New York.

The original Synanon House in Santa Monica, as seen from Del Mar St., 1973. (*Photo courtesy of Santa Monica Library Image Archives. Image reproduced from the Synanon Story Newsletter, December 1973*)

The Bay Ranch at Marconi Cove, owned by Synanon between 1964 and 1980. Originally a hotel, it became Synanon's "World Headquarters."

People's Temple cottages in
Jonestown, Guyana.
*(Photo courtesy of The Jonestown Institute,
http://jonestown.sdsu.edu)*

John Victor Stoen (seated), the innocent pawn
in a bitter custody battle. Jim Jones sent the
child to Guyana to avoid court orders to return
him to his parents and eventually ordered his
death in the midst of the Jonestown massacre.
*(Photo courtesy of The Jonestown Institute,
http://jonestown.sdsu.edu)*

Promotional flyer distributed by the
Center for Feeling Therapy, depicting
founders Richard Corriere and Joseph
Hart as Butch Cassidy and the Sundance
Kid, brandishing six-guns while leaping
over the tombstones of Jung and Freud.

A view of Bhagwan Shree Rajneesh's Rajneeshpuram commune in Oregon, photographed during a 1983 festival. (© 2003 Samvado Gunnar Kossatz)

Booking photo of Ma Anand Sheela, following the 1984 mass poisoning attack in Oregon.

Richard Nixon meets with Rev. Sun Myung Moon in the White House.

Scientology center on Hollywood Blvd.,
Los Angeles, California.

Individual taking a "stress test" using a
Scientology E-meter.

Former Scientologist Gerry
Armstrong, now among its
most active critics.

SECTION III:

Scoundrels, Charlatans and False Prophets

Chapter 8: Escape From Jonestown

(photo courtesy of the Jonestown Institute)

"Rattler Death Trap."

The banner headline fairly leaped off the page, a small part of the media crush that followed the 1978 attempt on my life. When I was well enough, my bed was wheeled into a hospital room bursting with microphones, cameras and suddenly inquisitive journalists.

I was stunned by all the attention. For years, I had been trying to warn the media about the growing menace of destructive cults, with little success. Apparently, all I had to do was nearly die.

There were many more dangerous cults out there, I warned the throng of reporters. People needed to understand that ordinary people manipulated into believing they are on some holy crusade can be turned into terrorists. I was (barely) living proof.

Two reporters present got the message. They started investigating another cult with stories of budding terrorism, this one stationed outside the United States. A month later, they decided to fly there and see it for themselves as part of an entourage with United States Senator Leo Ryan. They were among many in that group to return to the U.S. in body bags.

The stunning news broke only six weeks after the attack on me. I was home by then, watching a TV show that was interrupted by a breathless news bulletin: "900 dead in Guyana… news at 11." I knew immediately it was Jonestown and that "White Night" had happened.

*   *   *   *   *   *

James Warren Jones was born in 1931 in Crete, Indiana. His father was accused of being in the Ku Klux Klan and several childhood friends remember "Jim" as a "really weird kid" obsessed with religion and death. He held funerals for animals and allegedly stabbed a cat to death.

As a youngster, he studied Stalin, Marx, Gandhi and Adolf Hitler. In 1951, he joined the U.S. branch of the Communist Party; despite his association with that atheistic political philosophy, he continued to pursue a religious career. As a student pastor in a Methodist Church in 1952, he observed a faith-healing service at the Seventh Day Baptist Church. Impressed by the money that flowed from parishioners at the service, he founded his own church, the Wings of Deliverance Church, in Indianapolis in 1955, where he preached an odd amalgam of theology, socialism and communism. He later changed the church's name to the more apt People's Temple.

Jones' early life in Indiana was a model of rainbow liberalism. He was appointed director of the city's Human Rights Commission in 1960 and actively supported the NAACP. He and his wife became the first Indianapolis white couple to adopt a black child. They also adopted three children from North Korea and a Native-American child.

In 1965, convinced a thermonuclear war was inevitable, Jones unsuccessfully searched for a safe spot in Brazil, then bused his racially mixed flock of poor and working-class followers to Ukiah, California, thinking it to be somehow safe from fallout. Now out west, where new religions reigned, he started recruiting more well-to-do professionals.

By the early 1970s, Jones had rejected the Bible. Instead, he preached that he was the reincarnation of Gandhi, Buddha, Vladimir Lenin and Father Divine. "If you see me as your friend, I'll be your friend," he told followers. "If you see me as your father, I'll be your father, for those of you that don't have a father… If you see me as your savior, I'll be your savior. If you see me as your god, I'll be your god."

The politically ambitious Jones eagerly curried favor among local power brokers. He pledged his group's support to the successful election campaigns of San Francisco Mayor George Moscone, Dist. Atty. Joseph Freitas and Sheriff Richard Hongisto. Jones also established a relationship with President Jimmy Carter's wife and his eccentric sister, Ruth Carter Stapleton. Stapleton, the unofficial queen of the Age of Aquarius, actively courted new-age groups—including est and Synanon. She offered them a connection with her brother's administration through Dr. Peter Bourne, a special assistant to the president for health issues. Bourne later resigned after a story broke that he attended a party where cocaine was snorted.

Among Jones' biggest supporters were state senator Willie Brown, Vice President Walter Mondale and San Francisco councilman Harvey Milk, all eager to embrace the growing flocks of new-age—and voting age—true believers. When Jones' support helped Gov. Jerry Brown, Jr. get elected in 1975, "Father" was rewarded with the chairmanship of the state housing commission. Brown, rightfully dubbed Gov. Moonbeam, earlier wet-nursed the birth of Synanon along with his father, former Gov. Edmund G. Brown. He appointed Synanon's first lady, Betty Dederich, to his staff and offered another post to her megalomaniacal husband, Charles, which he declined. (Thank goodness Brown could never be elected governor again. What's that, you say?)

A master manipulator, Jones raised an average of $250,000 a month in donations, including $60,000 from the Social Security checks and liquidated estates of members. He used a variety of means to tap people's emotions and their pocketbooks.

Once, a blind woman was brought to a revival meeting the evening after she had been assaulted and robbed. She had suffered a broken arm, which had been set at a nearby hospital. To her amazement, Jones recounted in minute detail the events of her terrifying evening, apparently from a vision he had. Then, in front of the enraptured audience, he removed her cast and healed her arm as parishioners shouted praise and the woman sobbed in gratitude. Of course, none of those present had any way of knowing that Jones had rigged the entire thing, from the robbery and assault to the paramedics to the makeshift hospital where her perfectly healthy arm was treated. That night, she joined Jones' flock, as did many who witnessed the miracle, tossing in their homes and assets as they entered.

Eventually, press and IRS investigations accused him of bilking followers. As outside pressures mounted, Jones prepared to move his flock once again, this time to a remote, 27,000-acre commune in Guyana, which he immodestly named Jonestown. Jones had another motive for leaving, however, which was just petty and spiteful: He wanted to prevent a father—once his loyal, right-hand man—from executing a court order to retrieve his little boy.

*   *   *   *   *   *

My involvement with Jim Jones and the People's Temple originally came through my relationship with that father, Tim Stoen, and his battle to regain custody of his son from the renegade church-turned-destructive cult.

Tim Stoen graduated from Stanford Law School in 1964 and later became a deputy district attorney. But in 1967, engaged by the protests against the Vietnam War and the youth revolution brewing in the Bay Area, he quit to join the Legal Aid Society of Alameda County and help the flower children trying to change the world in San Francisco's Haight-Ashbury District.

Those were heady days for youthful rebellion. Due to the constant protests and confrontations with police, Berkeley students started carrying gas masks to the library. When student protestors in 1969 attempted to claim some UC Berkeley-owned land and turn it into a free-speech zone dubbed People's Park, Gov. Ronald Reagan sent squadrons of armed police in to reclaim the park and a bloody riot ensued.

Among the groups lending support to the protestors' efforts was the People's Temple and Jim Jones. Jones' good deeds impressed Stoen, a young man seeking spiritual and political enlightenment. Stoen saw a man who scrubbed toilets in his own church, who adopted a black child, who helped the poor and the addicted. So he provided legal aid to the group and gradually became more and more involved in its activities. He wrote of his political conversion to the temple's socialist vision.

In 1970, Tim moved into the People's Temple and married Grace Lucy Grech, whom he had met on a march against overpopulation and pollution at the San Francisco Civic Center. Despite typical cult pressure to abort pregnancies and eliminate "selfish" distractions, she gave birth to John Victor Stoen in 1972.

Jones, like Dederich, wanted children to be raised by the Temple, not by their parents. His control over Stoen enabled him to convince the young father to sign a document saying the Temple founder had sired the child. Simultaneously, to win the mother's approval, he elevated Grace to "elitist" status in the church. To gain further control of her, he urged Stoen to have sex with other women to relieve his stress and then told Grace about it, creating a rift between the couple. Jones wanted the bond between him and the women in his flock to be greater than their bond to their husbands.

Shortly thereafter, Tim Stoen was hired as an assistant district attorney in the Ukiah consumer frauds division and used his position to protect the temple. He discouraged attempts by ex-temple members to file complaints and got himself assigned to investigate alleged election fraud involving Mayor Moscone and the People's Temple. Naturally, the investigation withered away.

By 1976, Grace Stoen had grown disenchanted with the Temple. She was unhappy about being pressured into giving up her son to be raised by the community. Slowly, her eyes opened to the malice that surrounded her. She had to watch as her son was paddled, told his biological father was a homosexual and taught allegiance to Jones. Meanwhile, she was constantly berated; Jones once pointed a gun at her and threatened to shoot her if she fell asleep in a meeting. She also witnessed the beating of a 40-year-old woman who had claimed the temple turned members into robots. Jones had followed the same path as Dederich; drunk on power and surrounded only by toadying servants, he saw himself as a deity, with the right to punish as he saw fit.

In July 1976, Grace fled to Lake Tahoe.

*   *   *   *   *   *

Jones vowed that he would never return John Victor to her and threatened to take him to Guyana. When Grace considered legally divorcing Tim to strengthen her custody claim, Jones sent Tim to Jonestown so he couldn't be served with legal papers. There, Tim discovered that Jones had turned John against his mother.

Deprogrammer Ted Patrick once wrote that a brainwashed victim only had to be convinced of one lie, and then the brain would unravel the rest. Tim disappeared in June of 1977. When he resurfaced, he was telling anyone who would listen about the abuses at People's Temple and urging that the group be investigated. Stoen said he had knowledge of the temple's efforts to hide millions of dollars in charitable trust funds from the government by transferring the money to foreign banks.

By July of 1977, Jones had completed the move to the Guyana compound. The group left the same night an editor at *New West* magazine read Jones an article by Marshall Kilduff detailing allegations by former Temple members of physical, sexual and financial abuses.

As the truth about the People's Temple oozed out, most politicians broke ties with Jones. But a Temple rally against "Jones' enemies" was attended by Willie Brown, Harvey Milk and state assemblyman Art Agnos.

Tim and Grace Stoen began a custody battle for John Victor and in September 1977, a Guyanese court ordered the return of the boy to Grace. A few days later, that same court ordered that John Victor be arrested, a veiled attempt to get him out of the compound so he could be turned over to his mother. Despite the order, government officials refused to raid Jonestown to retrieve the child.

Fearing arrest on contempt charges, Jones set up a false sniper attack on himself so he could scream at his followers on a bullhorn that the enemy was at the door. So began the "Six-Day Siege," with Jones continually haranguing his flock about coming enemy attacks and surrounding Jonestown with gun and machete-carrying followers. Black activists Angela Davis and Huey Newton fired up the masses via radio-telephone, urging them to fight the "conspiracy." In radio broadcasts, Jones grimly insisted that "we will die unless we are granted freedom from harassment and asylum." A few members defected and would sign court declarations about mass suicide rehearsals. But it all seemed so surreal, authorities couldn't bring themselves to believe it would actually happen.

*   *   *   *   *   *

Stoen had heard about my skirmishes with Synanon and would frequently call to exchange notes, battle plans and ideas. There were obvious similarities between Synanon and the People's Temple— both pressured pregnant women to have abortions, both removed children from parents to be raised by the sect, both suffered from raging paranoia regarding outsiders and both waged bloody campaigns of violence against supposed enemies.

The similarities strengthened the growing bond between Tim and I. We pledged to help each other and after the snake attack, he offered to fly down and help cover my cases until I healed. The eerie similarities between Jones and Dederich, I later learned, weren't that unusual. It often seemed as if I was fighting the same man in all my cases.

Now cut off from the Guyana compound, the Stoens couldn't locate their five-year-old son. They joined with other relatives of Jonestown residents who shared their concern for the fate of loved ones still under Jones' influence. They interviewed Jonestown defectors, reviewed transcripts of short-wave communications between the Guyana compound and the group's San Francisco headquarters. While they met, surveillance teams sent by the temple were checking license plates outside to identify their "enemies."

Tim wrote to the U.S Secretary of State and the government of Guyana to get help. He went to Washington, D.C., to lobby for an investigation. In November 1977 a San Francisco court granted Grace Stoen custody of John Victor. Two months later, Tim flew to Guyana to take custody but again, the government refused to help. The Guyanese judge recused himself after a death threat, stating that a new judge would have to retry the case. A Guyanese official ordered Stoen to leave the country within 24 hours, even though his visa didn't expire for a week. While at the airport, he was surrounded by three People's Temple members who threatened his life unless he dropped his legal action. "If I went back, I thought I would probably be a corpse within 30 days," Stoen said.

Upon his return to Washington, D.C., Stoen briefed nine congressmen on his dilemma, including Leo Ryan, who, at the time, was working on a petition to free Patty Hearst. Stoen warned that any action by the Guyanese Army could result in harm to John or others. Jones then sent followers to eight of the congressmen to discredit Stoen. But Stoen's plea piqued Ryan's interest and he wrote a letter on Stoen's behalf to the prime minister of Guyana, as did several other congressmen, asking for help in rescuing John Victor and inquiring into the safety of American citizens in the compound.

Meanwhile, Stoen filed three separate actions for ex-members against the temple, seeking more than $56 million in damages. The group countersued, charging that Stoen violated its attorney-client privilege by using information obtained while he was representing the temple in a lawsuit.

The cases would never be tried.

Later that year, Tim went to search the Guyana jungle for his son. He was too late.

*   *   *   *   *   *

In Jonestown, the thought-reform process was relentless. Subsisting on rice and beans, commune members, many over the age of 50, toiled nonstop in the fields from early morning to late at night while Jones harangued them with lectures and sermons over a public address system. Public beatings and humiliations were standard punishments for any breach of loyalty.

Meanwhile, former member Debbie Blakely testified in a court case, Jones rehearsed a Doomsday plan—White Night—wherein they all would die, children included, for "The Cause." In early October, Stoen sent a telegram to the State Department warning of the possibility of mass suicide.

In November, Congressman Ryan and a 12-member entourage, including journalists, flew into a small airfield near the commune to investigate. It was a trip I might have taken also, had I not been home recuperating from the snake bite. I've always been tormented by the thought that I could have prevented those tragic events by steering Ryan away from some fatal mistakes. First, he shouldn't have taken journalists with him—it was sure to inflame Jones' raging paranoia. Cult leaders are obsessed with their image and can't bear the thought that negative press accounts could prevent them from being recognized as great men. And Ryan shouldn't have told Jones of his plan to leave with 16 of his followers who said they wanted out. This gave Jones ample time to contemplate the consequences and plan his reprisal.

Fearful of the tales the defectors would tell the journalists, Jones ordered an attack on the departing plane, killing Ryan and three newsmen—including the two who attended my hospital press conference—and wounding six others. I ended up representing the parents of a photographer who died in the massacre in a wrongful death suit, along with heirs of those who died in the actions that followed.

That night, having convinced his flock that an invasion by government forces was imminent, Jones urged them to die with dignity, as they had practiced, rather than be herded into prison camps. Jones often spoke of "translation," the process by which he and his followers would die together and transcend to another planet for a life of bliss. It's a common cult fantasy, one used by so many cult martyrs—from the SLA's Cinque to the Branch Davidian's David Koresh to Marshall Applewhite of the Heaven's Gate cult—to induce their followers to join them in death. The truth was simpler—having just orchestrated a mass murder, Jones would rather die than face prison and humiliation, and like other totalistic leaders, he wanted his followers to validate his choice by joining him.

As the poisoned Kool-Aid was passed around, Jones recorded the grisly mass suicide, convinced that history would look back on him favorably. On the tape, a father refuses to let his daughter die until he is bombarded with images of the terrible things the enemy would do to her. As he acquiesces, the flock applauds. "Mothers, you must keep your children under control," Jones shouts amid a tumult of shrieks. Gun shots can be heard, as the unwilling died with the willing.

Jones is further heard seeking volunteers to kill Tim Stoen. "He's responsible for it," Jones proclaims. "He brought these people to us... He has done the thing he wanted to do. Have us destroyed."

All told, 914 died; 276 were children, including John Victor Stoen, found poisoned in Jones' cabin. "Do you think I'd put John's life above others?" Jones can be heard asking on the recording. "He's no different to me than any of these children here."

It was the greatest loss of American civilians in a non-natural disaster until 9-11-2001.

Only 33 escaped. Survivors trekked almost 50 miles through the jungle to another town; fleeing church members who survived the airport attack, including five children, hid in the jungle for three days. The compound basketball team, including Jones' biological son, Stephan, 19, and adopted sons, Jim Jr., 18, and Tim Tupper Jones, 19, were playing a game in Georgetown, Guyana, and were thus spared. Jones' adopted daughter, Suzanne, 25, had defected earlier, prompting her father to denounce her as a "no good for nothing daughter."

Larry Layton, who posed as a defector and opened fire at the airport, injuring two people, was the only person convicted of the airport killing spree. The jurors in the case wrote the court asking for leniency, recognizing that Layton, too, was a victim. He was paroled in 2002 after one of his victims, Vern Gosney, made an impassioned plea for his release. Gosney had been one of the 16 defectors leaving with the Ryan party; he escaped into the jungle despite being shot three times. The early parole granted to Layton—compassion still eluding Leslie Van Houten and John Walker Lindh—again showed the remarkable inconsistencies of the U.S. legal system.

*   *   *   *   *   *

In the aftermath of the Jonestown massacre, the People's Temple plunged into bankruptcy and relatives of the dead filed lawsuits to claim the $9 million fund amassed from foreign banks and insurers. Representing people whose kin had been murdered was a new and unpleasant experience for me. The more clients you had, the more money you got. While I didn't have the biggest group, I had a significant amount, and my experience and knowledge in this field made me a lead counsel in the San Francisco proceedings.

In previous cases, I had worked slavishly and earned slave's wages —about 50 cents an hour in the nursing home case and probably less than that in the various Synanon judgments. Jonestown would be different. For one thing, my involvement in this case never approached the time spent on the earlier cases.

Among the attorneys jockeying for a share of the People's Temple estate was the legendary Melvin Belli, the King of Torts, who once convinced a jury that a bus accident turned a woman into a nymphomaniac. During his career, he would win $600 million worth of judgments. Knowing that funds would be limited, Belli made an immediate pitch for all of it, arguing that relatives of Jonestown members who committed suicide should get nothing. The money, he said, should all go to those shot at the airport. With a dramatic flourish, he proclaimed that if he couldn't prove the responsibility of People's Temple he would surrender his bar card, holding the card high in the air before placing it on the table.

In response, I swore that if I couldn't prove that Jim Jones in effect murdered his followers via brainwashing, thus making the estate liable in their deaths, I would turn in my bar card, which I similarly placed on the table next to Belli's.

Thanks to a great job by the trustee and its attorneys—and a sudden surge of common sense among the plaintiffs' lawyers—the who-is-going-to-quit duel never took place.

Given the multitude of personal-injury claims, litigating the circumstances of each death would have drained the pool. The only way for anyone to get any money was to find a compromise for settling all claims. Those who suffered the greatest harm—and couldn't be seen as contributing to their injury or death—received the most money, including those in Ryan's party who survived the attack at the airport and the families of those who didn't. A formula based on a point system was created for the other victims, relatives of those who died at Jonestown. It was one of those rulings that was necessary, but felt cheesy. If your loved one was a child you got more points; parents of a victim got more than siblings. The younger the victim, the higher the points. The trustee's final report cited me for my efforts to halt what would have been the largest and most wasteful mass trial of personal injury claims ever seen in a bankruptcy proceeding.

*　*　*　*　*　*

Epilogue:

I lost touch with Tim Stoen. No father could ever fight harder for his son, but Tim's war was now over and mine with Synanon would go on another decade. It is hard to be around sadness and John's death was the saddest thing I had ever experienced.

For a time, Tim served as corporate counsel for Pacific Energy & Minerals, Ltd., then went into private practice. He lost a bid for the State Senate in 1998 and later became a district attorney in Humboldt and Mendocino counties. Along the way, he lost the liberalism of his youth; he is now a Republican who opposes legalized abortions. Grace Stoen appeared in two documentaries about Jonestown and gave support to anti-cult organizations.

In April 1979, as his family requested, Jim Jones' ten pounds of white ashes were enclosed in a water-soluble envelope and tossed from a small plane into the Atlantic Ocean.

Chapter 9: Escape from est (Or How I Saved the LAPD)

As the Synanon battle dragged me ever deeper into the fog bank of cult life, I felt like some new-age anthropologist discovering a mysterious and uncharted world filled with strange and threatening indigenous tribes ripe for study. I read books and magazine articles voraciously, soaking up every bit of knowledge I could about totalistic movements and brainwashing. I kept files on different groups, thinking that someday, some of these cases might find me, as had Golden State and Synanon.

One of those groups was est, founded in 1971 by Werner Erhard and by many accounts, the most successful of the growing horde of for-profit self-help groups spawned by the human potential movement. Est's weekend seminars were, in my view, a viral pandemic spreading across the West Coast with ambitious plans for global expansion. The group's public profile was heightened by the inevitable flood of celebrities who rushed to take the training, including singers John Denver and Harry Chapin, actresses Valerie Harper and Cloris Leachman, Yoko Ono, political activist Jerry Rubin and futurist Buckminster Fuller (who had also been a fan of Synanon). So many top executives from film giant Warner Brothers took the training, some jokingly referred to the studio as W*erner* Brothers.

Not surprisingly, the group was also dogged by media scrutiny and controversy. Some viewed it as the latest in a string of California-based pop psychology fads that sprouted like crabgrass from the human potential movement. Even Erhard's eponymous authorized biography, written by his friend and self-described human potential scholar, William Bartley, noted that many viewed the training as a kind of "psychological Barnum and Bailey, catering to the affluent and narcissistic, radical-chic residents of West Coast spas and suburbs."

Others, however, saw it as a cult—and a potentially harmful one at that. In *Gods and Beasts, the Nazis and the Occult*, author Dusty Sklar described Erhard as L. Ron Hubbard's most formidable competitor, who used "Storm-Trooper tactics to bring people to enlightenment." This included, Sklar wrote, haranguing and insulting seminar attendees to the edge of despair and manipulating them through group dynamics to achieve an "est-ian" bliss.

After studying many of the growing body of books and magazine articles about est, comparing notes with experts such as Dr. Margaret Singer and interviewing former participants and staff members, I concluded that est was a money-making machine that practiced psychotherapy without a license and recruited an army of acolytes by persuading them to surrender their belief systems and devote themselves to serving Erhard. The real issue, though, was whether est achieved these ends through coercion and abuse. Bartley's biography, for example, called the training a "siege" that would "blow the mind" by breaking up its existing "wiring." Combined with the insults, humiliations and name calling reported by others, the est training seemed calculated to evoke pain by pushing psychological buttons— classic brainwashing tactics, in my opinion.

By my definition of a totalistic movement that people should be concerned about, I believed est qualified. Certainly, for many, the training had little impact, or wore off quickly. Some found the insights useful. But for a significant number it appeared that est became a way of life. Reports filtering out of est described some staff and some trainees who seemed to place est above everything else and to view Erhard as comparable to a deity.

While I'm not normally interested in a group's philosophy—other than to understand the carrot dangled before followers—Erhard's troubled me. It seemed to me he wasn't hawking the typical cult line of religious or political epiphanies. In fact, he derided logic and understanding as the "booby prize" and insisted est was not a belief system. But I saw est presenting many beliefs, such as the belief that only through its training could individuals become complete and attain true *"satisfaction"*—defined as a state achieved through bypassing the mind. Further, he seemed to believe the training was a necessary transformation all of society must undergo, from individuals to institutions. "The world as it is, in an untransformed state, is evil," Erhard once said, defining evil as trading aliveness for survival. And to "manifest and express" this conversion to aliveness, he added, "transformed relationships or families demand transformed institutions and organizations."

To me, that's as totalistic as it gets.

I was also concerned that est seemed to encourage people to ignore the Golden Rule of "do unto others as you would have them do unto you." In est's philosophy, you create your own universe and only you are responsible for everything in it, including being victimized; if your neighbor is attacked, that's his problem, not yours.

In "The New Narcissism," an article in Harper's magazine, author Peter Marin described one est graduate's proclamations that the poor must have wished for poverty and the North Vietnamese must have wanted to be bombed. Likewise, a woman raped and murdered in San Francisco was to be pitied for having willed it. Countering the graduate's statements with logic, Marin wrote, was fruitless, since she believed that reason was "irrational."

I couldn't begin to conceive of a world where rape happened because the victim somehow wanted to be raped. So you can imagine my concern when I learned that Trudy, on the recommendation of friends and without discussing it with me, attended an est weekend. It wasn't really surprising; Trudy is a sensitive soul who sought personal growth through the constant exploration of spiritual issues. And I wasn't very tolerant of such quests in those days—I had seen too many true believers victimized. I recall a meeting Trudy convinced me to attend where the group leader had the lights turned off for some touchy-feely exercises. When the lights came back on, I was in the kitchen eating turkey I found in the refrigerator. I have mellowed on this issue over the years, realizing that not all spiritual quests or those who pursue them are misguided and not all spiritual leaders are narcissistic manipulators.

But at the time, her participation in est worried me. Thankfully, once her peak experience faded, Trudy rejected est for her own reasons—among them, the group's relentless efforts to recruit her into est graduate programs.

Our fundamental differences on matters spiritual continued, however, and contributed to our first breakup. I was still feeling the sting of that loss when I was given the opportunity—as I viewed it—to save the Los Angeles Police Department from being brainwashed by Erhard and his minions.

*   *   *   *   *   *

Werner Erhard grew up in Philadelphia as Jack Rosenberg, a handsome and charismatic young man who, like many budding leaders of totalistic movements, had a difficult childhood. While there has been much dispute about the details of Erhard's pre-est life, the details summarized here come from his authorized biography--which he acknowledged he helped write and to which he contributed the foreword.

He had a contentious relationship with his father, who once punched him for skipping school. Both Erhard and Bartley acknowledged that he viewed his father as an Oedipal rival for his mother's attention. When the couple had other children, Bartley said, Erhard saw them as his replacements, which made him feel worthless and redundant. With that, Bartley added, Erhard viewed the Oedipal battle with his father lost.

His youth was also marked by a series of near-tragedies. He fractured his skull falling onto concrete, raising concern among his doctors about serious brain damage. He had to learn how to walk again, but after several months he recovered. Over the next two years, he got a ruler stuck in his throat, was badly scalded and fractured his skull again in an automobile accident. More than half of that two-year period was spent in various hospital stays. Bartley and Erhard both considered the possibility that he may have allowed some of these destructive things to happen unconsciously as punishment for his rivalry with his father over his mother.

When Werner broke his nose playing lacrosse in 1947, his mother refused to take him to the hospital--which he interpreted as an "ejection from childhood." Eventually, he began to see his mother as an enemy and distanced himself from parental control by staying with his grand-mother.

Drifting in and out of jobs, he finally found success as a car salesman and, by age 24, was married with four children. But he began feeling trapped in his marriage and started living dangerously. He began using an alias (Jack Frost) at work and engaged in extramarital affairs, eventually abandoning his family and fleeing west with a woman-- ironically named June Bryde-- he had secretly married under another assumed name (Curt Von Savage). Unfortunately, wrote Steven Pressman, author of *Outrageous Betrayal: The Real Story of Werner Erhard from est to Exile,* he entered into that union without the benefit of a divorce. And his new identity was compromised when his first wife discovered the false identification papers in the glove compartment of his car. So, as the couple traveled west, he chose the names Werner and Erhard from a list of prominent Germans in an Esquire magazine article. They obtained new false identity papers and rehearsed a false past.

The couple stayed for a while in St. Louis until moving (in a stolen car with its expired tags covered by mud) to Spokane, Washington, where Erhard sold encyclopedias for Grolier Inc. and later worked for Parent Magazine. Eventually, Erhard settled in California, the epicenter of the budding self-help movement, where he immersed himself in the study of Eastern philosophies, hypnotism, altered states of consciousness, autogenic responses, the human potential movement and Scientology. Looking for a fresh start, Erhard said he practiced "self-forgiving" and "self-acceptance" of his past; during this quest, he contended, he was even able to tap into memories of past lives.

His future soon arrived. As told by Bartley, Erhard was sitting in his car on a Marin County highway one day when he was transformed into "a different kind of being," someone who knew nothing, but at the same time, knew everything, who knew that everything had always been all right and would always be all right, no matter what had happened in his past.

At the time, he was a star trainer for Alexander Everett's and William Penn Patrick's Mind Dynamics, an early, for-profit encounter group that reportedly utilized more "aggressive" tactics than its competitors. The human potential movement had caught on with the madding crowd hooked on self-help gurus offering instant gratification at far less cost than traditional therapy. Hip, licensed therapists began billing themselves as holistic healers offering guaranteed short therapy programs, even if such guarantees violated the ethics code of the American Psychiatric Association.

Personal growth was becoming the hot product of the '70s and Erhard found himself smack dab in the middle of it.

*   *   *   *   *   *

Erhard decided in 1971 to leave Mind Dynamics, which crumbled two years later under accusations of practicing psychotherapy without a license, and launch Erhard Seminar Trainings, or est, with a small "e." Now, that checkered past became just another sales tool—demonstrating that even the most desperately lost soul could experience meaningful change by embracing his program. But had he truly transformed? The new Werner Erhard apparently still paid little attention to his children and admittedly still made space in his new life for cheating on his second wife, keeping a separate apartment and spending money she didn't know about.

Given such a sketchy background, who could have imagined that he would become a leading figure in the human potential movement? Even Erhard's authorized biographer described him as a "one-time liar, imposter and wife deserter" whose past was "thick with wives and nefarious deeds."

Ah, but the times were ripe for someone with his particular set of skills. Oozing the charm and self-assuredness of the car salesman he once was, Erhard became a psychological rock star and his creation grew exponentially by successfully pitching the idea that lives could be fixed in two long weekends locked in a hotel ballroom teeming with seekers who endured marathon sessions, with bathroom breaks permitted sparingly. As told by Pressman and others who attended, the est training sessions consisted largely of dismissive trainers who screamed profanities at participants, harangued them about the lousy decisions that plagued their lives and blamed their parents for the poor belief systems they passed on. The trainers demanded public confessions, applied liberal doses of ridicule and, in my view, ratcheted up group pressure until the participants broke down emotionally. They dismissed trainees as "assholes" who would remain so until they "got it." What was "it"? Did anybody really know?

But by the end of the second weekend, a ballroom full of exhausted people would invariably experience what they believed to be a peak experience. Whether they truly had, or just needed to get it because they had paid their money or had to go to the bathroom, who knows? Besides, even if they didn't get it, they could still pony up for any number of graduate programs and try again.

As the number of seminars swelled, est began raking in millions, aided by its low cost structure. Volunteers who had taken the training did much of the work, from cold-call recruiting to event logistics. According to *The Fuhrer Over est,* Jesse Kornbluth's 1976 take on the Erhard empire in *New Times* magazine, 3,500 est graduates volunteered as much as 40 hours a week each in 1976, when est was grossing an estimated $1 million a month. If they chose to work for nothing, this was how they created their "space." Besides, they benefited from greater contact with Erhard, who was busy filling his space with money and lots of it.

Some of that money belonged to the government, the IRS claimed. In the early 1990s, the Tax Court ruled certain deductions claimed by Erhard were based on sham transactions, but concluded there wasn't enough evidence to determine that Erhard knew they were shams. He was ordered to pay millions in back taxes, according to Pressman. Erhard reportedly got $200,000 back in a settlement of charges that the IRS released private information about est in violation of its internal rules. Erhard further contended the statements were defamatory.

But est's financial status didn't concern me as much as the content of its seminars. If Erhard and his trainers coerced, manipulated and abused people in order to control them, those acts should be considered crimes, I believed. As brainwashing expert Dr. Frederic Hacker wrote in his book, *Criminals, Crazies and Terrorists,* "rape of the mind is worse than rape of the body." Even Erhard's authorized biographer pointed out that the trance state that est participants allegedly achieved could be used for bad as well as good intents; it could induce either heightened freedom or psychological imprisonment.

Erhard never admitted to brainwashing his followers, but his seminar sounded to me like a near-replica of the Synanon Trip, a weekend-long version of the Synanon Game that was created to recruit outsiders to the group. Dederich admitted the practices used in the Trip were similar to Lifton's description of brainwashing; that is, to break a person's ego and force a conversion. I believed that was Erhard's aim: to control the environment, crush the ego, shed the skin of the former self and then rebuild it by implanting his cathartic vision.

I was convinced there were people involved who needed to be protected. Moreover, I felt a message needed to be delivered that countered Erhard's philosophy. It wasn't wrong to help thy neighbor and, as a society, we couldn't ignore wrongdoing and injustice because it might interfere with our achieving that blissful state of true satisfaction.

And, with his ambitious expansion plans, it didn't appear that Erhard would just go away. He offered free training to prisons and envisioned est being taught in schools. I believed it was only a matter of time before he started establishing live-in communes, a la Synanon and Jonestown. Could the Church of est, mass paranoia and withdrawal from society be far behind? In his authorized biography, Erhard insisted that est converts needed to dwell in communities populated by those who also had been transformed. (Ironically, when Synanon put its Marin County ranch up for sale, I was advised that Erhard had expressed interest in buying it.)

To stem this rising tide, I met with members of the State Medical Board, who basically agreed with my contention that the group was practicing psychotherapy without a license, but could do little about it, since the state billed the board for every investigation into an unlicensed therapist. An avalanche of est motions and appeals, they feared, would exhaust the board's limited budget. I suggested the board should sue the state for failing to protect its citizens, as the licensing statute intended. That was an interesting idea, one member conceded. Unfortunately, he added, the citizenry would rather have its gurus than tighter law enforcement. Hawaii's board at least made an effort to enforce the law, but settled, according to Pressman and other sources, for permitting the sessions as long as a psychotherapist or physician was in attendance— which, to me, was like having an ambulance on the sidelines at a football game. It can't prevent injury, only limit the damage.

I left with the distinct impression that I had interrupted their morning coffee break. I shouldn't have been surprised. California has done little over the years to stop unlicensed therapists operating under the banner of the human potential movement. A board member noted that there was even a bill pending that would, in effect, legalize the self-help movement. I lobbied against it; it didn't pass.

*   *   *   *   *   *

As the Synanon legal morass continued to drag on in the summer of 1978, I began to realize my life was in danger. Sadly, I was facing it alone. I missed Trudy terribly. About that time, the young mayor of Parlier, a small farm community north of Fresno, took the est training in San Francisco and believed he got it. He visited Erhard in San Francisco, I was informed, and told him Parlier was a young town struggling with growth and economic issues. Erhard apparently planned to save the day by training the entire community for free. When I learned of this, I feared that Parlier would become the first "estville" and Erhard would have a launching pad for any messianic ambitions.

After an appearance by Erhard, est trainers and graduates flooded into the tiny community. Meanwhile, a movement arose among skeptical residents to seek more information about these invaders. Having heard that an est trainer kicked a Bible during a seminar, many in this deeply religious Hispanic farming community feared they were about to hand over the keys to the city to an unwanted group. They eventually contacted Dr. Singer, who asked psychologist Jessie Miller and me to go to Parlier.

We wanted to stop Erhard here. If he could make the citizens of this small town believe they "got it," I was concerned Erhard might be able to use Parlier to market his program to other cities, presenting it as a shining example of est's success on a civic level. Through conformity and singular purpose, est might even generate improvements in the town, but at what price? Hitler made the trains run on time. That didn't make Nazi Germany a fun place. For me, the scene conjured visions of the movie *The Invasion of the Body Snatchers*, in which emotion and empathy-free aliens seek to conquer the world by taking over the bodies of humans.

So, on a warm summer evening, we arrived in a dusty town where English wasn't the primary language to do battle with the forces of Werner Erhard in the name of freedom of thought. Or so we imagined. I'd like to say I did something heroic—stole supplies, blew up vehicles and train tracks while kissing senoritas and building orphanages—but it wasn't that kind of fight. I did very little but answer questions and explain est's processes and goals, as I saw them, to a small committee of concerned citizens. But when it came time to act, they didn't need much help from us.

At a town meeting, an est trainer rhapsodized about the great things Parlier could accomplish with est training—tree-lined streets, successful farms, flowers blooming in refurbished plazas. When he paused, est graduates sprinkled in the crowd cheered vigorously and urged locals to join in. I feared the citizens of Parlier might be seduced. But, as Dr. Miller noted, Erhard might have had a better chance in Beverly Hills, Malibu, Marin, or some other hot-tub-filled community where the terminally bored mused about trendy psychological issues.

This was a street-savvy farming community that could spot nonsense. The people of Parlier, he concluded, just wanted food on the table and a roof over their families; they believed in Christ and didn't give a hoot about transcendence.

In the middle of the trainer's speech, a citizen interrupted in Spanish and said, in substance, the only problem Parlier had was est and when were they going to leave as asked? Before the night ended, the trainer tried several sales pitches. They all seemed to fall on deaf ears. The trainer said this was not an est meeting but a town meeting; then why, a town member asked in Spanish, are you the monitor? Appearing desperate, the trainer pointed out that the Los Angeles Police Department had agreed to let its officers be trained by est.

My ears perked. My work here was done; I was needed back home.

*   *   *   *   *   *

When I asked the LAPD if it was true, word of my inquiry reached two detectives in the department's Intelligence Division who opposed the training. But after being accused of abuses in several cases, including an unauthorized investigation into John Lennon, the unit had little clout, I was told. Rumors were circulating that Daryl Gates, L.A.'s new police chief, intended to disband the unit (He eventually did). The two intelligence officers, Lynn Cottle and Dale Hollis, felt helpless to stop the program from within and wanted me—as I interpreted it--to save the Los Angeles Police Department by keeping est out of it.

How could I refuse? So I wrote Gates, explaining my background and est's goals as I saw them. I expanded on that when I met with one of Gates' under chiefs—Chief Barry Wade. I told him that est was an imminent threat to the department because it could induce some officers to place their loyalty to est ahead of their loyalty to the department. I reminded him of the investigation that uncovered several Scientology moles on the force. Many of the officers trained by est might not be affected to any serious degree, and some might even have positive results from increased self-evaluation, I told him. But a significant number could end up under the group's control. Those officers might dedicate their lives to est, altering, perhaps forever, their life choices and commitments. Some might break up with their families and cast aside old friends. Some might quit the force. Ultimately, some officers could develop serious medical or mental health issues, especially if they decided years later that Erhard and est weren't what they seemed. Such results weren't uncommon among brainwashing victims. I pointed out Dr. Lifton's conclusions that the attempted brainwashing of American soldiers during the Korean War resulted in several psychotic breaks. And I showed him an article by Drs. Michael Kirsch and Leonard Glass in the American Journal of Psychiatry that reported findings of psychosis among est trainees. Finally, I expressed my opinion that the training was illegal under California law because it provided psychological services without a license.

Shortly thereafter, Gates issued a letter making it clear the LAPD didn't sponsor the proposed est training and had no opinion on whether anyone should attend. The sessions had been arranged by the Los Angeles Police Protective League, the policemen's union.

Ever the diplomat, I wrote Gates again, viewing his response as a very nice cover- your-ass letter. I repeated my request that he protect his officers, or at least warn them about the potential psychological danger. I offered to match Erhard's offer, providing free deprogramming right after the final est session.

I never heard back from anyone at the LAPD, so I contacted the union. The representative I talked to explained that union officials hoped the training would help their members build better community relations by showing their willingness to improve themselves through this popular program. The short-term image boost could certainly happen, I agreed, but at what long-term cost? I laid out all my concerns, as I had to Gates, told him about Parlier and briefed him on totalistic movements. He certainly seemed concerned and said he would look into it in more detail before continuing. But the first training session was scheduled for that weekend, he said, and since the hall had been rented and participants selected, they weren't inclined to cancel. I argued that they were putting officers at risk and that they had to cancel pending further investigation. I warned that even one training session could result in some officers suffering psychological damage and/or disrupted families. The potential harm was greater than the potential inconvenience.

He remained unconvinced, so I looked for another way to raise enough adverse public opinion to force cancellation of any further est training. So I called some reporters I knew from the networks, the Los Angeles Times, the now-defunct Los Angeles Herald Examiner and other outlets, and invited them to the Press Club for a briefing on the subject of whether the Los Angeles Police Department was about to be brainwashed. I brought in Dr. Hacker, as well as representatives from cult information clearing houses. I laid out some of Erhard's history and what was about to happen to unaware LAPD officers looking to show the public that they, too, could be "groovy." Was this really appropriate training for those dedicated to protect and serve? I asked.

I also asked Dr. Martin Reiser, the police department's head psychologist, to attend the first training session and report on what he observed. Afterwards, I gathered the press again. I wondered how police, who so often had to visit the scenes of brutal crimes, would respond to est dogma, particularly the idea that victims of crime were responsible for their own misfortune. I was told that est trainers had excised that message from the police training. In my mind, this confirmed one of my greatest fears about Erhard: He wasn't an ideologue. He cared more about profit and power and had no qualms about changing his sales pitch to fit different audiences.

I asked Dr. Reiser whether the est trainer used therapeutic practices. He said yes, calling it a "psychotherapeutic program." Then why, I asked, didn't he urge the officers in attendance to arrest the trainer for practicing without a license? He didn't answer. Did he witness the use of brainwashing techniques? He acknowledged the est training used "traditional methods of coercive thought control" and exerted "tremendous control" over the individual's environment during the training. He termed the tactics "aggressive" and "punitive." But he didn't see new beliefs being installed. Dr. Hacker filled in that blank. The simple message, he said, was: "est is great."

The media strategy produced better results than I had hoped for, not only raising the question of whether the LAPD was being brainwashed but whether the training was appropriate for the American public in general. This wasn't the message the police union wanted to send. Instead of building confidence in the police, the session may have increased the public's doubts. Police union board member Tony Amador, the Herald-Examiner reported, said the union wouldn't be scheduling further est sessions."And if they ask for letters of recommendation, they won't get it on our stationery," he added.

The Herald Examiner article noted that other institutions had turned down est, including the Los Angeles County Sheriff's office, the Fresno City Council and the little town of Parlier.

*   *   *   *   *   *

As time went by, the media increased the pressure on est. The movie *Semi Tough* took a satirical swipe at Erhard and the program and

Mother Jones magazine published an expose of the image-conscious Erhard's much-touted effort to end world hunger, the Hunger Project. The article—appropriately titled *Let them eat est*—concluded that much of the money raised for the project wasn't spent on feeding the hungry. Bartley acknowledged it wasn't designed to feed anyone, nor was it a charity program; it was aimed apparently, at transforming the public opinion that permitted the concept of starvation to exist.

Approximately a year after I stopped the LAPD est trainings, Drs. Kirsch and Glass, who had earlier studied the incidence of psychological damage from est sessions, presented a report on est to a Congressional subcommittee on human resources. The est training, they said, was "structured to promote regression" and "elevate the leader to a position of omnipotence." In that role, the leader would act "in an authoritarian, confrontational, and ridiculing manner that may produce anxiety, humiliation, and fear of future retaliation." This "fear of the powerful leader is contagious" and can lead participants to a "pathological identification" with the aggressor, they concluded.

To me, this was just another way of saying they were brainwashed.

*   *   *   *   *   *

Then, as the '80s approached, an est trainee fell silently during a session. It was reported that the trainer waved off those who tried to help, explaining that it was the ailing man's responsibility to work it out. He died.

The appeal of the est program was waning and the organization was beginning to fray. Don Cox, the former Coca-Cola executive and Harvard Business School professor who had given the company credibility when he was named est president, quit in 1980, later telling *People* Magazine that working for the hot-tempered Erhard was "like being in love and then being disappointed."

With enrollment declining, Erhard decided in 1981 to replace est with the allegedly kinder, gentler Forum. The Forum program did well, seemingly proving that successful encounter programs didn't require intense, Mao-like tactics; just offer a quick psychological fix and a chance at transcendence, throw in some catchy words and they will come. It's what Freud called the "herd instinct": once part of a group, many people are inclined to remain, no matter how irrational it becomes.

Erhard's second wife left in 1982 and told the San Francisco Chronicle that "Werner's ego and public image were the most important things in the world to him. Children, money or whatever are so far down it doesn't matter." Ironically, Erhard had told biographer Bartley that he could never afford the psychological trauma of a second marital breakup. "If I were to destroy another marriage," Bartley reported him saying, "I wouldn't be Werner Erhard anymore; I would be the liar Jack Rosenberg again."

The media siege peaked in 1991. An article in the February 17 issue of Newsweek magazine reported that in support of a lawsuit for wrongful discharge several people filed declarations charging Erhard with using abusive tactics to enforce obedience. Michael Breard, a former Erhard aide, claimed in the article that Erhard would scream obscenities at him if he didn't perform his tasks to the boss's liking. One of those tasks, he said, was to massage Erhard's feet in the morning. Erhard's daughter Adair, meanwhile, said "we were petrified of him," while daughter Celeste added: "He was a total control monster."

Then, on March 3, a segment of CBS' *60 Minutes* aired allegations that Erhard physically abused members of his family and incited others to do so. In one incident, Dr. Robert Larzelere, who gave up his medical practice to work for est after taking the training, and to whom Bartley's book was dedicated, said that he interpreted a verbal rant by Erhard against his wife as a request for someone to punish her; he said he attacked her in order to gain the leader's approval and love. Erhard's wife never confirmed nor denied the abuse allegations. She reportedly agreed to a nondisclosure pact in her divorce settlement. Also on the show, CBS reporter Ben Bradley stated Erhard's son, who wouldn't appear on camera, confirmed reports that his father hit him. A daughter accused Erhard of sexual abuse and also claimed that an unnamed sister had sex with Erhard and was in therapy over it. The show provided no corroboration from the unnamed sister or any other evidence supporting the claims of sexual abuse.

Erhard denied all charges and claimed the daughter who made the sexual abuse charge later recanted, but I haven't found any documentation supporting that claim. Erhard acknowledged the broadcast at least signaled that he and his family needed to heal. The issues of abuse in the Erhard family got even murkier when another daughter sued a newspaper that printed a story with similar accusations, claiming the reporter induced her to exaggerate her claims with promises of money and a book deal. While spokesmen for Erhard have pointed to this as proof of the alleged recantation, the daughter involved in the lawsuit wasn't the same one who spoke to CBS about the sex claim. The lawsuit was eventually dismissed.

When I saw the show, I wondered whether Daryl Gates had seen it and whether he thought about our little dust-up over est.

A year after the airing, Erhard sued CBS and non-family members who appeared on the segment. When CBS filed a motion to dismiss, he withdrew the suit. CBS never showed the program again, but the bad publicity took its toll. Amid reports of financial losses and a purported campaign to discredit Erhard by Scientology, which was allegedly miffed at Erhard for copying its technology, Erhard sold the Forum to Landmark Education, a company run by family members and former staffers, and moved overseas. At least this time, he didn't change his name.

And so, after a meteoric rise and fall, est ended and Erhard moved on. But it may have been the lead-in to the self-absorbed Me Generation and its proliferation of self-help movements. It may have even played a role in paving the way for the "greed is good" 80's, an era which has lingered to this day.

While it has never achieved the fame—nor the notoriety—of its predecessor, the Forum has survived and even, in its own modest way, achieved Erhard's global ambitions. But as much as things change, it seems, they can remain the same. Not long ago it was reported that the Forum closed its operations in France after hidden cameras recorded some of the same abusive tactics that contributed to est's downfall.

Epilogue*:*

Looking back, I don't know what part I played in est's demise. Perhaps I added a little more pressure to what was already a cracking dam. I take some pride, at least, in saving some LAPD families from grief, in spite of Gates. Eventually, Gates was forced out because of his inaction in the wake of the Rodney King beating and the riots that followed the not-guilty verdicts. Like Nero, he fiddled while his city burned.

Twenty years later, I became involved in a related case involving one of Erhard's closest operatives, who departed, created his own program and solicited former est/Forum devotees to join. Allegations of controlling people's lives and abuse followed, naturally, including charges that the founder had female members brought to him privately so he could teach them how to be worthy of a man like him. Each, it was claimed, was pledged to secrecy about the liaison, but word eventually circulated. Lawsuits were filed and the founder reached some quick settlements. I had the last of these cases, and finally got to sue a self-help movement for practicing therapy without a license. It involved a woman who claimed she was hospitalized for a psychotic episode after she discovered that she shared the founder with other women. Without proving that the group was practicing therapy, and not education, I wouldn't have had a case, since California doesn't allow suits arising out of consensual sex unless a duty to forbade exists.

The founder's bodyguard, I discovered, had previously been Werner Erhard's bodyguard. An ex-Los Angeles policeman, he told me he got involved with est by attending that lone est-LAPD training session in 1978. He "got it," and, as I warned Gates, it eventually cost him his wife—who left him (they had children) for the philandering founder of this new group.

"I am so sorry," I muttered. "I am so sorry. For you, your wife, your family. I could have stopped it. I could have found another way. I should have tried harder. Please forgive me."

He had no idea what I was talking about.

Chapter 10: Escape from the Cult of Cruelty

The long, winding road that was Synanon seemed to be nearing its end in 1980 with the completion of the bulk of the litigation. And when the men who tried to kill me finally pleaded no contest to the charge of attempted murder, the fear of retaliation started to wane.

But that meant the thrill was gone, too. Was life on the dark side of 35 years old going to be an agonizingly slow, downhill slide? How would I cope with the mundane, something I had scrupulously avoided my whole life?

Of course, I didn't know then that there were several new Synanon cases awaiting me, along with a stint assisting the Department of Justice on its tax case against the organization. For the moment, life was serene and I tried to convince myself that this was what I craved. But the truth was, I was still hooked on the danger and intensity and roller-coaster madness of it all. Clearly, nothing could approach that feeling again. How could it?

How wrong I was.

The *L.A. Times* called my next case "the longest, costliest, and most complex psychotherapy malpractice case in California history." Before it was over, I would attend more depositions, review more documents, interview more witnesses and invest more time than I did on Synanon. And I would learn still more about human frailties.

Once again, brainwashing was the issue. Only this time, I got into it by being one of the targets.

*   *   *   *   *   *

My first exposure to the Center for Feeling Therapy came in the summer of 1978, when I met two young women working for a nursery called the "Plant Pushers." They peddled flowers at office buildings and I was one of their best customers—principally because I kept killing the plants they sold me. They were friendly and nice, and over time we became friends. The fact that they were young and female may have had something to do with it, too.

While this was before I reached into my mailbox and saw my world spin out of control, my life still revolved around Synanon. In particular, I was in the midst of my complex scheme to free the three Butler kids. Nothing else existed for me. I met a stranger in the office one day and was shocked to discover that the firm had hired him weeks earlier and we had already been introduced.

It was in this semi-robotic state that the Plant Pusher girls found me one day, wearing my game-day scowl while eating lunch solo at the building's outdoor café. Why did I look so sad? they asked. I launched into a diatribe about the cruelty, violence and brainwashing at Synanon and my desire to free the Butler kids. They said I needed to relieve my stress and invited me to an open house at the Center for Feeling Therapy—a wonderful community where people lived in harmony, guided by brilliant therapists.

Sounds a lot like Synanon, I grumbled. They insisted that everybody at the center was happy and nobody was ever harmed. Now, you should know by now that skepticism is rooted in my nature, but so is curiosity. Could this group have found the magic formula? Had they succeeded where Synanon had failed? Had they created the utopian community the human potential groupies dreamed of? These questions troubled me, so I agreed to meet them before the open house at a restaurant in Hollywood, near the center.

When I arrived, they greeted me joyfully, with hugs. They took me from table to table, introducing me to other members. Each stood up and shook my hand and said how happy he or she was that I had come. I couldn't help but notice that at each table, there was one uncomfortable young person who was obviously, like me, a potential recruiting target waiting to be escorted across the street. Only, they hadn't seen the things I had seen. They had no idea that what they were experiencing was a classic cult recruiting strategy some called "love bombing."

After dinner, we were herded across the street and into the center's auditorium. A short film sang the praises of Richard "Riggs" Corriere, Joseph Hart and the center's other founders, who dedicated their lives to making the world better for everyone, with no thought given to personal gain. Missing was any explanation of the center's process or its therapeutic philosophy. Afterwards, a speaker described his life as a nerd before joining. Then he introduced the striking blonde he met and married after joining. Message received.

We were shuffled to a smaller room where a woman provided details of the center's "Associates Program." Apparently, after several months of therapy, we would become therapists, too, dispensing advice by phone or mail to non-members at $50 an hour, all of which, naturally, went to the center. Once again, those sensitive little hairs on the back of my neck were standing at attention.

In the midst of the crowd, my hand shot up. "It is illegal in the State of California for an unlicensed individual to give therapy and it is unethical to give therapy by telephone or mail," I advised the startled-looking speaker. After a momentary hesitation, she responded: "What we are concerned about here is not technicalities but helping people."

My Plant Pusher girls looked horrified, disgraced and scared. I saw angry faces looking at me and them. Apparently, since they had brought me, they were being held responsible for my insolence. It was time to leave.

As I drove home, I suspected the worst about the Center for Feeling Therapy. It looked like a Synanon clone. But even that wasn't close to the reality I would uncover before it was all done. I would litigate against the center's therapists for five years, trying to end what some have called the most horrific and brutal school of psychotherapy that ever existed. The hearings to revoke the licenses of the center's founding therapists lasted longer than any in California history. One of three books about the center was entitled *When Therapy Goes Insane* by Carole Mithers.

*   *   *   *   *   *

The Center for Feeling Therapy was another ugly stepchild of the human potential movement and America's hunger for psychological quick fixes. Richard Corriere was a University of

California at Irvine teacher and primal scream therapist. That branch of Therapy, conceived by Arthur Janov, held that we all suffered from repressed emotional pain—usually from childhood trauma—that could be released and re-experienced by, well, screaming. Talking therapies dealt only with the reasoning mind, Janov contended, and missed the emotional sources of our pain.

For a while, Janov's Primal Institute was the trendy thing to do for the self-improvement-obsessed and overflowed with applicants— especially after John Lennon sang its praises in a *Rolling Stone* magazine interview. While he was licensed only as a psychological assistant, Richard Corriere knew an opportunity when he saw it. Banding together with UC Irvine colleague Hart and other therapists, he left the institute, stuck a "Ph.D." after his name, and created the Center for Feeling Therapy in 1971, recruiting as its first patients many of their students at UC Irvine. It was hip, it was trendy and it led to book deals for Corriere and Hart and TV appearances with Geraldo Rivera and Johnny Carson, among others. The duo was self billed as the Butch Cassidy and Sundance Kid of psychotherapy, dancing on the tombstone of the outdated Sigmund Freud. They even made a poster of that image, complete with six guns blazing.

To circulate their message as widely as possible, the founders created Phoenix Associates. The patient-run publicity arm assigned patients to distribute flyers in the community promoting the founders' books and awarded prizes to those who handed out the most. When the founders lectured or appeared on TV, patients were planted in the crowd to whip up enthusiasm. Phoenix orchestrated patient call-in campaigns to talk shows; they raved about the center, but never revealed they were patients.

Soon, the young and rootless were flocking to the center, which promised to guide them to the love and success they never believed they deserved—and in just 90 days. What they found instead was psychological imprisonment worthy of a Russian gulag. Patients who even talked about leaving were accused of "planning to fail."

*   *   *   *   *   *

The center's victims were caught in the classic cult double-bind— bullied into thinking they were miserable and useless without the center's shelter, while simultaneously exalted as part of an elite group that made them better than outsiders. If this trap was sprung with enough manipulative skill, patients grew to believe that only in the center could they thrive. To make sure nothing contradicted that belief, the center discouraged contact with NIT (not-in-therapy) outsiders.

For a time, the pitch worked remarkably well. In its early years, only 20% of center patients ever left and 13% of those dropouts came in the first few months. If you were there for six months, you were theirs.

Welcome to the Hotel California. Much like the hellish resort featured in the Eagles' song—little-known fact: the song was about Synanon—you could check out any time you liked, but you could never leave. Like Synanon, the founders claimed that their participants needed to be permanently surrounded by other true believers for the therapy to work.

The founders publicly admitted that their system "washed" people into a new belief system; that they could make people believe that Atlantis was rising from the sea. If misused, they conceded, their therapy would be the equivalent of an electric saw cutting off fingers. But because their hearts were pure, this, of course, could never happen.

*   *   *   *   *   *

The thought reform process started even before arrival at the Center. To be accepted into the center, prospective patients were told, they had to write a detailed confession of their past failings, explain their great need for the center's help and vow to follow the program slavishly.

Upon arrival, each new patient was assigned to a therapist for an intensive, three-week program of marathon, sleepless sessions. The therapists immediately seized total control of their charges. Makeup and jewelry were banned, along with newspapers and television. They were badgered to reveal their innermost fears and declare their dissatisfaction with their former lives. As a final humiliation, many were forced to participate in some form of public ridicule, such as disrobing in front of other patients, who would critique their naked bodies

In therapy, as is common in all totalistic movements, they were told their misery stemmed from their parents, who were derided as "war criminals." Parental discipline denied the child's feelings. Rejecting a child's request for ice cream, for example, interfered with the child's true feelings and caused harm. Until people learned to live from their feelings, everyone was as insane as anyone in an asylum. To become sane, people had to express their true feelings and receive back true responses.

But all this feeling could get out of hand. Some center patients lost their jobs for expressing their true feelings too ardently. And therapy sessions could turn violent. In one taped session, Hart, who studied under humanism icon Carl Rogers, accuses a patient who bragged of winning a chess match blindfolded of "setting the other person up." When the patient denies this, Hart strikes him in the face and throws him around the room. Hart warns this is what a patient will get if he tries to set Hart up. Eventually, the beaten patient confesses; Hart calls him disgusting and demands that he confess all his crimes. Another victim claimed that Corriere repeatedly struck him in the back, kidneys and stomach for more than 30 minutes because he complained of boredom. During the beating, he claimed, Corriere taunted him: "Oh, the Harvard graduate is bored?"

Expressing feelings of anger towards another was called a "bust," similar to a Synanon "haircut." In both, a person must stand while another loudly berates his behavior. In the Center, a therapist could bust a patient by shouting, swearing or even striking. Often, other patients would join in. Patients were taught to bust each other outside the therapy sessions if they witnessed negative thinking. Some said they eventually learned to punish themselves for a negative thought.

What was a negative thought? Any perceived disloyalty, such as opposition to any center concept, qualified. A negative thought suggested that the person might still be crazy and any punishment that would save him was permissible, including hitting.

That punishment regularly featured heavy doses of humiliation. One woman criticized for her weight had to moo like a cow; another accused of being a "suck on the group" had to bring a black dildo to group and suck on it. A man accused of acting like a baby had to wear diapers, suck on a bottle and sleep in a crib. A woman said to be too promiscuous was ordered to submit to each member of the group; when she complained to Corriere and threatened to leave the center, she later stated, he assaulted her. One woman was ordered to insert her fingers in her vagina during a group therapy session, while another was given laughing gas and ordered to tell her sex fantasies to the group. Still another woman was ordered to bang her head against the wall until told to stop.

Therapist-controlled schedules determined when and how often people ate, saw friends or had sex. Permission was required to date or break up. Patients were told what they should wear, how much they should weigh and which television shows they could watch. As would finally occur in Synanon, child-bearing was discouraged, purportedly because it would interfere with the patient's therapy. In reality, the center, like Synanon, didn't want to care for children. In the nine years of the Center's existence, no member gave birth. Like Synanon, pregnant women were browbeaten until they agreed to undergo abortions. One woman who resisted was ordered to carry a heavily weighted doll around until she acquiesced.

The most loyal patients ascended to therapy group one—Corriere's group—which gave them power over other patients. Those considered least loyal were consigned to the "Tombstone" group, the final step before expulsion.

And then there was the sex. Always, there was the sex. Sex ran rampant at the Center. Sex was no more important than shaking hands, patients were told. To teach members how to live from their true feelings, they were sent to bars to ask for sex. For female patients, this led to a high incidence of venereal disease; for males, it led to a high incidence of getting slapped. Center couples were told how many orgasms they should experience. Even sexual positions were sometimes dictated. Therapists frequently had sex with patients they weren't assigned to. Having sex with a therapist was considered a stamp of sanity. Given that, who could refuse?

*   *   *   *   *   *

Despite its early recruiting success, the Center for Feeling Therapy was a house of cards built on some flimsy lies. When the lies were exposed, the house collapsed.

Actually, it took only one lie.

It started when Center therapists collected money from patients to build a gym. But no gym was built; instead, Corriere & Co. used the money to buy a dude ranch in Arizona. Patients were assigned to work there without pay while Corriere and friends played cowboy. Some patients slept in the barn. Therapists were also put to work to demonstrate that they were following the same path as the patients. They weren't overjoyed with the arrangement.

Back in Hollywood, stunned patients listened as a disgruntled therapist-leader confessed that all wasn't well at the Center and big changes were on the horizon. They would back off sluggo therapy—the hitting of patients—and the relentless demands to recruit new members.

In Corriere's group, therapist Jerry Binder encouraged patients to express their true feelings about the center founder, who was present, wearing his cowboy hat. This was unheard of and patients resisted. Finally, under Binder's persistent urging, a patient did the inconceivable, shouting that she was angry about her treatment by Corriere and the pain he had caused. Other patients slowly joined in and then, like wildfire, it ignited. The emotional release was so intense, reportedly, some patients vomited.

The anger and bruised feelings spilled out over two long days. As patients watched, therapists "busted" Corriere over their low pay and Corriere's grandiose ego and dictatorial ways. He was pressuring everyone to stoke the center's growth, but he was the only one getting rich, they complained.

They also cursed him for his ethnic slurs, particularly of Jews, who made up a significant portion of the community. One therapist told of being struck in the face. Others grumbled about inappropriate sexual behavior. Dr. Lee Woldenberg expressed the fear that he would be jailed for what they had done at the center. Since he was part of a cult, he argued, he wasn't responsible for what he had done to others.

At first, Corriere denied guilt. But he finally broke and apologized. He had once predicted that the center would close if his power was ever questioned. He was correct.

The admission led members to start questioning the two supposedly inalienable truths that the center was built on. One was that therapists lived happy lives because they had endured the same kind of humiliation and violence the patients were now undergoing. Second, the founders, thanks to their rigorous devotion to the center's therapy regimen, lived in perfect harmony inside the Compound, a bucolic patch of homes in Hollywood, where fences between properties had been removed to foster a commune-like feel.

Now, therapists made it clear that life in the Compound wasn't Shangri-La and therapists weren't happy about their treatment at the hands of the founders, either. Despite therapists' efforts to calm patients with promises of change, the atmosphere turned hostile, complete with vandalism and threats. On the heels of Hart's earlier resignation, a fearful Corriere fled to Aspen, Colorado.

The center had imploded.

By 1980, all of the estimated 350 patients of the Center for Feeling Therapy had bolted. For up to nine years, they had been told that if they lived from their feelings, social and sexual games would vanish, as would social inequality, racial discrimination and generational conflicts. What were they to believe now? Who were they to trust? If they ever really had treatable psychological problems, they had largely been ignored and were now, perhaps, even worse. They had been cut off from their prior lives and the outside world for years, made to believe that only within the center could they remain sane. They had surrendered their families and their autonomy to the center's control. In many cases, their life savings had been drained. How would they learn to make their own decisions again?

Of all the victimized people I've represented, I don't think I've ever seen a group more damaged. Their self-respect shattered, they felt betrayed and incredibly hostile, even, in some cases, towards each other, since the group included not just patients, but patients who had risen in the hierarchy to become therapists.

It made it difficult to build consensus. With the time pressures imposed by depositions and ultimately, trial, I had to be harsh and controlling at times to get things done. Sometimes, I suspected, I reminded my clients of Corriere, which revived nightmarish memories of the center. I explained that there was a difference—I was serving their best interests instead of exploiting them. I could only profit if they profited. It was clear that the center had so damaged these people they probably wouldn't start to heal until this was over and they could finally disperse, leaving their collective nightmare behind them. But I wondered if they would ever learn to trust again.

*   *   *   *   *   *

The behavior of the center's founders was outrageous, unconscionable. They shattered the Hippocratic Oath. To some degree, the therapists who were weaned from the patient population were also victims, but Corriere and Hart were intelligent men who, I believe, knew exactly what they were doing and why. They had to know that having sex with patients was unacceptable, how could they not? How could they believe that beatings and humiliation were therapeutic? That is like administering drugs while ignoring the warning labels.

While most cults at least maintained a façade that they were out to save the world, internal documents from the Center made it clear that for the Center's founders, it was all about getting rich—no matter what they said in their promotional material.

A manual for Center recruiters, written in part by Corriere, taught that the Center was a business and clients were investments. Recruiting of new patients was couched in terms of "sales" and "closing." Teams of patients—one dubbed the "Body Snatchers"—competed to recruit the most new clients, largely from high-income areas such as Brentwood, Beverly Hills or Westwood. Detailed financial information was gathered from new recruits so as to "max out" their ability to pay. Those expressing concern about the costs were encouraged to take out loans.

"If you can get a person to believe they need your product, they will move a mountain to get it," the manual stated. If that wasn't enough, center therapists were encouraged to create a false quota to pressure prospects into quick decisions, as in "I'm limited as to how many people I can take."

The founders had a master plan, to build a string of clinics—eventually worldwide—that would turn the center into the McDonald's of psychotherapy. The clinics would be manned by patients-turned-therapists and most of the profits would be funneled back to the founders.

Patients were trained to become therapists and to obtain some form of license—psychological nurse, psychological assistant—that would allow them to treat others. They would then operate clinics and aggressively recruit new patients, who in turn were encouraged to bring in loved ones so they could "work on their relationship." The loved ones were then pushed to stay on to work on their issues. Recruitment quotas were established and fines or punishments meted out to those clinicians who fell short. "Take your quotas seriously!" one memo urged. "You are responsible for numbers!"

New patients would eventually ascend to the therapist level and presumably go off to launch their own clinics. Eventually, the patients recruited to those clinics would be funneled back to the Center.

It was a giant, psychological pyramid scheme.

According to Center documents, handed over by a former Center clinician who sued, the founders anticipated that the Center would eventually house nearly 1,000 patients, who would generate $1 million in gross revenues annually. But that was just the beginning. They planned to open 38 clinics in Los Angeles alone in 10 years, charging an estimated $4,000 annually per patient. The clinics would spread from city to city after that. Eventually, the center projected, the clinics would gross more than $1 billion a year.

*   *   *   *   *   *

As in most cult cases, getting justice for my clients wasn't easy, since the issues weren't easy to understand or prosecute. I once asked a California Psychology Board investigator why they didn't revoke the license of Center therapists after they wrote books admitting to unethical conduct. His reply: "Who reads?" I piled a stack of center books, brochures, manuals and patient diaries on his desk. "Read this," I said.

Further, the Center had gone to great lengths to shield against potential lawsuits. According to Center documents, patients were asked to sign consent forms that would ostensibly restrict their ability to sue for damages. And therapists were instructed to avoid legal liability by carefully describing events in their therapy notes in misleading terms. Instead of writing about assaults and humiliation or "busting" someone for being a "creep," they were to write about an "intervention" to improve "behavior."

But the founders made several critical mistakes and left behind an arsenal of smoking guns. So I was confident when I filed a lawsuit in 1981 charging medical malpractice on behalf of more than 40 plaintiffs.

The Center instructed each patient to keep a diary about their therapy experiences, but didn't collect them before the patients left. When they were turned over to us, they filled about 120 bankers' boxes with enough gruesome details to titillate the Marquis de Sade. One female patient wrote a letter to her former therapist describing in chilling detail being worked to exhaustion, being bullied into having an abortion, being "chained" to a mate she didn't want and being yelled at and made to feel miserable when the relationship didn't work. When she attempted to leave, she was dragged back by other patients and shoved against a wall. She struck one of her attackers, who hit her back and threatened to kill her. "It seems like I've been wandering through a dark tunnel for a long time," she wrote. "I'm still in the dark, but I think there's a light up ahead. Maybe there's an end to it. I want so badly to feel good here again."

As her group therapist instructed, she never sent the letter. If she had, perhaps the infuriated former therapist would have brought an army of investigators—or the Marines or a SWAT team—to shut down the Center even sooner.

I obtained two other damning documents, including a letter sent by Hart just before he left the Center, asking UCLA expert Dr. Jolly West for information about brainwashing. This certainly made it appear that he was concerned about the issue or wanted to look like he was concerned. The other—you've got to love this one—was a dissertation on the center entitled "From Healing to Hurting," basically supporting our contentions and written by none other than Hart's brother John, who was seeking a license to practice psychotherapy.

Defense attorneys made an even bigger mistake by filing a defamation suit against Dr. West and a group of patients for statements made on "Cult of Cruelty," a *CBS News* special report on the center. The lawsuit had several impacts—all of them bad for the defense.

Dr. West, who held a counseling session for the patients after they left the center, had a strict policy against testifying as an expert witness. So, if he hadn't been sued, his opinions about the center as an abusive cult may never have been available to a jury. Moreover, the suit allowed my clients to involve their insurers, who would cover most of their costs, including my fee, thus insuring that I would get paid, win or lose. That gave me more leverage in settlement talks. It also exposed the defendants and their attorneys to a malicious prosecution case. I was glad to oblige.

In the middle of all this craziness, I got married. For some time now, I had wanted a family, but there were realities of my life and my commitment to these kinds of cases that made attachment difficult. And frankly, I wasn't over Trudy.

My bride was young, just divorced and a bit of a daredevil who could live with—and maybe even embrace—the danger in my life. But my obsession with my cases hadn't diminished. We got married over a weekend, skipped the honeymoon and I got right back to work. We really didn't know each other and the marriage wasn't destined to last very long. But it did produce Chaz, my son, and that made it all worthwhile.

*   *   *   *   *   *

For 18 months, the case made little progress, which I didn't mind, since it allowed me to finish two Synanon cases and help the Department of Justice with its tax case against the cult. When the case finally did get rolling, it was a court reporter's dream, with more than 225 days of depositions to record and sell to eight firms. And quick settlements weren't likely, since insurance carriers couldn't settle without the defendants' permission.

The pain felt by some of the therapists was nearly as palpable as that felt by their victims. In cults, some become such fervent believers they join in the abuse of others. As a result, they often suffer the most guilt and shame when finally deprogrammed. One such victim-perpetrator broke down crying during a deposition. To my surprise, the defense lawyers permitted me to take her into a separate room to soothe her. It was highly unusual, but I guess they realized that she needed help and I was probably the only one in the room who could give it. I told her that it was all right to cry, most people in her situation did. I told her that while she was a defendant, I knew she was a victim, too. "Everyone in that place was a victim," I said. I assured her that eventually, she, like the plaintiffs, would start to heal and return to a normal life. The defense lawyers never even asked me what I said. I always felt honored by their trust.

The defense argument was based on two basic points: If the plaintiffs did suffer from psychological problems, what was wrong with using blunt techniques to point this out? And if things were so horrible, why didn't they leave? Those who testified first struggled with the question. How do you explain why one would stay in such an inhumane place? There were two explanations—the one they believed then and the one they believed now. I instructed them to tell both. The former was a position molded and forced on them by the manipulative skills of the therapists, who convinced them they had to be there to survive. Finally freed from the brainwashing, the fears that kept them tied to the center evaporated.

But they still had to survive the brutal interrogation of defense attorney Lou Marlin, although I felt the atmosphere he created might make jurors see him as an extension of the Center's cruel therapists once we got to trial, thus making them more sympathetic towards my clients. My shaky clients also had to weather the appearance during their depositions of several of the center's founders, who, I suspected, hoped to intimidate their former patients into regressing to their former obedient states. I had to get a court order allowing one of my shaken clients to testify with his back facing the room, so he didn't have to look at them.

I tried to counter this with my best "Win One for the Gipper" speech. They should hope that all the founders showed up because then they could look them in the face—right in the eyes—and tell the truth. And, as someone said in the early days of Synanon, "then the truth will set you free."

And it did.

*   *   *   *   *   *

When we took Corriere's deposition, I rented a large room at the Riviera Country Club in Pacific Palisades so we could cram in as many plaintiffs as possible. If they saw him being forced to answer my questions, I believed, it would demystify him and jumpstart the healing process. His answers were unemotional and dismissive. I don't believe I have ever met a more cold and remorseless foe.

During Hart's deposition, a defense lawyer objected to one of my questions, claiming I was quoting from a book and should show the material to the witness. I shook with anger and shoved the book in front of me across the large round table with both hands, defying her to show me where I was quoting. Somehow—for the life of me I don't know how—the book took flight and would have thudded into the poor woman with considerable force if she hadn't managed to deflect it with her hand. I could never have done that again. I was sent home for the day, feeling shocked and embarrassed. I thought a lot about the incident. Maybe it was just the considerable stress I had been under for some time. But in that fleeting moment, I believe I somehow became a center patient-therapist, expressing my true feelings in a way that gave me strength I didn't really have.

The next day, I apologized profusely and gave her a gift. When she pulled a catcher's mask out of the gift box, everyone laughed. She took it well, which made me sorry I had to sue her later for malicious prosecution of the defamation case.

*   *   *   *   *   *

The end for the Center's defense started with James Von Sauer, a young defense attorney who wouldn't be a team player. Resisting pressure from others on the defense team, Von Sauer's clients, center therapists Paul and Patti Swanson, confirmed the plaintiffs' allegations and contended that they, as former patients, had also been victimized. It was a brilliant, gutsy move designed to save his clients from punitive damages, which weren't covered by insurance. Since it supported my clients' claims, he guessed—correctly—that I wouldn't even ask for punitive damages against his clients.

Eventually, other therapists who grew out of the patient base saw the wisdom of the strategy. Even a Lou Marlin client, Werner Karle, apologized and admitted for the record at administrative license proceedings that the Center was an abusive cult. He testified against the others and saved his license, getting off with probation and a temporary suspension.

There was still, however, one big hurdle to surmount. As part of the defamation case, the defense engaged Lee Coleman as an expert witness. Dr. Coleman had been a highly effective witness for me in the nursing home case, but when I asked him to testify against Synanon, he told me he was against the idea of suing religions for brainwashing. That's when I discovered that this man that I had so admired had been referred to me by a Scientology front group.

Now, he had been engaged by the Center defense team in the defamation case to argue that Dr. West wasn't qualified to draw any conclusions about the Center therapists because his lone meeting with ex-members took place after the Center's doors were closed and they were in crisis. That would fit with his anti-psychiatry beliefs.

But the defense hadn't briefed him fully on what was in the Center's documents—a veritable cornucopia of quack psychotherapy. If they had, they would have known that he could be turned. In preparing for the deposition, I read everything Dr. Coleman had ever written and struck pay dirt with an article in which he determined that a home for boys used brainwashing techniques. Having acknowledged its existence there, surely he couldn't deny its use here.

I considered ambushing him with this, but when he showed up for his deposition, it was like seeing an old friend. So before the deposition, I pointedly told him that I had read everything he had ever written, hoping he would realize that I had read the brainwashing article.

Having been shown internal center documents, he did turn, ultimately telling me the Center was the worst psychotherapy group he had ever encountered. That, of course, prompted the defense to drop him as a witness. But since he had been deposed, we could have called him to testify if the case had gone to trial. It didn't.

By late 1986, there wasn't much left in the malpractice case but negotiating the final terms of the surrender. The defamation case was later dismissed and our subsequent suit for malicious prosecution was settled for a significant sum. The exact financial terms of the settlements were sealed at the request of the therapists and their lawyers.

I left all those details to the other lawyers and took off for a much-needed skiing vacation and belated honeymoon with my wife and our nearly one-year-old son. In a mountain restaurant in Utah, I saw my son take his first steps.

*   *   *   *   *   *

Epilogue:

Corriere and Hart had their licenses revoked on Sept. 27, 1987, after a marathon, 94-day hearing before administrative law judge Robert A. Neher, who described the activities at the Center as a "gothic maelstrom."

Corriere later reinvented himself as a personal coach and counselor based in Aspen and New York City; he wrote a book called "Life Zones," which he promoted on CNN during a break in his license revocation hearing, which later embarrassed CNN. His current online resume describes him as a "technology-driven entrepreneur," but makes no mention of his role in the Center for Feeling Therapy.

Likewise, those years are missing from the online resume of Joseph Hart, a university administrator in Oregon.

In his ruling, Judge Neher said the Center purported to offer treatment by the world's "premier psychotherapists" in a set-up that allowed the therapists "to solicit money, sex, or free labor from patients" and to coerce them into "obsessive devotion. By any definition it was a cult," he concluded.

The case also set a precedent that would have a broad impact on tort law. When we alleged that Sluggo Therapy constituted battery against our clients, a charge that, if upheld, would allow us to pursue punitive damages, the defense moved for judgment. The court granted their request, ruling that it may have been malpractice, but couldn't be battery because the participants gave their consent to the procedure. I filed a writ with the Appellate Court to reverse the ruling, contending that their consent was based on fraudulent representations that the treatment was for the participants' own good and that the Center concealed their true intent to use Sluggo Therapy for control. The court rarely hears such pre-judgment writs, reasoning that the issue might eventually be settled or judgment accepted, making the court's work unnecessary. But the court accepted my writ and ruled in our favor, setting a precedent that would allow a battery charge for any consented touching if it was based upon fraud.

After the Center's breakup, one former member, now a publisher, wrote that Corriere had been lecturing his therapy group on the virtues of Adolph Hitler. "If Hitler had won World War II," Corriere told his patients, according to this account, "he would have eventually done good for the world, because all human beings, deep down, want to do good."

That was Maslow's Humanist theory.

Chapter 11: Escape from the Moonies

Fresh from the Temple University School of Law, 27-year-old David Molko passed the Pennsylvania Bar Exam and decided to reward himself with a trip to San Francisco. Knowing that the city in 1979 was a melting pot for off-kilter cults, he was on the alert for proselytizers.

At a bus stop, he chatted with a group of 21 young men and women who said they were socially conscious people who lived in an international community that existed solely to stimulate discussion of important issues. While he was suspicious, they assured him the group had no religious affiliation, so when they invited him to dinner, he accepted. After a lecture on general social issues, a slide show about Boonville—the group's serene rural getaway—and plenty of fawning attention from his friendly and caring young hosts, an impressed Molko agreed to visit, unaware that he was headed to an indoctrination center for the Unification Church.

He was promptly herded into a van with 11 other recruits and transported to Boonville, where he was deposited in a barracks-like building and handed a sleeping bag. By morning, the building was teeming with recruits—and their shadows, members of the group who accompanied them wherever they went, including the bathroom.

The first day was crammed with activities: calisthenics, breakfast, a lecture on morals and ethics, lunch, more exercise, more lectures, dinner, testimonials, singing and group discussions. By the end of the day, Molko was exhausted and uncomfortable, but he was convinced to stay for the important discussions to come.

The next few days were exactly the same, right down to the lectures, which were repeated verbatim each day. The hectic schedule, with little sleep and little time for reflection, continued day after day. Speakers discussed brotherly love and social problems, with frequent references to God and prayer. When he asked again about the group, he was told it was named the Creative Community Project and drew its teachings from many philosophical sources, including Aristotle, Jefferson and the Rev. Sun Myung Moon. Molko again asked to leave on Friday, when the group headed to another retreat, Camp K. He was again convinced to stay a few more days. The exhausting exercise-and-lecture routine continued at Camp K throughout the weekend, with additional group discussions in which recruits were pressed to confess past mistakes. After the weekend, the group returned to Boonville.

On the 12th day, the recruits were finally told about the group's connection to the Unification Church and Rev. Moon. Deceiving recruits in this way was necessary, group leaders said, because of all the negative press the church had received. They even had a name for it —"Heavenly Deception." It was a church doctrine that permitted lies and deception in the name of saving souls or advancing the Kingdom of God on earth.

By now, the exhausted Molko was disoriented and depressed and didn't know what to believe. He agreed to stay to work out his confusion.

For the next five to seven weeks—the days passed in a confused jumble—Molko received "advanced training" at Camp K that changed little from his initial training. By the time his parents arrived from Florida to urge him to leave, the brainwashing was nearly complete. Told that his parents were agents of Satan, he refused to leave. Eventually, he was deemed fit enough to sell flowers and bear witness for the church in San Francisco. As a sign of his commitment, he donated $6,000 to the church.

Church leadership urged him to take the California bar exam so he could serve the church as a legal advisor. But as he left the final session of the exam, he was abducted by deprogrammers hired by his parents. For three intense days, the team challenged the Moonie programming while holding him prisoner in a motel room, providing him with facts about the Unification Church and surrounding him with familiar family love. Eventually, they convinced him to renounce his association with the church.

In June of 1979, 19-year-old Tracy Leal, daughter of trial attorney Stanley Leal, completed an unhappy freshman year at San Diego State

University and set out to visit Humboldt State University in Arcata, Calif., with an eye towards transferring. While waiting to change buses in San Francisco, she was approached by a Unification Church member, who similarly concealed his affiliation, and fell into the same trap Molko did. For nearly three months, she went through the same brainwashing regimen at Boonville and Camp K, with some extra training in Boulder, Colo. Eventually, she, too, ended up selling flowers on the streets—this time, in Los Angeles. She, too, was reclaimed by deprogrammers hired by her parents.

One of the deprogrammers was David Molko.

*   *   *   *   *   *

Thus began what I consider the most important case of my career. It would alter the legal landscape regarding cults and brainwashing, but along the way, it proved to be the legal version of the *Perils of Pauline*, with the case constantly clinging precariously to a ledge high above a deep ravine, with almost everyone expecting a calamitous fall. Everything seemed to be against us and I frankly didn't think we could win. But with the stakes so high, we had to win.

Both Molko and Leal sued the Moonies for fraud and the psychological damage caused by the group's brainwashing tactics. The church filed a cross-complaint against Molko and deprogrammer Neil Maxwell, alleging the church's federal and state civil rights were violated by their efforts to break the psychological chains that bound Moonies to the church.

I wasn't involved in the litigation at that point, but given the intense scrutiny cults were getting in the wake of Synanon, Jonestown and the Center for Feeling Therapy, the issue of brainwashing was ripe for judicial review. Certainly, there was no clear-cut judicial position on the subject, but the existing case law wasn't promising. Patty Hearst tried to use brainwashing as a defense in her criminal trial, but the judge didn't support the theory, the jury didn't buy it and she was convicted. A trial court in a case (Katz) that also involved the Moonies granted conservatorship over adult children to their parents because they were allegedly brainwashed, but an appellate court overturned the ruling in 1977, arguing that California law didn't permit the granting of an involuntary conservatorship based on a claim that the person was brainwashed. It was, unfortunately, the right decision—the statute permitted a conservatorship only in cases where the subject couldn't care for himself or posed a danger to himself or others. That hadn't been established. Moreover, the appellate court also stated in dictum— which means it was a finding not necessary to the decision—that the initial hearing to determine if the followers were brainwashed violated the constitutional guarantee of religious freedom by challenging the validity of the church's beliefs. That, in my view, was just plain wrong. Beliefs weren't the issue, just the methods used to impose those beliefs.

While a finding in dictum didn't necessarily establish this principle as a legal precedent, it effectively became one as courts started citing it in other cases. Arguably, this gave cults carte blanche to do whatever they wanted to impressionable recruits.

While I had alleged brainwashing against Synanon, the People's Temple and the Center for Feeling therapy and other cases, I always made sure there were other winnable claims, since I couldn't be sure that higher courts would permit me to sue for brainwashing. They, too, could dismiss it as a violation of the defendants' constitutional rights; protection of religion is, after all, in the Bill of Rights, and persuasion, no matter how coercive, could be considered protected free speech, whether religious or not. Or they could simply rule it was an unproven theory; in those days, most people preferred to think that people in cults had mental problems and everyone else was immune.

Law makers, meanwhile, ignored the topic entirely, preferring not to be exposed to the political fallout from a bill that would affect not only destructive cults, but all religious groups. Of the Moonie followers placed in conservatorships set up in the prior case, three eventually renounced the sect; the fourth suffered from a mental illness. To me, those were positive results that not only showed that brainwashing was real, but that its effects could be reversed. That alone could have justified the passing of a new law. The unchallenged appellate ruling effectively left kidnapping and deprogramming as the only avenue left for parents seeking to rescue their children.

It's a heart-tugging quandary for parents. Kidnapping is illegal and the tactics used by deprogrammers to wean victims away from destructive cults can be brutal. If applied to people who aren't truly brainwashed, the process can lead to psychological damage. Yet I have talked to young people who say it saved their lives. What would I do if I was the parent? I once heard that even a judge resorted to hiring a kidnapper. These are complicated issues the legislature should have tackled, but never did.

Because of the ruling in the prior Moonie case, the Molko and Leal cases were nonstarters. Neither trial judge would accept testimony from experts explaining that the church's sophisticated indoctrination tactics rendered both plaintiffs incapable of exercising their own judgment. Both judges couldn't get past the fact that the plaintiffs stayed even after learning of the church's deception and testified that the church had "satisfied" their personal concerns. And, leaning on the dictum in the Katz case, both judges ruled that the lawsuits were unconstitutional inquiries into the validity of religious beliefs.

At that moment, I realized that I could no longer seek damages for a client who had been brainwashed by a destructive cult. Before I could ever get the issue into an appellate court, it appeared that the cause— and this little legal niche that I had turned into a career—had been lost.

So I offered my services pro bono to the attorneys handling the Molko and Leal case, hoping for rewards in the afterlife (I certainly wouldn't mind 72 virgins of my own). I helped write a petition for Leal asking the California Supreme Court to hear the case and Ford Greene wrote one for Molko. Getting a case in front of the high justices was no sure thing. They aren't required to review any decision; you must convince them that an important legal or social issue requires clarification for the benefit of society.

I argued that the lurid recent history of dangerous cults cried out for a reevaluation of the finding in the earlier Moonie case. For the sake of public safety, the court needed to determine whether thought reform existed and, if so, under what circumstances could victims seek legal redress.

The High Court agreed to hear the case.

*   *   *   *   *   *

That this precedent-setting case involved the Moonies was, perhaps, poetic justice. After all, many credit Rev. Moon as the principal importer of Mao Tse-Tung's thought-reform practices to the United States.

Born in 1920 in Sangsa-rin-myon in the North Pyongan province of North Korea—then under Japanese control—Moon was one of 13 children. Moon's family went into bankruptcy proceedings while he was still a child, which may explain his preoccupation with amassing wealth. The family converted from Confucianism to the Presbyterian

Church when Moon was 10 years old. While praying on a mountain top at age 15, Moon claims Jesus told him he had been chosen to bring God's kingdom to Earth. But when he started preaching his interpretation of the bible in North Korea, he was arrested in 1946; he claims he nearly died from the beating police gave him.

His five years in a prison labor camp exposed him to Mao's thought-reform theories. Upon his release, in the midst of the Korean War, he began to build his own church, the Holy Spirit Association for the Unification of World Christianity, with a goal of eventually ruling the world—literally. By 1955, he had 30 church centers and three years later started spreading his gospel to Japan and later, to the United States. He relocated here in 1971. The church recruited aggressively, adapting Mao's tactics in Rev. Moon's own unique way; his "love bombing" and "Heavenly Deception" practices lured a steady stream of impressionable youths who would donate their savings and then hit the streets to raise even more money.

His Unification Church stood firmly against communism, which won him some early U.S. fans on the political right. In 1974, he gambled that Richard M. Nixon would survive Watergate; Moonies prayed and fasted for the beleaguered president for three days in front of the Capitol Building, for which Nixon thanked Moon publicly.

The church continued to grow, recruiting in 120 countries by 1975. But people were noticing his extreme views, including his call to end the separation between church and state. A report on the church compiled by U.S. Rep. Donald M. Fraser contended that Moon was a political tool of the North Korean CIA. A book by the staff director of Rep. Fraser's committee charged the church with financial corruption. Other reports alleged the church was involved in manufacturing munitions. In 1976, Moon was denounced by Charles Wilson, a California congressman, who inserted two negative articles about Rev. Moon in the Congressional Record and noted that the Unification Church leader owned a 22-acre estate in Tarrytown, N.Y., which included a mansion valued at $850,000. "As for his religion," Rep. Wilson said, "if that is what it is, it is regarded as being as weird in Korea as it is here."

In 1982, Moon launched the *Washington Times*, a daily newspaper in our nation's capitol. While he hired legitimate journalists, many considered it a propaganda tool for the church. Several of its original editors resigned, claiming editorial interference by Moon and his aides.

That same year, Rev. Moon was convicted of filing false federal income tax returns and was sentenced to 18 months in the Federal Correctional Institution in Danbury, Connecticut.

*   *   *   *   *   *

While the legislative branch is charged with drafting laws, some are made by the judiciary, through decisions that define our inherent rights. For example, a legal journal article arguing for the protection of our right to privacy led to judicial decisions defining those privacy rights and establishing when people could sue for having them trampled. Here, we were asking the state high court to confirm the existence of brainwashing and establish the right to sue those who would use it to force their beliefs on others.

This was my version of a holy war, with the souls of what could be thousands of future thought reform victims at stake. Was brainwashing a provable fact, and if so, was it protected by the first Amendment or were there circumstances that would permit victims to sue? If we could convince the California high court, whose precedents carried considerable weight in other states, we could change society.

The motivation for most brainwashing was to suck money from victims; if cult leaders understood that their money could be taken away, they might abandon those tactics. A positive ruling would also reinforce the need for more education about brainwashing and cults.

If we lost, I feared that cults would multiply and spread. And I would be taking fender bender cases. Yeah, it was huge.

With my involvement in the Center for Feeling Therapy litigation, it first appeared I wouldn't be able to pursue the Molko appeal and I tried unsuccessfully to find a law firm that would do it pro bono. But the Center litigation was settled much quicker than I expected and suddenly, I was experiencing something alien: free time. So I decided to do the Molko brief myself.

Some heavy hitters weighed in against us. Religious groups and other organizations claiming spiritual origins—including, naturally, Scientology and Synanon—backed the Moonies. The American Psychological Association, under pressure from many lobbyists for religious groups, submitted a brief written by a former California attorney general claiming brainwashing was an unproven theory. Then, they withdrew it.

On our side was Ford Greene, Stanley Leal and me. Leal was representing his daughter. I was arguing for my once and future clients —and my career. But Greene had an even more compelling reason for his involvement.

In 1974, his 18-year-old sister Catherine disappeared, eventually turning up in a Unification Church camp. Greene went to Boonville to see her, but she was continually surrounded by Moonies. So, when a church leader invited him to attend a training session, he agreed, hoping it would get him closer to his sister. In doing so, he ignored his fears about Moon, whose speeches sounded "Hitler-like" to him. At the training camp, he was exposed to the Moonies' "love bombing" tactics. Visions of Hitler Youth danced in his head, but self-doubt crept in as church leaders poured on the love. He eventually succumbed, becoming a Moonie, which he later blamed on low self-esteem, a common trait in young people. Eventually, the church's persistent demonizing of outsiders as Satan's spawn prompted him to leave after eight months. He became an outspoken critic of the church and a cult deprogrammer. He testified in congressional hearings on Rev. Moon and went to law school so he could carry on the fight in court.

But he was never able to get his sister out. When he tried to deprogram her, she sued him as well as other family members. They finally had to accept that she was gone, no longer a part of their lives. She was eventually married off in South Korea in one of Rev. Moon's mass weddings.

*　*　*　*　*　*

Greene and Leal wrote briefs on behalf of their clients. With no client, I had to be hired by an interested party seeking standing to present a friend-of-the-court brief. So I convinced the Cult Awareness Network (CAN) to permit me to file the brief on its behalf and the Supreme Court granted us permission to do so.

It was the most important brief I had ever written and I needed to nail it. There is an old saying: bad facts can make bad law. Likewise, if lawyers frame the issues incorrectly, bad precedents can be set. Both the trial and appellate courts ruled that concealing the true identity of the Unification Church wasn't relevant because the plaintiffs stayed on for personal reasons, even after they knew the truth. But I believed the plaintiffs' testimony during their depositions was never placed in the proper context. The courts didn't understand that the personal reasons they cited for staying were based on beliefs that had been forced on them by the group.

Molko and Leal had answered honestly and, following their lawyers' standard instructions, had limited their answers to the narrow framework of the questions posed. They should have added that those beliefs had been forcibly imposed on them, in part through the persistent lies told by their handlers to get them to stay, thus giving the handlers ample time to brainwash them into believing that they needed to stay permanently. The ruling rewarded the cult for successfully deceiving their victims. We had to challenge the doctrine of "Heavenly Deception" and make the courts understand the damage it caused.

The constitutional debate also needed to be reframed. The validity of the Unification Church's beliefs weren't on trial; the system used to force them on the unsuspecting was. To win that debate, I needed to overcome the burden of the finding in the Katz conservatorship case. And to do that, I needed to convince the court that brainwashing was real. Then, the court could define what the law should be, even if it felt the evidence in this particular case didn't fit a claim of brainwashing.

Knowing the reluctance of judges to restrain religious freedoms in any way, I offered the High Court an out. If the justices would just rule that religious organizations which concealed their identities or denied their religious origins couldn't then assert their rights to protection under the first amendment, we could then define victims' rights in another case—hopefully, one of mine.

It wasn't going to be easy. With the help of a young law graduate, Tony Ellrod, I spent months in the Pepperdine University law library locating every state or federal case that addressed the issue of brainwashing. And this was before computer data bases. We had to go through file cabinets organized by subject matter and keyword books. We then took the cases we found and searched the case law books to find other cases in which those initial cases were cited. We summarized the facts and rulings of every relevant case. We scoured legal journals for articles that supported our view that brainwashing was a scourge and civil remedies were needed.

We found a number of precedents that confirmed our thesis that there was a substantive difference between the freedom to think, which is protected absolutely, and the freedom to act, which isn't. We also pointed out that this wasn't a case brought by parents seeking to remove their children from the church (as in the prior Moonie case); it involved former members themselves accusing the church of fraud and of damaging them personally.

I also found considerable precedent for the right to sue religious groups for harmful acts, even if they were religiously motivated. A California court allowed a priest to sue his superiors for imprisoning him in order to force a confession of sins. A Pennsylvania court allowed a member to sue his church for interfering with his marriage and business interests by ordering the congregation to shun him. And a Washington court permitted an alienation of affections claim by a husband who was accused of being "full of the devil" by his pastor, who also counseled his wife to leave him.

*   *   *   *   *   *

I was proud of the finished product, which was quite lengthy. But it almost got left at the starting gate. The Cult Awareness Network sent a copy to its New York attorney, Herbert Rosedale, who decided it was too long and analytical for time-constrained high court justices. He dashed out a quick, eight-page policy argument that deleted the legal analysis and case review. I was furious. We needed the analysis to overcome the burden of the existing legal precedents, a fact he failed to recognize. Rosedale convinced CAN to submit his brief. I believed my brief was critical, but without a recognized interested party to sponsor it, I couldn't present it.

Henrietta Crampton saved the day. While she was a member of CAN, she was also president of its predecessor, the Citizens' Freedom Foundation. I had frequently advised Ms. Crampton on cult issues and we became friends. When I told her about Rosedale and asked her to trust that my brief was needed to win this fight, she decided to go against CAN and Rosedale and hire me to file a brief for the foundation. The court granted our request to file another brief.

But, since I didn't represent one of the plaintiffs, I still had no standing to make oral argument. So I asked Greene and Leal to give me the time they were allotted to rebut the other side's opening statement. I was better at rebuttal than opening statements anyway. Rarely do lawyers surrender precious argument time, especially in a case like this. But we all saw one advantage. I was the one who had brought the brainwashing issue into the public arena by fighting Synanon and I was the one who got bitten by a rattlesnake for doing it. It had been a big national news story and made me an object of curiosity for the justices. They would want to judge me for themselves—was I right or wrong?

It was an unusual move—perhaps unprecedented—but the attorneys—and the justices—eventually agreed to let me do the rebuttal.

*   *   *   *   *   *

There were two times in my life that I felt fear while packing for a trip. One, in 1981, was for a flight to Visalia to take Charles Dederich's deposition after his conviction on charges of conspiring to murder me. The second, in 1988, was when I was preparing to leave behind my wife and three-year-old son to stay at a hotel room in San Francisco the night before oral arguments in the Molko appeal.

I didn't believe we could win. Greene wasn't optimistic either; during dinner, neither of us smiled much. It was like being at a wake. I didn't get much sleep that night.

We were challenging an established precedent handed down by a respected judge. Further, we were arguing a case record that might not be sufficiently clear on key facts. And we were battling the reluctance of the judiciary to restrain religious freedoms in any way. I hoped the court would at least consider the alternatives I put in the brief to salvage what we could from the rubble of defeat.

Thankfully, the Justices declined and addressed all the issues in the case head-on.

*   *   *   *   *   *

The day dawned on one of the most exhilarating experiences of my life. I had argued before in the appellate courts, but there was something majestic about appearing before the highest court in the state. Lawyers were announced by name and asked to step forward to their seats, like Knights of the Round Table. The Justices sat like kings, high above the proceedings. Everywhere there were television cameras and reporters with pens and notebooks poised. I was filled with pride just to be there, especially with a case I felt could make history.

Greene hit hard on the facts of the case, contending they proved that Molko and Leal didn't become Moonies voluntarily, but were brainwashed. Stanley Leal didn't have any experience in this kind of fight, but as the suffering father of one of the victims, he made the anguish of a parent touched by brainwashing palpable. When he spoke before the court, his obvious distress communicated the reality that this could happen to anyone, even lawyers or judges. His daughter was taught that he was an agent of Satan. Who wanted to be the next parent to feel that pain?

And by the time Ford was halfway through his opening statement, we were all smiling.

Because appellate-court justices frequently interrupt presentations to ask challenging questions, it was often possible to tell how they were leaning by what kind of questions they asked. In this case, they were asking Greene all the right ones. Not only that, they were grilling the church's lawyers mercilessly. Obviously, our briefs had done their job.

By the time I got to bat, no home run was needed. All I really had to do was stay the course and say yes to the questions asked. But I did close by saying that by establishing a clear right to sue organizations for brainwashing the court would discourage those groups from maintaining indoctrination centers like Boonville for fear of facing huge damage judgments. And money, I said, was what these groups were all about. Further, it would reassure parents about the safety of their children's religious choices, thus diminishing the need for kidnapping and deprogramming.

We were greeted outside the courtroom by a swarm of popping camera bulbs and inquisitive reporters. Arm-in-arm, Ford and I giddily provided our version of the *Ghostbusters* motto: "We came, we saw, we kicked their ass."

*   *   *   *   *   *

The court issued its formal ruling in October of 1988. My son was still too young to understand his Dad's exuberance. The justices ruled that the "marginal burden" placed on churches' exercise of free religion was justified by the state's duty to protect families from the great stress and financial losses they endured when members were "unwillingly subjected to coercive persuasion as a result of fraud and deception."

The justices decided there was sufficient evidence to rule that by the time the Moonies had identified themselves, they had rendered Molko and Leal "incapable of deciding not to join the Church, by subjecting them, without their knowledge or consent, to an intense program of coercive persuasion (thought reform)." The jury, said the court, could conclude that "such conduct is extreme and outrageous when it exceeds all bounds of decency usually tolerated by a decent society," therefore making the Church liable for punitive damages as well as compensatory damages.

To my great satisfaction, the ruling proved that Rosedale was wrong. The court not only wanted to review the past cases cited in my brief, it quoted most of them. It also quoted from an excellent legal journal article I had included from Richard Delgado, a USC law professor, which showed the damage caused by brainwashing: "While some individuals who experience coercive persuasion emerge un-scathed, many others develop serious and sometimes irreversible physical and psychiatric disorders, up to and including schizophrenia, self-mutilation, and suicide."

In an important conclusion, the High Court also rejected the dictum stated in the previous Moonie case, noting its ruling didn't burden one's right to believe, but only burdens the effort to recruit new members by deceptive means.

It was nearly a total triumph. In only one instance do I believe the court erred. Leal contended that she was falsely imprisoned when the Moonies brainwashed her into believing that if she left, her family "would be damned in Hell" and she would lose her ticket to heaven. The justices rejected the claim, arguing that threats of divine retribution were protected religious speech.

But this contradicted the rest of their decision. No one claimed that it was wrong to teach such beliefs, or determine whether they were valid, only that the belief was forced on the plaintiffs by an intense brainwashing regimen, which was made possible by the fraudulent concealment of the group's true identity. If it was wrong to bully people into beliefs that made them join or donate money, why wasn't it wrong to bully them into believing they couldn't leave? Somehow, the justices failed to connect the same dots on that issue they had in the other causes of action.

Shortly after the decision, the Unification Church settled with Leal and Molko. I didn't get a dime, but I did get some great thank-you letters, including one from Professor Delgado that hangs on my wall.

As for the virgins, we'll see.

Did we change society? You bet. While the ruling didn't fulfill my fantasy of obliterating all destructive cults—they're forces of nature that will always be with us, like tornados or earthquakes—the ability to make cult leaders pay for brainwashing the unsuspecting finally put a damper on the explosion of cults that grew out of the confusion and spiritual quest of the '60s.

Far fewer cases came my way. I heard less often from the media, which had less to report; only a handful of today's cults have approached the size and notoriety achieved by their predecessors. And the de-programming business went the way of buggy whips and typewriters.

As for the Unification Church, it is still with us, although not nearly as visible as it once was. Prior to his death, Rev. Moon remained politically active into his 90s, sponsoring such events as the Million Family March, a sequel to the better-known Million Man March, and the 2001 Inaugural Prayer Luncheon for Unity and Renewal, a gathering of 1,400 ministers and civic and political leaders, many of whom had no idea who their host was, and weren't particularly overjoyed when they found out. The event was part of the ceremonies leading up to the inauguration of George W. Bush.

In 2002, celebrating the *Washington Times*' 20th anniversary, Rev. Moon said the newspaper "is responsible to let the American people know about God" and "will become the instrument in spreading the truth about God to the world."

But the newspaper reportedly has never been profitable despite the nearly $2 billion Rev. Moon poured into it by 2002. Ronald Reagan reportedly read it religiously while he was in the White House, but over the years its appeal dwindled along with its coverage, staff and readers. On November 2, 2010, Rev. Moon and a group of former *Washington Times* editors purchased the paper from Moon's son, Preston Moon, for $1, saving it from a proposed shutdown.

*   *   *   *   *   *

Epilogue:

In 2008, Rev. Moon turned over leadership of the church to another son, Hyung Jin Moon. But even in retirement, the aspirations of a man who called himself the second coming of Jesus Christ certainly weren't any less lofty. On July 8, 2010, according to a Unification Church website, Rev. Moon delivered a speech at an event ambitiously named "The Providential Convention to Proclaim the Word that Firmly Establishes the True Parents of Heaven, Earth and Mankind." In the speech, Moon revealed that God had scheduled a D-Day three years hence in which family members from the spirit world would return to Earth and eight generations would live as one family. This event was going to have a huge impact on the world as we know it. Secular elections were to disappear, all people were to become one family through cross-cultural marriages and we would all enjoy tranquility and happiness in the sacred reign of peace.

But Rev. Moon died in 2012 and the prophecy's D-Day has passed with nary a word from the spirit world. Thank goodness. Who needs all those relatives moving in.

Chapter 12: Escape from Rancho Rajneesh

He moved about, going to Crete where he was arrested. He tried Switzerland, Sweden, Great Britain and Canada, but was refused entry. Ireland let him stay for two weeks as long as he didn't speak publicly. When he landed in Madrid, the Guardia Civil circled the plane. He was tossed out of Dakar; when he gave a speech in Uruguay, he was banished. Jamaica gave his group 12 hours to leave.

I tried to warn them.

It all started with a case I really didn't want. Learjet heiress Patricia Lear had agreed to publish a collection of the philosophical musings of her Indian guru, the Bhagwan Shree Rajneesh, who founded a controversial commune in Oregon noted mostly for its sexual liberties and the founder's fleet of 93 Rolls Royces. But they had a falling out and the guru sued Ms. Lear to prevent publication. She hired me to countersue for a loss of expected profits.

I was certain the commune was a destructive cult, but this case wasn't about the abuses typically linked to totalistic movements. It was more of a business dispute and I had bigger fish to fry, cases where people faced physical harm and lives were at stake. But an Oregon attorney I respected asked me to take the case so I did, hoping a replacement could be found later.

As I got more involved, however, my concerns about the commune's activities grew, particularly as I got to know Ma Anand Sheela, the sect's powerful second-in-command. She was arrogant, hostile and profane. When an NBC reporter asked her about allegations of ethnic slurs by her guru, her answer included a reference to the Holocaust as "500 Jews in an ashtray."

In our talks and my review of interviews she had given to both print and broadcast journalists, I saw a familiar dark storm cloud boiling on the horizon. In Ma Sheela's view, someone was always out to get the commune, which justified any actions it deemed necessary to achieve its goals. I'd heard this kind of paranoia and rationalization before, at Synanon, the People's Temple and the Center for Feeling Therapy. I knew in my bones that violence was inevitable in this once-serene corner of the Pacific Northwest.

Hoping that my past history and expertise would carry some weight, I informed local authorities of my fears. Naturally, they asked for proof. I had none. All I could say was that I knew cults and I knew evil and I knew the warning signs of impending violence. The similarities to other cults that had turned to violence were unmistakable. But nobody wants to think it could happen in their idyllic community. Really, I think they considered me a bit nuts.

Two weeks later, I learned I was wrong: violence wasn't about to break out, it already had. That's when it was revealed that Rajneesh's followers had poisoned more than 700 people living in surrounding communities with a virulent strain of salmonella. And investigators uncovered far more ambitious plans in the works, including a stillborn plot to crash a bomb-laden plane into a county courthouse, an eerie precursor to 9/11. Meanwhile, Sheela compiled an ever-growing list of potential assassination targets, including state and federal prosecutors, county officials and dissidents among the guru's followers.

Eventually, this crime wave led to the dissolution of the commune, prison sentences for several followers and the forced exile of its leader.

*   *   *   *   *   *

Born Chandra Mohan Rajneesh in 1931, Bhagwan was the eldest of eleven children of a cloth merchant living in a small village in the Raisen District of Madhya Pradesh, India. He was an atheist in his youth; he later dabbled in hypnotism, explored socialism and eventually claimed to have achieved spiritual enlightenment in 1953 following a mystical experience in the Bhanvartal Garden in Jabalpur.

In the 1960s, he took the name Acharya Rajneesh and started issuing dire warnings of a "third and last war" and the need for a "new humanity." He started lecturing and receiving visitors in 1970 and by

1971, he was the spiritual teacher to a group of loyal sanyassins, or followers. He changed his name again, this time to Bhagwan Shree Rajneesh.

The budding guru depended upon the kindness of wealthy women to build his spiritual empire. Ma Yoga Laxmi, his secretary and first disciple, used her fortune to spread his word. Greek shipping heiress Catherine Venizelos, aka Ma Yoga Mukta, helped fund the purchase of property in Koregaon Park, Pune, for his first ashram. And later, Ma Anand Sheela got her husband, wealthy American businessman Marc Silverman, to purchase land for the Oregon ashram for $5.75 million.

As new-age spiritualism flourished in the '70s, Indian gurus, with their air of meditative wisdom, were all the rage. Even the Beatles had their own personal guru, the Maharishi Mahesh Yogi, the father of transcendental meditation, who was also targeted by anti-cult organizations. Soon, Westerners seeking spiritual enlightenment flocked to the Pune ashram, donning flowing orange robes—a holy color in Hinduism—to soak up Bhagwan's teachings, stock up on clothes, jewelry, ceramics and organic cosmetics at the arts and craft center and join in the meditation and encounter groups conducted by human potential movement therapists visiting from the U.S.

Amidst all this joyous self-realization, controversy dogged Rajneesh. Stories of unfettered sex at the ashram led to him being dubbed the "sex guru" by the press. Reports also started leaking of physical aggression. Richard Price, co-founder of the Big Sur, California-based Esalen Institute, which existed to exalt these new-age groups, allegedly suffered a broken arm during an eight-hour encounter-group session with Rajneesh sannyasins armed with wooden weapons. Some balked at the violence, but others rationalized it as the price of enlightenment.

In 1979, with a mountain of bad press piling up about violence in cults, Rajneesh publicly admitted the violence but swore that it had ended, having "fulfilled its function" in evolving a spiritual commune. The Bhagwan's avowal didn't quell concerns about his community. Stories also spread of Western sannyasins raising money for the movement through prostitution and drug-running—allegedly with the Bhagwan's approval.

But still they came, some 30,000 visitors a year, to hear Rajneesh's pungent mix of spiritual guidance and political ramblings—leavened by a healthy ration of dirty jokes more suited to a Las Vegas lounge act.

In his lectures, Bhagwan chided socialism for socializing poverty and dismissed Mahatma Gandhi for worshiping poverty. He also criticized institutionalized religions such as Hinduism, making him increasingly divisive in his homeland. Fed up, the Indian government in 1974 rescinded the ashram's tax-exempt status, leaving it with an estimated $5 million tax bill.

Clearly, it was time for Bhagwan to take his act on the road.

*   *   *   *   *   *

After speaking daily to followers for nearly 15 years, Rajneesh suddenly stopped talking in 1981, launching three years of public silence and satsangs, or spiritual readings. His silence didn't stop him from applying for a U.S. visa that year, claiming a medical emergency —basically a painful prolapsed, or burst, disc—that allegedly would threaten his life if he wasn't allowed to emigrate to the U.S and get American medical treatment.

Waiting for him in Oregon was the 64,229-acre Big Muddy Ranch purchased by Marc Silverman and renamed "Rancho Rajneesh." He arrived in August and by November, the former atheist applied for permanent U.S. residency as a religious worker, which was refused on the grounds that he couldn't lead a religion while ill and while living in a self-enforced silence. Legally, it was a ridiculous position, violating the First Amendment right to freedom of religion. It was reversed three years later.

The good folks of Oregon weren't too happy with their odd new neighbor, who kept issuing dire proclamations of an impending nuclear apocalypse sometime in the 1990s. Or that perhaps two-thirds of humanity would be decimated by AIDS, as Sheela said Bhagwan also predicted. He, like Scientology's L. Ron Hubbard, had an obsessive fear of germs and required his followers to wear both condoms and rubber gloves during sex.

Bhagwan insisted he didn't teach any belief, but encouraged followers to essentially live in the present, without regard to concerns about God or an afterlife. He urged followers to let go of the desire for reward, because work is its own reward, an odd statement for a man who lusted after luxury cars and diamond-studded watches.

Within a year, local authorities launched a series of legal battles with the commune. The county tried to enforce land-use laws limiting population growth and construction at the ranch. To circumvent those restrictions, the commune incorporated as a city in 1982. But that vote was challenged by the state, which contended that a religious entity couldn't legally control a city (state officials apparently never visited Salt Lake City).

As the area's immune system sought to reject this invading virus, Rajneesh and his followers grew stubborn, confrontational and paranoid. Not coincidentally, this period also marked the rise to power of Ma Anand Sheela. Sheela left her native Baroda, India, at age 18 to get an American education at Montclair State College. She returned in 1972, joined the Pune community with her wealthy new husband (who took the name Chinmaya) and quickly rose through the ranks. In 1982, Rajneesh granted her power-of-attorney after she promised to build him the utopian community he envisioned at Rancho Rajneesh; a year later, she announced that he would speak only to her.

From this unholy alliance grew the roots of terrorism.

*   *   *   *   *   *

Sheela, surrounded by a cadre of loyal women called "moms," anointed herself the "Queen" of Rajneeshpuram. She met every day with Rajneesh and ran the commune with an iron hand, using housing and work assignments to reward allies or punish opponents. One of the sect's top attorneys found himself pursuing a new career as a bulldozer driver after a clash with Sheela.

The most feared punishment was banishment. Since most of the members of the commune had sold their possessions—donating the proceeds to the guru—and severed all ties with the outside world, they had nothing to return to if expelled.

During the Lear litigation, I had frequent telephone conversations with Sheela and was struck by her misplaced sense of self-importance. When the commune won some legal decision, she delighted in calling me so I could hear the raucous celebration in the background. Her constant battles with the surrounding community reminded me chillingly of Synanon's fights with its various neighbors and the violence that followed.

She accused the surrounding communities of bigotry, warning that those who opposed the commune would pay. "If they touch any one of our people, I'll have 15 of their heads," she threatened, "and I mean business."

When the Wasco County board of commissioners demanded that the commune adhere to all those zoning and permit requirements, it was a clear sign to Sheela that the commissioners were out to get Rajneeshpuram. So, in 1984, she attempted to get two sannyasins elected to the board. To enhance their chances, she bused in 2,000 voter-eligible transients from all over the country, promising them free food and beer. She heralded it as a humanitarian gesture to reduce homelessness.

After a judge ordered registration hearings for the transients, however, some left. Others, it turned out, suffered from mental illnesses and became unruly and combative, prompting Sheela to dump them into the neighboring communities. She then offered to retrieve them and transport them back to their original homes if authorities allowed Rajneeshpuram to build its utopian community. Oregon rejected the offer, instead coughing up an estimated $100,000 to bus the transients back home.

As tensions increased, I knew violence was inevitable. And while Oregon law enforcement officials didn't take me seriously, there was someone who did.

Win McCormack, the publisher and editor of the local Oregonian newspaper, reported aggressively on the activities of the Rajneeshees. McCormack had good reason to be wary of the group and to heed my warnings. For four years, he had been my client, one of the many victims of the Center for Feeling Therapy. He particularly hated the center's Richard Corriere, who he accused of browbeating the mother of his unborn child into an abortion by forcing her to carry around a heavily weighted doll. McCormack believed Corriere should have been arrested for murder.

When McCormack left the Center, he returned to the serenity of Oregon to heal. But once again, a dangerous cult was at his doorstep. He became interested in Rajneesh in 1983 when hearing of his propensity for anti-Semitic statements, a stark reminder of Corriere. As he investigated, he discovered more similarities, such as the encounter groups that broke down followers' personalities and reprogrammed them. But the commune's brand of abuse seemed even more controlling and violent. He dubbed it the "Center on steroids" in his monthly column "Rajneesh Watch."

*   *   *   *   *   *

Bhagwan ended his period of public silence in October of 1984, resuming daily discourses. This apparently created a rift with Sheela, who saw this as an attempt to reduce her power. Her paranoia growing, she saw threats everywhere and started to compile a list of assassination targets from among those who opposed the commune's plans. Included were county commissioners, along with U.S. Atty. Charles Turner and Oregon Atty. Gen. David Frohnmayer, who were pressing legal cases against the sect.

Sheela and other followers did manage to poison a couple of officials, who survived, and obtained handguns in Texas and false identification cards in New York as part of a plot against the two prosecutors, but the plan fizzled. Affidavits of ex-members stated the murder conspirators belonged to a group known as "the 38," an Uzi-toting brigade who had been trained in "commando tactics" in much the same manner as Manson's family and Synanon's Imperial Marines.

The hit list also included sect members who opposed Sheela, or were perceived as threats. Helen Byron made the list when she won a $1.7 million judgment against the guru—she said she loaned him the money to purchase Rolls Royces, while Bhagwan called it a donation. A group of wealthy Los Angeles donors—including the wife of the producer of *The Godfather*, were similarly targeted, because they flaunted their wealth and resisted Sheela's rule. Sheela even included the guru's personal physician, Swami Deveraj (formerly George Meredith), his dentist and his caretaker, wary of their influence on the commune's leader. At a social function, Ma Shanti Bhadra, one of Sheela's moms, approached Deveraj and, while hugging him, jabbed him with a syringe loaded with poison. Deveraj became gravely ill, but survived.

As with so many other cults, the frustration of not getting their way had boiled over into criminal activity. As the board of commissioners election neared, Sheela sought to prevent local residents from voting by dispatching teams of commune residents to add some lethal salmonella seasoning to salad bars in restaurants and a grocery store in the county seat of The Dalles. One Rajneeshee was assigned to smear the poison onto fixtures in the men's room of the county courthouse. Sheela later claimed that she and one of her moms, Ma Anand Puja, a nurse, discussed the bioterrorism plan with Rajneesh leadership.

They even discussed using a more potent salmonella strain which causes typhoid fever, but backed off, fearing it would raise suspicions and trigger an investigation. Apparently, they believed that severe tummy aches on a massive scale wouldn't raise an eye-brow.

More than 700 people fell ill, though all survived. Once authorities concluded that deliberate poisoning was the likely cause, it wasn't difficult to pinpoint the most likely suspects. Investigators soon discovered a "germ warfare" laboratory at the commune, where Ma Puja experimented with toxic brews. Salmonella samples found there matched bacteria isolated from the salad bars.

The investigators also discovered something more alarming: Puja's "Moses Five" project, a failed attempt to cultivate a live AIDS virus. That discovery led some to theorize that Sheela and Puja, in their fanatic devotion, were attempting to ensure the fulfillment of the Bhagwan's prophecy that two-thirds of the planet's population would be wiped out by AIDS.

Sheela's group also allegedly fire-bombed a county records office in The Dalles in the bizarre belief that this would halt county efforts to stop development at the commune.

*   *   *   *   *   *

In September of 1985, Sheela—and most of her cronies—suddenly resigned and departed for Europe. Bhagwan held a press conference and accused them of the attempted murder of his personal physician, poisonings of public officials, bugging of the commune (including his own home) and the biological attack on The Dalles. Sheela's robes, along with 5,000 copies of the Book of Rajneeshism—which she had published—were burned by 2,000 Rajneesh followers.

While Bhagwan insisted he was unaware of these crimes until Sheela and her supporters left, other sannyasins claimed she was merely a convenient scapegoat. Bhagwan was behind everything, they contended, and blamed her only as revenge for leaving.

Investigators found an extensive network of wiretapping devices throughout the compound. In an interview on *60 Minutes*, Sheela admitted to the bugging, saying she feared Rajneesh was planning to blame her for the commune's crime wave. She denied the other charges and called the Bhagwan a liar who directed every criminal act she committed. Bhagwan "exploited people by using their human frailty and emotions," she said.

A month later, a federal grand jury charged Bhagwan and several other disciples with conspiracy to evade immigration laws. Noting that he never sought outside medical attention for his alleged medical emergency after arriving here, the Immigration and Naturalization Service concluded that he had lied about it on his visa application. Soon thereafter, Bhagwan and some sannyasins were arrested on a North Carolina airstrip attempting to flee the country in, of all things, a rented Learjet. On board, authorities found $58,000 in cash, 35 expensive watches and over $1 million in jewelry. Instead of photos in a Rolls Royce, the world now saw the sex guru pictured in handcuffs.

Bhagwan was only prosecuted for the immigration fraud, which also included charges of arranging sham marriages in order to obtain U.S. citizenship for followers. He pleaded no contest to the charges and got off with five years probation, a $400,000 fine and deportation.

He was never charged with the poisoning or murder plots, but some law enforcement investigators who listened to hundreds of hours of tape recordings believe charges should have been filed. Frohnmayer, the attorney general who made Sheela's hit list, called Rajneesh and Sheela "genuinely evil," adding that the guru's philosophy was not "disapproving of poisoning."

*   *   *   *   *   *

The capture and prosecution of the conspirators dragged on for years. But the sentences handed out were oddly light compared to other notorious cult cases, another example of the uneven application of justice in cult-related cases. Here, the courts, to their credit, obviously took into account the undue influence of a manipulative cult leader in judging his followers. But they failed to adequately punish those responsible.

Two moms, Sally-Anne Croft and Susan Hagan, were extradited from Britain in 1994 and convicted a year later for their participation in wiretapping and the plot to murder Turner, the U.S. attorney. Both got five years in prison and were released after serving two years. In December of 2002, mom Phyllis McCarthy, aka Ma Yoga Vidya, pleaded guilty to immigration fraud and conspiracy to commit murder, and was sentenced to one year in jail and fined $10,000. She was released in ten months. In court statements, Ms. McCarthy, like so many other ex-cultists I have encountered, expressed regret that she wasn't tough enough to resist the brainwashing at Rajhneeshpuram. She called her time with the group "psychological torture."

Several others were convicted on a variety of charges; many who pleaded guilty got only probation. A few of those indicted remain fugitives. Rajneesh corporations agreed to pay $400,000 to cover Oregon's investigative costs, $500,000 to cover damages owed by four restaurants involved in the poisonings, an additional $400,000 to the restaurant owners and $5 million to the Oregon state victim's fund.

With its leadership scattered, the Rajneeshees abandoned the commune, eventually selling it to Dennis Washington, a wealthy Montana rancher, for $3.95 million. Washington donated the property to a Christian group, Young Life, for a summer youth camp.

*   *   *   *   *   *

Sheela was arrested on October 28, 1985, in West Germany and extradited to the U.S. in February 1986. Sheela and Puja pleaded guilty in Oregon state court to a variety of assault and conspiracy charges related to the poisoning of County Judge Bill Hulse and County Commissioner Ray Matthew. They each received 20 years in prison and $400,000 in fines on the various charges.

In federal court, Sheela and her co-conspirators admitted to the attempted murder of Swami Deveraj, the poisoning of two county officials, setting fire to a county office, wiretapping and immigration fraud, among other charges. Sheela and Puja were sentenced to 24-year terms in federal prison and fined $470,000 each.

All told, Sheela received three concurrent, 20-year terms in prison. The State of Oregon allowed Sheela to serve her time in Pleasanton, Calif., a minimum-security, federal prison for nonviolent, white-collar criminals. But she and Puja were released after only two and a half years for good behavior and immediately left for Europe before the U.S. Department of Justice could notify the state that it planned to file additional charges against the pair after their release.

I believe Sheela should have served the full 20 years; she was no brainwashed puppet for a manipulative cult leader. She lusted for power. She was Goebbels to Bhagwan's Hitler.

At least she lost her green card.

*   *   *   *   *   *

In Europe, Sheela managed restaurants in Germany and then Portugal. She fled to Switzerland to avoid extradition when she was tipped off that American authorities wanted her on new charges.

Arriving in the Swiss town of Basel in 1990, she was nearly penniless, but still managed to convince a Swiss court to grant her immunity from extradition on future criminal charges (a legal maneuver Roman Polanski also found quite useful recently). The Swiss instead agreed to try her, and although she was found guilty, she was sentenced to time served—the 2 1/2 years she spent in Pleasanton.

Now free of legal entanglements, she started building a new life. A local employment agency got her a job walking a retired man's dog for 10 Swiss francs an hour. She soon became the man's caretaker and eventually started a health-care business by taking three elderly ladies into her own home. The business grew and Sheela published a book about home health care management.

Here's a tip for customers of Sheela's home health-care facilities: Don't eat the salad.

*   *   *   *   *   *

After his followers in India reached a settlement with the government concerning back taxes on the Pune ashram, Rajneesh returned to his homeland in late 1984, receiving a hero's welcome by his disciples in New Delhi. They denounced the United States and declared that "either America must be hushed up or America will be the end of the world."

After visas for non-Indians in his entourage were revoked, Bhagwan flew to Crete where he was arrested. He tried Switzerland, Sweden, Great Britain and Canada, but was refused entry. Ireland let him stay for two weeks as long as he didn't speak publicly. When he landed in Madrid, the Guardia Civil circled the plane. He was tossed out of Dakar; when he gave a speech in Uruguay, he was banished. Jamaica gave his group 12 hours to leave.

In January of 1987, he returned to his original ashram in Pune, now reinvented as a "multiversity" with therapy, meditations and a dizzying array of colored robes. Bhagwan claimed his health was failing because U.S. authorities poisoned him during the incarceration that followed his arrest.

In 1988, the guru turned to Zen and soon thereafter renamed himself yet again. After a speech in April, 1989, the newly anointed Osho resumed his public silence; he died on January 19, 1990, at the age of 58, allegedly of heart failure. His epitaph was eerily like that of Heaven's Gate cult leader Marshall Applewhite seven years later, stating he had no life nor death, but "Visited this Planet Earth between Dec 11, 1931 – Jan 19, 1990."

Following his death, revisionist history began in earnest. Suddenly forgotten was his involvement in the Oregon crime spree, including what was widely labeled the first act of bioterrorism on U.S. soil (actually, the U.S. military's delivery of smallpox-infected blankets to Indians preceded it by more than 200 years).

Some Indian scholars exalted him as a spiritual leader in the mold of Gautama Buddha and Mahatma Gandhi; he was hailed as one of the ten people who had most changed India's destiny. A 2006 festival celebrated the 75th anniversary of his birth. His entire body of written work was placed in the library of India's national Parliament in New Delhi; his books have been translated into 55 different languages and have attained best-seller status in Italy and South Korea. An estimated 650 books quote his views on all facets of human existence.

By 2008, there were a reported 60 Osho locations in Nepal with 45,000 initiated disciples. The Osho group runs stress management seminars for corporate clients such as IBM and BMW. Bhagwan's ashram in Pune is now the Osho International Meditation Resort, billed as a "sacred space" for discovering one's true self. It is popular with tourists, attracting 200,000 visitors a year, including entertainers, actors, politicians, media and the Dalai Lama. (I was once asked at a lecture how to identify a destructive cult. I answered, only half in jest: "Count the number of Hollywood celebrities in attendance and if there is more than five, you get the hell out.")

Despite these postmortem hosannas, I believe Rajneesh had all the qualities of a sociopath: an unrealistic sense of self-importance and uniqueness; a need for constant attention and admiration; a penchant for outright lying; and, most importantly, a complete lack of empathy.

*   *   *   *   *   *

Epilogue:

Patricia Lear's case was an uphill battle and I never took it to trial. Since Ms. Lear now considered Rajneesh a destructive cult leader, how could she be harmed by not publishing his book? And how do you calculate lost profits in a new business with no track record? So, when Bhagwan's lawyer made a reasonable settlement offer, I recommended my client accept it. I didn't feel I could do better in court. But Pat turned it down. While she had that right, I no longer felt comfortable accepting her money; the cost was too high for the likely benefits she would get. More importantly, the Center for Feeling Therapy trial, where I was representing 40 clients claiming psychological damage, was about to start. I thought the trial might take as much as a year, so I bowed out. (It actually was settled in much less time.)

Here's what I remember most about the case.

When I attempted to schedule Rajneesh's deposition in Oregon, I was informed by his attorney, Swami Prem Niren, the former Los Angeles defense lawyer Philip J. Toelkes, that I first had to agree to some ground rules, to wit: I must take several special showers, wear a robe, bow and question from a kneeling position.

Here was my counteroffer: I told him I would not shower for several weeks and show up in sweat clothes, having just come from the gym and a two-mile run. And I expected Bhagwan to shake my hand. "He may be God to you," I said, "but he is not to me."

Bhagwan actually made a motion in court seeking to enforce his rules; it was hard not to laugh. The motion was denied.

I lost touch with Ms. Lear after that and don't know if she continued to pursue her claim. But I am confident she found the shutting of Rajneeshpuram and the arrest and deportation of Bhagwan more exhilarating than any financial award.

SECTION IV:

The Beat Goes On

Chapter 13: Escape from L. Ron Hubbard Way
Part 1: From Xenu to Xenophobia

In 1977, I decided to do some research on the Church of Scientology. While I didn't yet have a case, from all I had heard, it was only a matter of time. So I compiled a list of articles about the organization, most of them pretty critical. But when I went to my local library to check them out, the Scientology article had been ripped out of every magazine I picked up.

As Butch Cassidy said to the Sundance Kid: "Who are those guys?"

Had Scientologists been dispatched to every library and newsstand in the country to keep the general public from reading about their long history of misdeeds? What else were they capable of doing?

Throughout the '80s and '90s, I attempted to lay bare the secrets of Scientology's past through litigation. If I could get key documents unsealed, the public could see the organization's history of criminal acts and abuse, the bizarre life and beliefs of its founder and its outlandish claims that its "auditing" process could cure everything from carbuncles to catatonia to cancer.

Regrettably, my efforts weren't particularly productive and Scientology continued to grow into one of the richest and most successful cults in U.S. history. Thanks to its recruitment of high-profile entertainers such as Tom Cruise and John Travolta, it has become a pervasive presence in American life, although its claim of having eight million members is widely disputed (a 2008 survey by a City University of New York team put it at closer to 25,000).

How ironic that after all that, many of the secrets I tried to expose were eventually revealed in a TV cartoon show.

*   *   *   *   *   *

The story of human misery, as told by L. Ron Hubbard, science fiction writer-turned-creator of Scientology and pieced together from documents and accounts of former Scientologists:

Once upon a time—presumably about 75 million years ago—in a galaxy far, far away, the evil warlord Xenu ruled over the Galactic Federation, which consisted of 26 stars and 76 planets. Despite that abundance of space, the federation apparently suffered from a serious case of overcrowding. To relieve the problem, Xenu—with the help of evil psychiatrists (a redundant phrase, according to Scientologists)—concocted an elaborate plan to capture a billion people, paralyze them in an alcohol-and-glycol compound to capture their souls and banish them to earth, known then as Teegeeack, in space transports that looked oddly like DC-8s (which shouldn't be surprising, since Hubbard's vision of Xenu's realm looked a lot like 1950s America).

Upon arrival, Xenu's minions dumped the bodies into volcanoes all over the world and dropped hydrogen bombs to incinerate them in a horrific "wall of fire." Their souls escaped, but retained these terrible memories in something known, for some reason, as R6 implants. Those troubled souls, or "thetans," inhabited the bodies of newly born earthlings, infecting them with all the physical and psychological miseries contained in those transient vessels.

Fast forward to the present. Anyone seeking to cure the disorders those pesky thetans have burdened him (or her) with for the past 75 million years need only hook up to a Scientology e-meter—basically a box with two cups attached that measures galvanic skin responses, much like a lie detector. When the e-meter's needle jumps, it is measuring the "mental mass" created by the "thetans" in the subject's body. The more thetans you have, the more miseries you're afflicted with. But, through a series of questions asked by the box's operator, it can somehow exorcise those demons, restoring the subject's ability to act independently of his physical body, cause physical events to take place by sheer will and cure the illnesses and psychological disorders of others. In addition, he will become all-knowing and claim dominion over life, thought, matter, energy, space and time.

And he might start looking just like Tom Cruise.

It reportedly takes about $100,000 to achieve this miraculous omnipotence, but that has proved to be a moving target. After too many people reached the rarefied air of clarity, originally defined as "Operating Thetans III," new levels of clarity started to appear. Now, one must pony up to reach OT-VIII to obtain clear status. And the wealthier the person being audited, the more thetans he seemed to have and thus, the more auditing he required, noted Bent Corydon, a former Scientologist, in his book, *L. Ron Hubbard: Messiah or Madman?* One man, a geologist, engineer and entrepreneur, spent $450,000 to be cleared, Corydon wrote.

For an additional $6,500, ex-members said, a clear person would be allowed to carry around the sacred information that explained the "true secret" of all human problems in a briefcase handcuffed to his wrist, just like the *Blues Brothers*. Naturally, he would be sworn to secrecy, Corydon said, since revealing this powerful information to someone who isn't ready could result in pneumonia, lack of sleep or even death.

By the way, in case you wondered, the arch-villain Xenu, who started all this *mishigas,* was captured by opposition forces after a six-year battle and confined in an electronic mountain prison, where he remains today. There has been no word on visiting hours.

*   *   *   *   *   *

By now, you might be asking yourself, how did Hubbard know all this stuff from 75 million years ago, when there were no Twitter accounts? Scientology's explanation, naturally, is that Hubbard was there—the only person to survive the "wall of fire," thanks to his auditing "tech," which was powerful enough to neutralize the threat of hydrogen bombs. However, he did suffer a broken back, knee and arm.

Of course, another possible explanation is that Hubbard made it all up. He was, after all, a writer of science fiction, and let me emphasize the word "fiction." How different is Xenu from *Star Wars'* evil emperor? In a letter allegedly written by Hubbard to his wife Mary Sue, and frequently cited by Scientology critics, he tells of "drinking lots of rum and popping pinks and greys" during his writing of Xenu's epic tale. Scientology, of course, denies the existence of the letter.

The debate over the letter symbolizes Hubbard's life, of which there are two, polar-opposite versions: Scientology's and the one dug up by inquiring minds.

First, the Scientology version:

Lafayette Ronald Hubbard was born in Tilden, Nebraska, on March 13, 1911, the son of an ex-sailor and a school teacher. Hubbard was a child prodigy who rode a horse before he could walk, could read and write by the age of four and was a "blood brother" of the Blackfoot Indian tribe by the age of six. When he was 17, his father re-enlisted in the Navy and the family became military gypsies in Asia and the South Pacific. He learned about Eastern philosophies from Buddhist lamas and old Chinese magicians and about Freud from a Navy psychoanalyst. (He reportedly found Freud's ideas lacking.) He traveled in Manchuria's Western Hills and beyond, sharing campfires with Mongolian bandits, Siberian shamans and magicians descended from the age of Kublai Khan.

Hubbard went on to study nuclear physics at George Washington University before launching a successful career as the author of about 140 pulp science fiction short stories. As the commander of a squadron of Navy corvettes in World War II, he earned 21 medals for valor including the Purple Heart, given to those wounded in battle. He returned from the war blinded and lame, having been twice pronounced dead, all of which he cured with the mind-control techniques he developed.

Most of that romantic and inspiring saga is widely disputed. Another version of his life comes from a variety of sources, including Hubbard biographies by former Scientologists (Corydon's book and *A Piece of Blue Sky* by Jon Atack), documents obtained by a third biographer, Russell Miller (*The Bare-Faced Messiah*) and the *Los Angeles Times* through federal Freedom of Information Act requests and a vast array of documents collected by a former Hubbard aide, which the Church spent years trying to suppress.

Collectively, they sketch a much different portrait of Scientology's founder. Those claims about his early youth appear to be myths, for the most part. His communion with wise men in the Orient also appears greatly exaggerated. According to his youthful diary, Hubbard actually didn't think much of the Orient. The "gooks" were lazy and ignorant, he wrote, a "Chinaman drags things down" and there are too many "Chinks that smell of the baths they didn't take."

Hubbard failed the Naval Academy entrance examination before attending George Washington and his study of nuclear physics consisted, according to his school transcript, of one class in "atomic and molecular phenomena," which he flunked. He dropped out of college.

As for his service record, his command of a PC-815 submarine chaser operating off the coast of Oregon ended after he fired off 37 depth charges and claimed that he crippled two Japanese submarines. A Navy inquiry found no evidence of an enemy presence. He also lost his only other command after anchoring off the uninhabited Coronado Islands near San Diego and conducting an unauthorized gunnery practice, sparking a protest from the Mexican government.

This shouldn't have surprised Navy command after an unflattering assessment a year earlier by Naval Attaché L.D. Casey, who concluded that Hubbard "pretended competence without authority" and "tried to carry out assignments for which he was not qualified."

Veterans Administration records revealed Hubbard wasn't injured during the war—although he was hospitalized at war's end for an acute duodenal ulcer. He received only four minor medals and no Purple Heart.

*   *   *   *   *   *

After the war, Hubbard befriended John Whiteside Parsons, a founder of the Jet Propulsion Laboratory and an ardent believer in the occult, specifically the Thelema religion founded by English magician Aleister Crowley, who preached "do as thou wilt." Thus inspired, Hubbard and Parsons reportedly created a kinky ritual intended to summon the incarnation of Babalon, the "Mother of Abominations," who was sexually free. In the ritual, Parsons whipped up a vortex of energy with his "magical wand" in order to summon something called "the elemental." Translation, according to one historian: Parsons masturbated in the name of spiritual advancement while Hubbard—referred to as "The Scribe" in the diary of the event— scanned the astral plane for "signs and visions."

But the relationship ended badly. After the two launched a yacht-selling business, largely with Parsons' money, Hubbard took off on a world cruise with part of the inventory, leaving Parsons holding only a $2,900 promissory note. Crowley claimed Parsons had been conned. Scientology accounts contend Hubbard's actions were aimed at ending "black magic" in America.

On August 10, 1946, Hubbard married—which was inconvenient, since he already had a wife. The situation was resolved in 1947 when his first wife found out and divorced him. Now living in Laguna Beach, California, Hubbard wrote fiction to supplement his meager war disability allowance.

But he apparently wasn't making much money, because on August 31, 1948, Hubbard pleaded guilty in a San Luis Obispo, California, court to charges of petty theft for passing bad checks. He was fined $25. Scientology claims he was a Special Police Officer with LAPD, studying society's criminal elements.

After several publishers rejected a psychology book he was writing in which he claimed to have discovered the source of man's problems, an abbreviated version showed up in *Astounding Science Fiction* magazine. The magazine's editor, John W. Campbell, recruited Dr. Joseph Winter to help Hubbard develop the article into a book. It took 30 days to finish *Dianetics: The Modern Science of Mental Health*, which sold 55,000 copies in three months, despite being trashed by the scientific community.

According to Hubbard's book, the brain records every experience as "engrams" that trigger emotional and physical problems and can only be "cleared" by his e-meter. Auditing could restore withered limbs, mend broken bones and erase wrinkles. In fact, he proclaimed, the treatment would eliminate all physical ailments, which were really psychosomatic. He would later claim, in a *Journal of Scientology* article, that he cured eight cases of a psychosomatic illness: leukemia.

A totally clear subject also had a perfectly functioning mind with an improved IQ and photographic memory. But when Hubbard, with considerable fanfare, introduced the first "totally clear" person to a skeptical audience of reporters and scientists at the Shrine Auditorium, the poor woman reportedly failed to answer several simple questions designed to test her all-knowingness.

Despite that humiliating setback, the business continued to grow. Across the U.S., 500 Dianetic auditing groups were set up. Famed author Aldous Huxley was audited personally by Hubbard.

Meanwhile, Hubbard's personal life soured. His rocky, affair-ridden second marriage ended after Hubbard attempted to have his wife, Sarah, declared insane and seized their year-old daughter, Alexis. Sarah filed for a divorce in 1951, accusing him of bigamy and abuse, including sleep deprivation, beatings, strangulation, kidnapping and exhortations to commit suicide. Hubbard wouldn't return Alexis until Sarah signed a document stating her claims were "grossly exaggerated or entirely false" and that she considered Hubbard "a fine and brilliant man."

Truth be told, Hubbard never had much success with family. He married three times. His oldest son, L. Ron Jr., denounced Scientology in 1959 and, fearing harassment, changed his name. He eventually co-authored Corydon's biography of his father. Hubbard's youngest son and heir-apparent, Quentin, died in 1975 from an apparent suicide, although questions about the cause of death have circulated for years. Although a hose ran from the window of his car to the tailpipe, no traces of carbon monoxide were found in Quentin's body.

*　　*　　*　　*　　*　　*

In 1952, Hubbard created the Hubbard Association of Scientologists International, or HAS, to promote his new "Science of Certainty"—Scientology. A year later, he incorporated the Church of Scientology, despite previously expressing hostility towards religion and stating flatly in his book, *The Creation of Human Ability*, that Scientology wasn't a religion.

But, realizing the financial advantages of a tax-exempt entity, he had a spiritual epiphany. The rebranding also had legal benefits, according to HAS officials, who wrote that the first-amendment protection given to religious entities would shield the new church from attacks by the medical profession.

Some auditors promptly donned clerical attire, complete with collars.

With his new legal protections, Hubbard aggressively attacked his critics, who he labeled "suppressive persons." Under his new "fair game" policy, he wrote that "SPs" could be "deprived of property or injured by any means by any Scientologist without fear of punishment." In addition, they could be "tricked, sued or lied to or destroyed."

Litigation was Hubbard's primary weapon. "The purpose of the suit is to harass and discourage rather than to win," Hubbard wrote in an internal memo, adding that this harassment should be sufficient enough to cause the "professional decease" of the target, "or, if possible, of course, ruin him, utterly."

The sect was soon immersed in litigation with victims of the fair game policy, medical authorities and the IRS. The group's leader blamed it all on a conspiracy cooked up by psychiatric front groups and the government officials they controlled. So he created the Guardian Office (GO), headed by his wife Mary Sue, and charged it with gathering intelligence on perceived threats—which largely meant a hunt for evidence of "lurid, blood sex crime" committed by enemies.

Had he tipped over into serious mental illness? Suggestions of mental instability had dogged Hubbard as far back as his Navy days. In 1947, according to VA records, he requested psychiatric treatment for lingering melancholia from his military service. On February 3, 1959, an FBI report stated that "competent medical advisors recommended that Hubbard be committed to a private sanitarium for psychiatric observation and treatment of a mental ailment known as paranoid schizophrenia." A 1965 report by a board of inquiry in Victoria, Australia, where regulators accused Scientology of brainwashing, blackmail, extortion and damaging the mental health of its members, concluded that Hubbard was of "doubtful sanity, had a persecution complex and displays paranoid schizophrenia with delusions of grandeur."

Scientology was eventually banned in Victoria, Western Australia and South Australia, and the British denied foreign Scientologists entry in 1968, classifying Hubbard as an "undesirable alien."

In response, Hubbard, in typical paranoid cult fashion, curled his organization up in a ball and withdrew from the world. He wrote that Scientologists would be required to "disconnect" from any organization or individual—including family members—deemed to be suppressive. In "Keeping Scientology Working," a communications office policy directive, he wrote that people joining the sect "joined up for the duration of the universe."

So naturally, when he took to sea with an armada of yachts to evade all the critics and legal problems, he signed his crew to a billion-year contract covering "this and all reincarnated lives" and set sail for faraway ports surrounded by the Commodore's Messenger Organization (CMO)—primarily young errand girls dressed in hot pants and halter tops who catered to his every wish and served as liaisons with the Guardian Office.

While Hubbard and his family lived like royalty in posh quarters, the Sea Org crew inhabited squalid, roach-infested cabins below, Miller reported in *The Bare-Faced Messiah*. To ensure their continuing obedience and loyalty, Corydon wrote, Hubbard applied lessons from *The Brainwashing Manual*—yes, that's really the title— allegedly written by a Russian secret policeman. The manual recommended techniques for suppressing individualism, self-determinism, creativity and imagination in favor of conformity and allegiance to the state. "These willful and unaligned are no more than illnesses which will bring about disaffection, disunity, and at length, the collapse of the group to which the individual is attached," the manual stated.

According to Ronald DeWolf, aka L. Ron Hubbard Jr., the manual was actually authored by his father.

*   *   *   *   *   *

While Hubbard roamed the seven seas, government investigations and legal skirmishes continued to pile up. There are too many to relate here, but here are the highlights:

The Food and Drug Administration seized 100 e-meters as part of an investigation that led to charges of misrepresentation and practicing medicine without a license. The litigation dragged on for more than eight years, until Federal District Judge Gerhard A. Gesell concluded in 1971 that the organization's claims for the e-meter were fraudulent and that the devices could only be used in "bona fide" religious counseling. Even then, warning labels had to be attached advising the user that they offered no medical benefits.

While the ruling appears to give Scientology carte blanche to defraud the public, as long as it is done in a religious context, Judge Gesell, I believe, was sending a more subtle constitutional message: You are free to believe whatever you want spiritually, but let the buyer beware.

Judge Gesell made his low opinion of the device and the organization clear in his ruling, chiding Scientology for the "extravagant false claims that various physical and mental illnesses could be cured by auditing...this was and is false—in short, a fraud... there is absolutely no scientific or medical basis in fact for the claimed cures."

Unfortunately, as Judge Gesell also noted, "the government did not move to stop the practice of Scientology and a related 'science' known as Dianetics when these activities first appeared and were gaining public acceptance. Had it done so, this tedious litigation would not have been necessary. "

*   *   *   *   *   *

What Howard Hunt was to Richard Nixon, Michael Meisner was to L. Ron Hubbard. Like Hunt, the architect of the Watergate break-in, Meisner was a dirty trickster for Scientology.

Meisner and Gerald Wolfe were caught in a restricted area of the federal court in Washington, D.C., in the spring of 1976, according to a narrative in Judge Charles Richey's ruling in the case. Their purpose, Judge Richey wrote, was to steal IRS files relating to Scientology. Unwilling to do jail time, Meisner, a high-ranking official in the Guardian Office, escaped from the group and produced a titillating affidavit for the FBI.

Here are some of the dirty deeds outlined in Meisner's affidavit and an estimated 50,000 documents seized by the FBI during court-ordered searches of two Scientology buildings:

- In Operation Snow White, the Guardian Office bugged an IRS office where high-level meetings took place and planted a mole on the agency's secretarial staff to steal documents.

- After her book, *The Scandal of Scientology*, came out in 1971, Paulette Cooper was deluged with a dozen Scientology lawsuits. But that was the small stuff. According to Cooper, a Scientologist posing as a flower delivery man choked her lookalike cousin, who was staying at her apartment. Operation Freakout sought to have Ms. Cooper imprisoned or committed to a mental institution.

  The most bizarre tactic was Operation Dynamite, in which Guardian Office agents broke into her apartment and used her paper, with her fingerprints on it, and her typewriter to author bomb threats against the Church. Also planned, but never carried out: a bomb threat against Henry Kissinger. Police actually arrested Cooper, but eventually learned of Scientology's "fair game" policy before going to trial. Attempting to save face, they offered to drop charges if she agreed to a year of psychotherapy. By then, the frazzled Ms. Cooper was drinking and smoking too much, had lost her boyfriend and certainly could have used a bit of therapy. She accepted the deal.

- Scientology launched a sex smear campaign against Gabriel Cazares, the mayor of Clearwater, Florida, after he spoke out against a land grab in his city orchestrated by groups linked to the church. They also tried to frame him for a bogus hit and run. He sued and the case was settled out of court.

- As part of an effort to get Scientology critic Larry Tapper removed from his post as a deputy in the California Attorney General's office, Scientology sought to have forged checks from a doctor under investigation for drug violations deposited in Tapper's bank account. In Operation Snapper, the group sent an obviously pregnant woman dressed like a nun into a state office to loudly denounce the married Tapper for seducing and abandoning her. The campaign didn't work, but when I mentioned to Tapper three years later that I had FBI documents relating to a plot against him, he asked if it involved a pregnant woman; when I confirmed that, he asked me to send the documents to him ASAP so he could show his wife.

In December of 1979, 11 members of the Guardian Office were convicted on charges of stealing government documents and obstructing justice. Mary Sue Hubbard was sentenced to five years in prison; she served one year.

Both Meisner and Cooper sought to hire me to sue Scientology. But in each case, either the timing or the circumstances weren't right. Meisner's calls came right after the rattlesnake attack; by the time I got back to him, he was already in witness protection. I believed Ms. Cooper had a better chance to get a quick settlement—which is what she needed after her lengthy ordeal—with a lower-profile attorney that Scientology didn't regard as an enemy. She eventually settled.

$$* \quad * \quad * \quad * \quad * \quad *$$

While searching through 21 battered cardboard boxes at a Scientology facility in Gilman Hot Springs, California, for evidence to refute the group's critics, Gerry Armstrong got quite a shock. The boxes were filled with faded photos, worn documents, memorabilia, baby clothes— and what he viewed as proof that Hubbard's life and Scientology's claims were a tissue of lies.

Feeling that the truth would make Scientology stronger, the long-time Sea Org legal, public relations and intelligence officer started gathering evidence from FOI requests and visits to places and schools named in Hubbard's biography, eventually compiling 250,000 pages of documents. But his attempts to set the record straight led only to his assignment to the Rehabilitation Project Force, where Scientology doubters and other miscreants were sent to live in harsh, boot camp-like surroundings in order to get their minds right—an echo of Synanon's Slug Camp. After two years, he fled. "I realized I had been drawn into Scientology by a web of lies, Machiavellian mind-control techniques and fear," he said.

Armstrong claimed he became prey to the group's fair game policy. He alleged that his property was stolen, he was assaulted and his family was threatened. Scientology also filed suit to retrieve the 25,000 pages of documents he had copied and taken when he left. But Judge Paul G. Breckenridge Jr. ruled that Scientology did practice fair game, describing the organization as "schizophrenic and paranoid," and that Armstrong was justified in taking the documents for his own protection. The documents in question, along with testimony in the case, the judge noted, revealed Hubbard's "egoism, greed, avarice, lust for power, and vindictiveness and aggressiveness against persons perceived by him to be disloyal or hostile."

As part of an $800,000 settlement agreement, Armstrong agreed to keep the documents sealed and not speak about Scientology. He only signed, he said later, because his attorney advised him the gag order wasn't enforceable. He donated the proceeds to people he thought needed it more.

I filed a motion in the case, arguing that the court couldn't allow Scientology to seal documents others might need to prosecute the cult or defend themselves against the group's legal assaults. The court agreed, allowing us to review the case file at the courthouse, where I got my first glimpse at the world of Xenu. But an appellate court reversed the decision, ruling that we had filed after a six-month deadline for setting aside a judgment. I was ordered to destroy my notes. I couldn't understand how the court could set a six-month deadline on a judgment when the public had no way of knowing when the clock started and wouldn't even be interested in the information until they were sued or otherwise harmed by Scientology.

Armstrong violated the gag order after being publicly vilified by the church in 1992, believing that such an unprovoked public attack would surely nullify it and permit him to defend himself. Scientology promptly sued. Armstrong hired Ford Greene to defend him and he asked me to help. I argued that upholding the settlement's gag order was akin to paying a murder witness to keep quiet. Also, while it was true that those involved in legal actions with Scientology could still depose Armstrong, each deposition could cost thousands of dollars, a distinct disadvantage for poor plaintiffs. Besides, by forcing those facing Scientology to show all their cards to opposing counsel at depositions, instead of getting the information in private interviews, the ruling represented a violation of the litigants' right to a fair trial by denying them the right to prepare their case in secret.

While I felt legal precedent was clearly on our side, the court upheld the agreement. In my view, the court overlooked the public good in order to lighten judges' workload, handing down a ruling that encouraged more settlements and fewer trials.

Over the next decade, a defiant Armstrong admitted to violating the gag order more than 200 times through web postings and aid to those involved in litigation with Scientology. After a series of fines, damage awards and finally, a threatened jail term, Armstrong fled the country and continues to tell his tale.

*　　*　　*　　*　　*　　*

That wasn't my only legal brush with Scientology. I also represented Corydon, the Hubbard biographer, in some interesting litigation.

For many years, Corydon ran what was essentially an independent Scientology franchise in Riverside, California, tithing 10% annually to the church. But in 1982, with Hubbard in exile on the high seas and the cult in the throes of management upheaval, Scientology sought to centralize control of "mission holders" such as Corydon. Stung by the loss of autonomy, Corydon split from the church. He reopened as the Church of Scio Logos, which continued to use e-meters to audit its parishioners. Scientology sued, claiming the historic building that housed Corydon's church, which was worth millions of dollars, was paid for by the tithes of Scientology parishioners and was held in trust for them. We countered that the building should indeed belong to the parishioners and the majority of them wanted to join Corydon's new church.

I saw the case in part as an opportunity to demonstrate that I wasn't anti-religion, or even anti-auditing. I was representing a church that performed audits and was fighting for its right to exist. The head of the church also claimed he was being harassed under Scientology's fair game policy for being a suppressive and what Hubbard termed a "squirrel"—someone who alters the church's "tech" for his own gain. I wasn't fighting against religions, I was fighting against abuse.

Ultimately, I felt the outcome of the case hinged on the wishes of a majority of the congregation. I feared that Scientology might harass or shun them, in an attempt to intimidate them into returning to the fold.

Other legal issues complicated the suit, however. Scientology unsuccessfully sued publisher Lyle Stuart Inc. to halt the release of Corydon's biography of Hubbard. But as the war raged over the book, Corydon agreed to debate two Scientology PR men on radio.

Responding to accusations leveled against him during the debate, Corydon, knowing of the group's policy of using "black propaganda" to attack foes, stated Scientologists were trained to lie about perceived enemies. The Scientology debaters sued him for defamation.

I didn't see the defamation case as much of a threat. It was a debate on the radio, making the participants public figures permitted to state opinions without fear of legal consequences—unless it could be proven that the accuser maliciously made accusations he knew to be untrue. That seemed highly unlikely, given Scientology's documents on black propaganda.

But the cost of litigation, as ever with Scientology, worried me. I knew that some recent rulings had held that insurers didn't have to defend suits where, to be successful, it had to be shown that the defendant had acted intentionally. Libel against a public figure fell into that category and I feared Corydon could lose his insurance defense. So I negotiated a buyout of Corydon's insurance policy—enough to cover the costs of the litigation.

Eventually, a settlement of all litigation was negotiated by attorney Toby Plevin. Scientology dropped its lawsuits and Corydon's church kept the building.

*   *   *   *   *   *

Claire Headley came from a family of Scientologists, including her mother, her uncle and some cousins. Her first exposure to the church came at the age of 4 and at age 16, she claimed, she joined after being promised an education, three weeks of vacation annually and regular family visits.

None of that happened, she alleged.

For the next 15 years, Ms. Headley claimed she worked slavishly through seven-day, 100-to-150-hour work weeks. She said she was kept awake to work for days on end and allowed only brief naps at her desk or on the floor. She stated she was restricted to the Scientology compound, which was surrounded by a barbed wire fence. Gates were guarded at all times and to leave, she said, she needed to submit a written request, get it approved by three different officials and submit to a "security check" interrogation of the reasons for her excursion.

Shortly after joining Scientology, she said she received three weeks of training; it was the last hint of education in her 15-year sojourn with the group. She married, but stated she was pressured into submitting to two abortions. She said she acquiesced after seeing the punishments dished out to resisters: withheld food, months of hard labor, demotions; and forced separation from friends and family—even spouses.

For many years, she couldn't conceive of leaving Scientology. What would she do? Where would she go? She had essentially been raised by the church; she had no money, insurance, housing, high school diploma or job prospects.

Nevertheless, she finally took the plunge in 2005. Shortly thereafter, she received a bill from Scientology demanding payment of $46,500 for her so-called "freeloader debt," the supposed difference between the discounted cost of her auditing procedures and the amount charged to outsiders.

In 2008, she consulted an attorney. Before then, she said, she didn't realize she had any legal recourse. She filed suit for damages, claiming that she was held in involuntary servitude for all those years and unable to comprehend until she left the wrongfulness of Scientology's actions.

But the suit ran aground in U.S. District Court, where Judge Dale S. Fischer ruled that Scientology was protected by the first amendment guarantee of freedom of religion. "Inquiring into these allegations would entangle the court in the religious doctrine of Scientology," the Judge explained in the ruling.

I couldn't believe it. Judge Fischer's wrong-headed decision flies in the face of the landmark California Supreme Court decision I fought for in the Molko case. Once again, a judge was ignoring an accused destructive cult's abusive actions because he considered it a challenge to the constitutional guarantee of religious freedom.

Did we have to go through this all over again? To remind the court of the precedent-setting Molko decision and other cases involving similar allegations against Scientology, I filed a friend-of-the-court brief in support of the Headley appeal. "The issue at hand here is the ministerial exception, which bars courts from resolving employment disputes involving ministers, all in the name of supporting religious freedom," I wrote in the brief. "But this exception would not apply to the dropping of witches into barrels of water in old Salem to determine guilt… It does not apply to Mormon blood atonement used to massacre innocent settlers, Muslim justification of 9/11, the forced suicides of members of the People's Temple or the attacks on enemies by Synanon's Imperial Marines. And, as ruled in previous cases, it does not allow Scientology to use coercive practices such as its 'fair game' policy, its 'billion-year contracts' and its usurious 'freeloaders' debt' to take away an individual's freedom to leave the church."

Denying people the right to leave a church, I argued, is just as much a violation of the first amendment as denying them the right to join a church. And challenging the methods used to coerce someone into changing their beliefs isn't the same as challenging the belief itself. Let me say it again: I am not anti-religion, I am anti-abuse.

And Claire Headley's claims, if true, clearly indicate abuse.

Alas, because of my illness, I hadn't been aware of the case until recently and couldn't file my brief before the designated deadline, as Scientology noted in its motion to squelch the brief.

The court read, but didn't officially accept, my brief and in July, 2012, rejected the appeal. The court ruled that the facts, as presented, didn't fit the plaintiffs' argument that Scientology had violated the federal slavery law. But the court agreed with my argument that the plaintiffs had sued under the wrong law and might have fared better had they framed the legal argument differently. The slavery claim had always been a Hail Mary strategy, drafted only because the plaintiffs had missed the statute-of-limitations deadline for filing the claim under more appropriate state statutes. Because of this, the court never got to hear and analyze a claim for brainwashing, which, if upheld, would have preserved the Molko precedent.

*   *   *   *   *   *

In some cases, the aggressiveness and persistence of Scientology has prevailed over less-resolute foes.

Take the IRS, for example.

For 20 years, the agency had successfully litigated against the church. The IRS won rulings upholding its refusal to grant Scientology tax-exempt status because of its business model and the exorbitant salary paid to Hubbard. In 1980, the IRS placed a lien on Scientology's Los Angeles headquarters, the former Cedars of Lebanon complex. Scientology unsuccessfully appealed each defeat; one court ruled that in retaliation, the organization deliberately jumbled two million pages of tax-related material so as to cost the IRS time and the taxpayers money.

In 1984, Scientology's new intelligence agency, the Office of Special Affairs, created "The National Coalition of I.R.S. Whistle-blowers" to accumulate evidence of alleged abuses by the IRS. The *New York Times* reported the group hired private investigators to probe the personal lives of senior IRS officials involved in Scientology litigation. Scientology filed multiple lawsuits against the agency and its officials.

The agency buckled in 1991, according to news reports, agreeing to restore the church's tax-exempt status in exchange for the group's promise to drop all litigation against the agency and pay a negotiated percentage of its back taxes. A year later, an IRS official agreed to keep the bulk of Scientology's financial statements secret, despite the agency's legal obligation to disclose the information it gets from tax-exempt organizations. The IRS reportedly agreed to grant tax exemptions to all 150 Scientology entities in the U.S.

In October of 1993, Scientology paid the IRS the agreed $12.5 million in back taxes and dropped all lawsuits brought by Church entities and individual Scientologists against the agency. Afterwards, the *New York Times* reported, David Miscavige, Scientology's chief executive officer, held a "victory rally" attended by 10,000 cheering Scientologists in the Los Angeles Sports Arena, declaring he had defeated the secret master plan of the "pea-brained, psych-indoctrinated mental midgets" to use the IRS to destroy Scientology.

*   *   *   *   *   *

The watchdog Cult Awareness Network routinely named Scientology as "public enemy no. 1" in the cult world. "Scientology is quite likely the most ruthless, the most classically terroristic, the most litigious and the most lucrative cult the country has ever seen," CAN director Cynthia Kisser told *Time* magazine in 1991.

In 1993, members of Scientology filed 21 lawsuits against CAN, contending they were improperly denied membership in the organization. CAN prevailed in each case.

But in another case, CAN was found guilty of conspiring to violate the civil rights and religious liberties of Jason Scott, a Pentecostal represented by Scientology lawyer Ken Moxon. The $1 million in damages awarded to Scott, added to the cost of defending against all the litigation, drove CAN into bankruptcy, where it was acquired by Scientologist Steven Hayes in 1996.

So caveat emptor. If you call the network for information on cults, be aware that you are probably talking to a Scientologist.

*   *   *   *   *   *

Hubbard, named a co-conspirator in the Meisnergate prosecution and pursued by countless lawyers seeking to depose him, spent his final years living like a fugitive, first at sea, then, in a string of U.S. safe houses and finally, in a luxury motor home parked on a 160-acre ranch in Creston, California. He died of a massive stroke on Jan. 17, 1986.

As with many expired cult leaders, Hubbard didn't just die, he decided to "drop his body" because it became "an impediment to his work." Scientology reports that he is carrying on his work on another planet, having "learned how to do it without a body."

Often, when the founding guru of a cult dies, the cult tends to disperse. But the Church of Scientology anointed a new leader, David Miscavige, and continued to grow.

Some likened it to going from the frying pan to the fire.

Miscavige was a second-generation Scientologist who started assisting in auditing sessions at age 12 and dropped out of high school to join Sea Org at 16. Perhaps serving as a surrogate for the sons Hubbard lost, Miscavige became his closest assistant and by 1979 was appointed head of the CMO, responsible for enforcing the leader's policies.

With Hubbard in hiding, Miscavige took control of the organization. Like most despots rising to power, he replaced most of the church's upper and middle management, including Mary Sue Hubbard, who he reportedly convinced to resign.

In a 1991 cover story, *Time* magazine described Miscavige as "ringleader" of a "hugely profitable global racket that survives by intimidating members and critics in a Mafia-like manner." Since 1986, the magazine said, authorities in France, Spain and Italy raided more than 50 Scientology centers leading to charges against more than 100 of its overseas members that included fraud, extortion, capital flight, coercion, illegally practicing medicine and "taking advantage of mentally incapacitated people." Reports of beatings and other abuse administered by Miscavige have proliferated.

And then there are those mysterious disappearances.

Heber Jentzsch, a witty, well-liked public relations man for the church, was seen by Miscavige as a threat, according to former Scientologists. Mike Rinder, one of the most recent officials to leave the church, wrote that Miscavige frequently belittled Jentzsch and struck him on at least ten occasions and eventually imprisoned him. In 2010, Rinder wrote that Jentzsch hadn't been seen for years.

Jentzsch is officially listed on the California Department of Justice Missing Persons Database. Both Jentzsch and Miscavige's wife, Shelley, who hasn't been seen since 2006, are listed on the Federal Missing Persons Database and the LAPD, it has been reported, has opened a missing person case on each.

*   *   *   *   *   *

Close encounters with Scientologists:

Cathy Lee Crosby sat next to me in a class at USC. She was a typical USC sorority girl—blond, blue-eyed, with long, bronzed legs. She was elegant, but down-to-earth and we became friends. Over the years, as she became a professional tennis player and later, an actress— she was TV's first Wonder Woman, before being replaced by Lynda Carter—we would occasionally run into each other.

One night, I saw her on a TV talk show, praising Scientology. When I spotted her at Los Angeles International airport some time after the rattlesnake attack, I pulled her aside. Because people listened to celebrities, I asked if I could show her documents detailing the organization's criminal behavior and abuse. I told her about FBI documents that showed the group's intention to destroy careers by illegal means.

Whatever the church did to insure its existence didn't interest her, she said. She was getting "benefits" from her association with the organization and that was all she cared about.

I was disappointed; this wasn't the Cathy I knew at USC. But her attitude was only too familiar—it was the voice of the Me Generation, denying any responsibility for helping others.

I have heard reports that she left the church, but she didn't respond to an inquiry I made seeking confirmation.

*   *   *   *   *   *

In the mid-1990s, a friend asked if I would speak to his sister, who had spent a considerable amount to be audited by Scientology with no apparent results. I did, basically making her aware of some general history. Soon thereafter, I got a letter from Scientology attorney Tim Bowles accusing me of saying derogatory things about the organization. None of it was true.

When I read her the letter, the woman was aghast, admitting she had mentioned that she had spoken to me during a Scientology audit security check. (During these checks, auditors routinely ask if the person has met anyone who spoke negatively about Scientology.) She insisted that she never said those things and wondered aloud why Scientology would say she did. "Here's a better question," I said. "Had you not been told that auditing is privileged and confidential?" Yes, she replied. "Then whether true or not, how could they break confidences and put what you allegedly said in a letter to me?"

According to my friend, she departed from Scientology.

*   *   *   *   *   *

In 1998, at a first-date lunch, a lovely ballet teacher asked me what my legal specialty was and I proudly told her. At the end of the date, I asked if I could see her again and she declined. "I'm a Scientologist," she explained, hesitantly.

I told her I understood. "Trust me," I warned her. "Don't tell them we met."

*   *   *   *   *   *

My most direct confrontation with Scientology occurred in 1995, at a health fair in my home town of Pacific Palisades, a tiny beach community snuggled between Santa Monica and Malibu. As I strolled through the booths for traditional and new – age health providers and advisers, a man asked me if I would like to be interviewed on the subject of psychology.

Boy, did he pick the wrong guy.

What kind of questions? I asked. He showed me a list of questions clearly displaying an anti-psychotherapy bias. "You're Scientology," I said. No, he insisted, they were just a group of actors spreading the word about psychotherapy abuses. I said, "No, you are Scientology." He continued to deny it while simultaneously trying to lure me up on his stage. Finally, he confessed they were Scientologists but weren't representing the church that day.

Angry that the group had not revealed its true nature, Arnie Winnick, president of the local Chamber of Commerce, decided to ask them to leave. If you do, I told him, they will possibly bankrupt the city by dragging it through years of litigation for religious discrimination. "You're not equipped for this," I said. "Let me handle it. This is what I do."

During a pause in the group's skit about the controversial electroshock treatments given to 1940s actress Frances Farmer, I addressed the very interested crowd. "The people speaking here have the right to do so. They also have an interest in denouncing mental health professionals. They have that right. You have the right to know who is speaking. So I am telling you this is from Scientology. You can walk away or continue to listen, but at least now you will be clear as to the source."

The crowd started to scatter. About 15 minutes later, several police officers told me the Scientologists were accusing me of interfering with their First-Amendment rights. Not true, I told them. I only exercised my own rights. A bit later, one of the officers returned. "Go get them, Paul," he said.

As I sat alone on a curb eating a hot dog, two of the Scientologists approached. "We know it's you, Paul," said the woman, as if confronting a legendary devil.

*   *   *   *   *   *

So now we come to the part you've all been waiting for: Tom Cruise. What a guy. In his heart of hearts, L. Ron Hubbard desperately longed for acceptance and believed celebrity endorsements would hasten the process. So in 1969, the Scientology Celebrity Center International was founded in Hollywood. Among the celebs reportedly targeted were Edward R. Murrow, Marlene Dietrich, Ernest Hemingway, Howard Hughes, Greta Garbo, Walt Disney, Henry Luce, Billy Graham and Groucho Marx. Those efforts were unsuccessful.

But with the advent of the Me Generation and the quest for spiritual and psychological quick fixes, the tide turned. The church eventually recruited stars such as John Travolta and Kirstie Alley, among others. Travolta reportedly credited Dianetics with lifting him from a deep depression after the death of one-time lover Diana Hyland, who played his mother in the 1977 film *The Boy in the Plastic Bubble*.

And then they landed Cruise, the Top Gun.

Cruise followed his first wife, actress Mimi Rogers, into Scientology around 1990. He reportedly believes auditing cured his dyslexia. Whatever the reason, he dove in with a passion, co-founding a much-criticized, post-9/11 program to offer rescue workers "detoxification therapy" based on the works of L. Ron Hubbard. He also got considerable media abuse for denouncing Brooke Shields' use of anti-depressants to recover from post-partum depression. Chemical imbalances don't exist, he said. Shields' response: "His comments are dangerous. He should stick to saving the world from aliens." Cruise later apologized.

But Cruise's passion for Scientology began to look more and more like madness. There was, of course, the infamous couch-bouncing freak-out on the *Oprah Winfrey* show. Then there was the Scientology-produced video interview that became a YouTube must-see with over seven million hits, despite efforts by both the church and Cruise to get it removed from the web. (The organization claims the web version was edited from three hours of video intended for Scientology members.)

When I saw the tape, I heard echoes of Charles Dederich and other cult leaders with his you're-in-or-you're-out and you're-either-for-or-against mantra. His periodic cackling and rants rival Charlie Sheen's incoherent ramblings about "winning" and "tiger's blood" for manic video of the decade honors.

Cruise speaks of what a privilege it is to be a Scientologist who can "create new realities." Scientology is the authority on drugs, the mind, criminals and world peace, he says. "You are aboard, or you're not'."

Cruise's ramblings could come back to haunt Scientology. He seems to endorse Scientology's "tech" as a scientific cure for what ails people, something the courts have expressly forbidden. That opens the organization to allegations of fraud. And his rant about the future elimination of "suppressives" could be interpreted as a confirmation that the fair game policy is alive and well and could also provide many with legal recourse against the church and even him, personally.

While envisioning a world without "suppressives," he spoke eagerly of confronting them. He ominously advises people not to run from suppressives, but to "shatter and suppress" them. He dares suppressives to face him.

Call me Tom, we'll do lunch.

*   *   *   *   *   *

As you can tell, Tom Cruise bothers me. Scientology bothers me. What bothers me most is that I wasn't able to affect the course of the movement, or at least expose its secrets so people could make informed choices about whether or not to get involved.

Then one night, I saw a video of the animated TV series *South Park*.

All the secrets I argued the public had a right to know about were there, skewered in a cartoon parody first aired in November, 2005. In "Trapped in the Closet," the 137th episode of the subversive series about a bunch of kids and their parents in a fictional small town, little Stan, looking for something "fun and free," wanders into a Scientology center and is revealed by auditing to be the reincarnation of L. Ron Hubbard. A mob of Scientologists, including Cruise and Travolta, gather outside Stan's house that night, urging him to accept the mantle of church leadership. After Stan trashes his acting ability, Cruise locks himself in a closet, believing he has disappointed the new prophet. Travolta, Nicole Kidman (Cruise's second wife) and others try to coax him "out of the closet." Travolta ends up in the closet with Tom and now both are being exhorted to "come out of the closet."

Meanwhile, the church's president recounts the tale of Xenu for Stan's parents as a caption flashes repeatedly on the TV screen—"This is what Scientologists actually believe." When Stan, in his new role as prophet, says that to really be a church, they can't charge money to help, the president confesses that the church is a money-making scam.

A scheduled rebroadcast of the episode was reportedly cancelled when Cruise threatened to back out of his publicity tour for *Mission: Impossible III*, which was produced by a subsidiary of Viacom, which also owns the TV network that airs South Park. Isaac Hayes, a Scientologist, and the voice of the show's Chef character, quit. His departure was commemorated in a subsequent episode, when Chef was struck by lightning, burned, impaled, shot and mauled. South Park's cheeky creators, Trey Parker and Matt Stone, responded to the controversy by issuing a statement declaring themselves "servants of the dark lord Xenu."

The episode, of course, still lives on the Internet, where it has been viewed an estimated three million times. On Comedy Central, which has aired the episode many times, it is listed as one of "10 *South Parks* That Changed the World."

Meanwhile, new threats to the church's continuing prosperity were looming in the vaporous realm of the internet.

*   *   *   *   *   *

Epilogue:

In 1997, after a heated debate and many objections from residents, the Los Angeles City Council voted 8-to-3 in favor of changing the name of Berenda Street to L. Ron Hubbard Way. Some 7,000 people attended the April, 1997, ceremony, where speakers praised the church as having "greatly contributed to and enhanced our City through its outreach and community services programs and projects." They honored Hubbard for his "humanitarian works, which are contributing greatly to helping eradicate illiteracy, drug abuse and criminality."

Meanwhile, the New York Times Square Alliance saluted Scientology for its help in beautification and in fighting crime and drug addiction, hailed its fight to overcome religious persecution and lauded the techniques Hubbard developed to help people with personal problems. Apparently no one with the alliance read any of the court rulings that declared Scientology's auditing process fraudulent or described fair game abuses. Among those who came to praise Hubbard instead of keeping him buried were U.S. Rep. Charles Rangel and United Nations Undersecretary General Maurice Strong.

What's next? The Adolph Hitler Railway in Germany?

P.S.: During the final editing of this book, Scientology began airing a TV commercial touting its growth and good deeds, under the heading: "Who Is Scientology?"

Now you know.

Part 2: Anonymous, the Virtual Vigilante

(Photo courtesy of Paul Williams)

"We are Anonymous / We are legion
We do not forgive / We do not forget
For every one that falls / Ten shall take his place
We are the face of chaos / The harbingers of judgment
We laugh in the face of tragedy / We mock those in pain
We ruin the lives of others simply because we can
We are the embodiment of humanity
With no remorse, no caring, no love and no sense of morality
We have only the desire for more
We are everything / We are nothing
And now, quite simply, you have our attention
Expect us."

> *—Anonymous*

For most of its existence, Scientology has been the big bully on the block.

Those who dared to criticize the organization for its abuses, its adjudicated fraudulent claims of medical miracles and its Mondo Bizarro view of world history were intimidated physically, psychologically and legally. Even L. Ron Hubbard's son felt compelled to change his name and embark on his own personal witness protection program upon leaving the cult, fearful of the abuse doled out to escapees under the organization's ruthless "fair game" policy. Scientology attempted to frame journalists and public officials for bogus crimes and enmeshed anyone else who opposed them in long-running and costly lawsuits.

But in recent years, the cult has been a bit more docile in its interactions with the outside world. That may have resulted, in part, from a maturation of the organization and its tactics in response to widespread criticism. It may be partly due to a changing of the guard in the post-Hubbard era. But many have given at least partial credit to Anonymous.

Who or what is that?

Imagine if you will a worldwide organization of cyber-protestors constructed like an amoeba. It reaches out in in all directions, with portions occasionally breaking off to coalesce around targets that have angered someone with ties to the organization. A clarion call goes out for a coordinated attack and around the world, computers whir to life. Those with access to the collective's coded online forums can choose to join the attack, which could involve anything from puckish pranks—ordering the delivery of a stack of pizzas, c.o.d., to a foe's facility—to mean-spirited mayhem—hacking into a major corporation's computers and posting the private financial information of its customers.

These attacks have prompted some to label Anonymous cyber-terrorists seeking to impose its radical political agenda on the world by organizing the ever-growing mass of Internet geeks into a cohesive political force. Others see them as online merry pranksters lacking the organization and the attention span to wield true political power. "We are legion," proclaims the group's own propaganda, but what does that mean? Millions? Thousands? Or maybe just 23 dudes bored with *Mortal Kombat*.

It's impossible to tell because they are, well, anonymous.

This loose collective of web denizens has been very busy over the past three years, haranguing a wide variety of targets with online pranks and in some cases, live protests. These attacks are usually accompanied by the online posting of a sinister-sounding video—complete with that creepy, electronically-altered voice frequently heard in kidnapping movies—explaining Anonymous' gripe with that organization and what punishment it intends to mete out.

What's their motivation? For some, it is the protection of the free flow of information on the internet; for others, a sincere desire to protect society from sinister and corrupt forces. Still others just want to share bootlegged (and thus, free) video games. And some just do it for the laughs.

Simply put, there is more than one face to Anonymous. Like the amoeba, it can divide and reproduce many times—some of its offspring are playful, some sincere and some destructive. Sometimes, they wind up fighting each other. And it has become clear that often, one tentacle of Anonymous has no idea what the other tentacles are doing.

Consider the battle between Sony Corp. and a group claiming to be Anonymous. It started when Sony tried to prevent users of its PlayStation 3 device from bypassing the company's operating system —known as jail-breaking the device. That enables independent game designers to develop their own games for the PS3. That's the party line of the internet crowd, anyway. But the more likely motivation for the majority of protestors was the ability to play bootlegged copies of Sony games distributed through file-sharing services. In retaliation for Sony's efforts to shut them down, the group hacked into Sony's computers and posted the private information of thousands of customers.

But Anonymous vehemently denied any role in the hack, saying that the company was using the group as a scapegoat to cover up weaknesses in its computer network's defenses against hackers. Or, the group speculated, maybe it was a radical splinter faction of the larger Anonymous collective, acting independently. Who really did it? Who knows? Oliver North would have been proud. Talk about your plausible deniability.

*   *   *   *   *   *

In 2003, the massive Internet imageboard 4chan provided the web-addicted with an online community where they could anonymously discuss, analyze and prank on topics near and dear to them—such as anime, manga, music, video games and pornography. This anonymous community started spreading to other discussion forums online. In these back channels of the Internet, anger grew over attempts by mainstream corporate interests to restrict free online access to its proprietary music, movies and video games. So participants began to organize cyber-protests and soon, those protests spread to a wide variety of targets, including the military and the CIA. One major front involved the banks and credit card companies who staunched the flow of donations to WikiLeaks, the online repository for leaked documents from whistle-blowers, which had come under government fire for posting secret cables hacked from State Department computers.

Meanwhile, in another corner of 4chan's wide world of forums, former Scientologists and other spiritually-based activists sought ways to expose the church's abuses. Many of these online Scientology critics had been exchanging chatter on the cult since the early 1990s through the alt.religion.scientology newsgroup on Usenet, an early version of today's discussion forums.

Now, with this growing sense of anonymous empowerment sweeping the net, these people, so long on the defensive against the belligerent behemoth, saw an opportunity to play some offense. When the Tom Cruise video was leaked to the Internet on Jan. 14, 2008, Scientology immediately filed a copyright infringement claim against YouTube and demanded that the video be taken down. In response, members of the "bigger, darker" Anonymous group formed Project Chanology to protest what they saw as an assault on free speech, says —how to put this—an anonymous Anonymous source.

It was a grudge match made in Internet heaven. On one side, the Internet trolls, champions of openness, transparency and unfettered freedom vs. Scientology, a highly paranoid and litigious organization that zealously guards its privacy. And Anonymous proved an elusive target for Scientology's usual bullying tactics; how do you physically or legally intimidate an enemy you can't identify?

At this point of its existence, Anonymous was mostly into sophomoric pranks. They shut down Scientology websites by overwhelming them with traffic and flooded Scientology centers with prank calls, bogus faxes and a whole bunch of unpaid-for pizza deliveries. In a video entitled "We Run This," Anonymous cheekily asked Scientology if they were having "as much fun as we are." The video chronicles its campaign to drain the church of money and constituents and concludes: "Thank you for playing the game."

In a video seminar, Gabriela Coleman, an assistant professor of anthropology at New York University specializing in new media, admitted that Scientology's aggressive attitude towards critics had long made her reluctant to write about the cult—until the emergence of Anonymous. "Anonymous has allowed me to be more public about this material," she said.

But some long-time Scientology critics wanted more than pranks from this emerging new force. Mark Bunker of XenuTV.org, in a video message to Anonymous, lauded them as exciting and passionate people. But he urged the group to abandon its hacker pranks and focus on political action. Surprisingly, Anonymous embraced him, dubbed him "Wise Beard Man" and took his advice—sort of.

On Jan. 21, 2008, the anti-Scientology wing of Anonymous posted a video on YouTube officially declaring war on the church. A week later, a new video called for live protests at several Scientology locations around the world. On Feb. 10, an estimated 700 protesters appeared at 93 different Scientology sites (including a one-person protest in Japan).

Several protests followed, although, truth be told, these demonstrations seemed more like oddball tailgating parties than serious political activism. They consisted mostly of a bunch of surprisingly orderly and playful people brandishing relatively inoffensive signs while wearing those creepy, Joker-like masks from the movie *V for Vendetta*. No one felt compelled to call out the National Guard.

Other protests—both live and virtual—ensued, but who, actually, was doing the protesting? In March, a group allegedly affiliated with Anonymous hacked into computers at an epilepsy support forum, sending flashing computer animations supposedly intended to trigger migraine headaches and seizures. Anonymous denied involvement, accusing Scientology of launching the attack to sully the collective's reputation.

As the group got more involved, it started discovering a "mountain of dirt" on Scientology and connecting with critics and whistleblowers persecuted by the group over the years, the source recalled. "We came to a monumental conclusion: Scientology was a motherfucking evil like nothing Anonymous had ever scrutinized for targeting before," the source added. "We had to show them who the final boss of the internet was and give them their well-earned dose of bitter medicine. Nobody else had ever managed to stop Scientology with a full frontal attack. So the game—and yes, to us, it's totally a game—became to make history, to show the world what we can do."

According to the source, Anonymous does it for the "lulz," or laughs. When Scientology's end comes, as they are confident it will, Anonymous will "be on the sidelines, pointing and laughing our asses off as the bad guys get raided/arrested and the victims get set free," the source said.

The group's cheeky attitude shines through in "The Rules of the Internet," posted on 4chan. Some of the 47 rules: Anonymous never forgives; Anonymous can be a horrible, senseless, uncaring monster;

everything that can be labeled can be hated; nothing is to be taken seriously; nothing is sacred; the more beautiful and pure a thing is, the more satisfying it is to corrupt it; No real limits apply here—not even the sky.

In some ways, Project Chanology acts like a disgruntled franchisee, embracing the brand recognition of Anonymous while grumbling about the group's darker, more militant factions. One Anonymous writer called the larger collective "the underbelly of the internet" and likens Project Chanology to "a cancerous pimple in the armpit of the bigger Anonymous collective with a mind of its own." Project Chanology members see themselves as "white hat" hackers, meaning they eschew illegal hacking and the "shock-and-awe" tactics of militant factions such as LulzSec and AnonOps, who "do stupid stunts that can send their butts to jail," the source explains. "We hold hard and firm to an extra moral code of helping, not harming, people."

To counter the cyber-terrorist image of other factions, Project Chanology protestors are known for waving signs offering "free hugs" at its demonstrations.

This person says the group is leaderless and governed by consensus. Those who get out of line, or exhibit a hunger for power are quickly swatted down, a philosophy expressed in the motto, "Anonymous devours its own." As soon as anyone shows signs of "true arrogance"—as opposed to the faux arrogance the group portrays as part of its image—"trolls turn on trolls right quick," the source says. "We go to war against ourselves on a regular basis to put anybody who gets a big head in check."

To instigate action against Scientology, Chanology members can go to a private chat room and post a document or news story accompanied by a brief summary of the issue and a question intended to provoke debate. At this point, no opinions are allowed. The debate begins if two or more people responding to the posting express differing opinions. The online debate continues until the group decides which opinion will prevail. If that decision doesn't spark any ideas for action, it is discarded as worthless.

This process, the group contends, has allowed it to seize control of the court of public opinion, build a platform for former members to tell their stories and, through its Operation Reconnect, help reunite families torn apart by Scientology. It has also spread the word on hitherto underpublicized lawsuits filed against the cult.

There are hints, also, that the group may have gotten the attention of the FBI, although the relationship is a bit murky. While it would appear on the surface that the FBI has the Anonymous movement in its crosshairs, based on a handful of arrests of hackers affiliated with the collective in New York and Great Britain, it isn't clear if the agency is after the whole movement or just its more militant hacker parts.

For example, the Anonymous source claims that the FBI is slowly warming to the idea of a full-fledged investigation of Scientology and has been open to hearing tales of fraud and abuse. The source cautions that the FBI won't cop to the probe publicly. Nevertheless, I found a curious document on the social and publishing weblog Scribd which says, in essence, that the FBI will neither confirm nor deny the Scientology probe, but if you're a victim, witness or perpetrator of a Scientology-ordered crime, here are the procedures for reporting it.

The document featured the logo of the Cultwatch Rapid Response Unit, which bears a striking resemblance to the Anonymous logo. And it contained a link to Project Chanology's "Why We Protest" site.

*   *   *   *   *   *

So what are we to make of this amorphous collective? Are they an association of Lone Rangers, masked vigilantes roaming the Internet countryside protecting the little guy from the evil and corrupt? Is this the Cyber *Revenge of the Nerds*, lashing out against an establishment that has taunted and bullied them in the physical world but now finds itself the 90-pound weakling in the virtual world? Or are they a bunch of video-game-addled slackers playing cyber-James Bond with their secret decoder rings? Are they a ray of hope for the future, a beacon warning of new forms of cults and brainwashing threatening future generations, or just a bunch of dim bulbs of little consequence?

The answer, of course, is all of the above. For an organization that professes to have no leaders, whose various factions operate independently of each other, there is room under the virtual tent for all manner of people and motives and tactics. It is difficult to assess the group's numbers and inclinations because its participants dwell largely in the shadows. And as its prominence grows, so, apparently, do copycats and subversive splinter groups.

Certainly, the Project Chanology faction of Anonymous has had some impact. After all these frustrating years, Scientology may finally be in some danger, because its victims might now outnumber its membership and the internet—thanks in part to Anonymous—has connected them.

In the end, though, whether Anonymous eventually becomes a force or a flop depends on its response to adversity.

The first threat to the Anonymous movement is ennui. Internet geeks have famously short attention spans. Can this geek gang maintain its structure and operate effectively for the number of years it will take to create real political change? Already, the source says, Project Chanology's numbers have dwindled—cut in half after a year and now down to a much-smaller group of die-hard regulars.

At some point, the organization may have to emerge from the shadows and take actual shape in order to wield true political power. That would be fine with some. The basic concept of anonymous protest isn't universally embraced by netizens. Both Randi Zuckerberg, former marketing director of Facebook, and Google CEO Eric Schmidt have warned of the dangers of online anonymity. "Anonymity makes people think they can do whatever they want," Ms. Zuckerberg said in a *Huffington Post* interview. "People behave a lot better when they have their real names down."

Supporters counter that anonymity is needed to protect the disenfranchised—from political dissidents to victims of sexual abuse—against the bullying tactics of the rich and powerful and connected. Which raises a question: Would the group be as bold out in the open?

As an ardent supporter of First Amendment rights, and as a part-time journalist for many years, the subject of anonymous sources is a troubling one. It has always been my belief that a free and independent press plays an important role as a watchdog of government and corporate abuses. And anonymity has always been an important tool in the exercise of a free press. Would we have learned about the dangerous forces behind the Watergate break-in without anonymous sources? The press—and thus, the public—has benefited from a long string of whistleblowers who probably wouldn't have come forward without the cloak of anonymity.

Anonymity has certainly protected the collective from Scientology's wrath and its success in exposing the cult's abusive past has similarly shielded others who might have felt the sting of the cult's aggressive tactics in past years.

But for journalists, this has always been a two-edged sword. Anonymous sources can also embellish and even lie without fearing consequences. More than one good person has been ruined by disreputable anonymous sources. The Bush administration used anonymous CIA leaks to expose covert CIA operative Valerie Plame and get back at her husband, former Ambassador Joseph C. Wilson, for his essay accusing the president of misleading the nation about the origins of the war in Iraq. But in days gone by, you could at least be reasonably assured that major journalistic organizations like the *New York Times*, *Washington Post* and *Wall Street Journal*, with their multiple layers of editors and lawyers, would insist that any story based on anonymous sources be corroborated by on-the-record sources and documentation before it was published.

Ah, but in today's cyber world, filled with unsupervised bloggers and amateur citizen journalists, all that stands between would-be reporter and reader are a keyboard, a monitor and a network of computers and servers. While most of the old news-gathering titans are still around, even they have been hampered by dwindling resources and the Internet-prompted need for speed. Thus, much of what people absorb from the Internet is unsubstantiated rumor and outright propaganda masquerading as journalism.

And frankly, all too many readers don't even care to differentiate, as long as the rumors and propaganda are titillating enough and fit their preconceived notions.

This brings us back to Anonymous. Can we trust that this blob of a movement won't spin out of control and turn into a destructive, cyber-cult monster?

My communication with the group started with an article I posted on my website about Scientology. Soon thereafter, I started receiving hosannas from e-mailers professing to be part of Anonymous. I began corresponding with a representative of Project Chanology, applauding the group's efforts to alert the public about the dangers of Scientology.

As our correspondence developed, my admiration was mingled with dashes of concern. Clearly the group was struggling with the vigilante dichotomy: To be successful in bringing down a powerful and corrupt foe, they felt they needed to be as zealous and ruthless as the enemy.

I disagree. When fighting rule breakers, it is important to stay within the rules and ideals you are fighting for. You put a fire out by pouring water on it, not fuel. I worry that on the road to exterminating its foe, Anonymous, or some of its factions, may morph into a destructive cult itself. In the first major article written about the group back in 2008, David Kushner, writing in *Maxim*, made an interesting observation about Anonymous and Scientology: "...as highly sophisticated, clandestine organizations, they have more in common than either side would care to admit."

Zealousness and righteousness run rampant can lead to cult-like behavior. I started noticing dabs of cult-speak sprinkled into our online conversations. You're with us or against us. Good vs. evil. Us vs. Them. We operate on hate. The anonymous Anonymous source spoke of "civil wars" between factions and expressed fear of retribution for overstepping. "I would be easy prey for harsh pranks that could ruin my career if I unknowingly do or say the wrong thing that pisses off the wrong troll," the source confessed. These "civil wars" between Anonymous factions seeking to demean and expose each other evoked visions of a cyberspace version of the Synanon game.

The insecure bond themselves to causes, turning into self-appointed guardians of a perceived "holy grail." Some Anonymous members have expressed fears that the more malicious among them have become a virtual black ops special forces faction. *TRON* meets the Synanon Imperial Marines. It isn't unusual for a group fighting terrorists to become terrorists. Their leaders become pathological, they separate from society and adopt an "ends justify the means" philosophy. They identify enemies whose only crime has been to criticize the group and its tactics—even those among them who dare to question tactics. It's a short hop from there to believing that God has sanctified your cause and that any action that furthers your campaign is now acceptable.

When I suggested that Project Chanology ditch the larger, more menacing collective and proceed on its own with its ideals intact, my source's response was instructive: "I readily admit that what the darker channer world calls fun is not harmless; but were we to swear off all things from the big channer world, drop all Anonymous symbolism, we would be fair game for being attacked again. We would be seen as traitors." I found the use of the term "fair game" intriguing.

The anonymous Anonymous source is a true believer who has been involved in a variety of charitable organizations and political causes and should know that reason should never be surrendered to hate.

Charles Dederich once said that Alcoholics Anonymous was built on love, while Synanon was built on hate. "Our way works better," he insisted.

Time has proven that he was wrong.

Chapter 14: Escape from a Seaside Sect

In the story I'm about to tell you, the names have been changed to protect not only the innocent, but the guilty. This was one of my most troubling cases.

It involved a small cult located in a quaint little beach community in California and its attempt to rob a 10-year-old boy of the million-dollar inheritance left him by parents who had just died in a tragic plane crash.

Clearly, these weren't nice people.

But the bigger issue here had to do with the legal system and the odorous things lawyers sometimes must do to get justice—or a reasonable facsimile thereof—for their clients. Specifically, this case raises the question of whether a lawyer is ever justified in suspending freedom of speech and the public's right to know in order to settle a case on favorable terms for a client and whether the courts should validate such agreements or hold them unenforceable as being against the public good.

The subject here is gag orders, which are commonly negotiated in civil cases, especially those involving big corporations. Typically, the defendant dangles a huge settlement offer under the plaintiff's nose; in order to get it, however, the plaintiff must promise to never again speak ill of the defendant or reveal to anyone what the defendant did. The plaintiff gets his money, the judge is delighted with the quick resolution that eases his crushing backlog of cases and the lawyers all get paid.

Everybody's happy, right?

Unfortunately, this means that often, perpetrators of the worst crimes can avoid exposure and prosecution.

Let's say 10 people have similar lawsuits against a big corporation. The corporation offers a big settlement to the one with the strongest evidence if they agree to a gag order, making that evidence unavailable to any other litigants. And the courts, shockingly, approve. Basically, it's the same as paying a witness to a murder to refuse to testify.

Some judges argue that these witnesses can still be deposed or subpoenaed to testify. But without the ability to interview them privately to find out how useful they might be, poor litigants must pony up thousands of dollars in court costs to speak to each potential witness. It's discriminatory and an impediment to justice that shouldn't be permitted.

To someone who believes that the freedom to speak freely and the public's right to know what its government and major institutions are up to are absolutes in a democracy, who still fancies himself a part-time investigative journalist, this is a heinous act that makes the plaintiff and the lawyer accomplices to the crime and any future violations the defendant may now get away with.

To be clear, I don't object to gag orders in extraordinary circumstances, such as a nuisance suit where the court has determined that the charges are suspect and injurious. Likewise, I have no problem sealing the financial terms of a settlement agreement, but what purpose does the system serve if settlements legally silence witnesses in cases where the defendant has perpetrated a crime? What is gained when the facts that spell out the perpetrator's misdeeds are hidden as part of a deal to avoid trial? How is society warned? Where is the deterrence?

Certainly, if all cases went to trial, the system would collapse from the overload. Lawyers are duty-bound to seek settlements. But if settlements hide the truth and subvert justice, then the court isn't protecting the interests of the public. Of course, some people think the system should just be a dispute-resolution center, with no wider responsibility to serve the interests of society. A judge once told me I should just represent my client and not society.

If you've read this far into the book, you know how I feel about that.

That's why I almost never agree to a gag order on the facts of a settlement. I say almost, because the Seaside sect case was one of only two times I ever did it. In each case, though, I reserved my right to discuss the facts of the case, hoping that someday I could use them as a teaching tool. In the end, I had to remember that my primary duty is to get my client paid, whatever my social agenda.

Still, both of those decisions left me with a bad taste.

*   *   *   *   *   *

I have seen ample evidence of man's cruelty to his fellow man throughout my life. But the acts of this cult were truly unconscionable and they didn't involve illicit sex or bloody violence. To me, it proved that for some, there are no limits to their willingness to exploit the vulnerable.

Here are the facts of the case, as detailed in the settlement brief:

The day after their parents' plane crash, Ronald's older brother took the distraught child to a meeting of the Seaside Sect, of which he was a member. Followers gathered around the boy, cooing words of sympathy. The cult leader strode into the middle of the gathering, placed his hands comfortingly on the boy's shoulders and told him that his parents' karma dictated that they earn lots of money and die young so their wealth could benefit mankind. And with the help of the sect, the boy would be the vessel that would assure the fulfillment of his parents' destiny.

By donating his inheritance—roughly $1 million after taxes and probate costs—Ronald would make the world a better place and guarantee his parents a better life in their next reincarnation.

But since Ronald was a minor, the cult couldn't simply take his money. So they would start by taking the money of his older brother, already a true believer. And when the brother was old enough, he would become Ronald's guardian. Ronald was placed with foster parents who were sect members. He went to schools where the teachers were also true believers. His brother went to law school and became the sect's attorney. When Ronald turned 18, the brother, as guardian for his estate, would turn the money over to the sect. But the brother made a big mistake: he started transferring some of the money before his brother turned 18.

Eventually, Ronald noticed that the sect's leader might not be all there. He witnessed several nonsensical rants and once saw him shouting at walls. Scared, he left the sect with his girlfriend. In Berkeley, he heard about brainwashing expert Margaret Singer and went to her for counseling, which she provided.

She also referred him to me.

Meanwhile, the sect also faced a similar allegation in another case; the cult's leader was publicly denying the charges and attacking the character of the claimants. But I felt there were aspects of this case that might change his attitude. First—and I say this as humbly as possible— I was now involved. I had earned a reputation for successfully suing cults. I knew what they did and how they did it and they knew I could prove it. The cult's leaders thus couldn't dismiss the case as the ravings of crazy, anti-cult conspirators. I hoped that would nudge them towards settlement talks.

The cult's Achilles Heel was the brother. As the guardian for Ronald and his estate, he had a fiduciary responsibility to protect the boy. But he was also the sect's attorney. You didn't need a law degree to realize there was a pretty glaring conflict of interest there. He faced disbarment and possible criminal charges. Transferring the boy's assets to the sect before he turned 18 was a major violation of his responsibility as the boy's guardian. So a major theme in the lawsuit was the brother's breach of his multiple fiduciary duties and the wrongful depletion of his brother's assets under his stewardship. In addition to asking for repayment by the sect, we asked for payment by the brother—plus punitive damages. We didn't even need to get into the touchy issues of brainwashing, religious freedom or whether churches could be forced to refund donations, although we tossed them in to add some glitter.

Before filing the lawsuit, I showed it to the attorney representing the sect, who agreed to settlement talks before the filing. I believed the sect would do almost anything to keep the lawsuit from becoming part of the public record, thus giving the media an opportunity to latch onto it.

Of course, the cult leader could go to trial and let the brother fall on his sword. But I didn't think he would. Few assets are more valuable to a cult than a home-grown zealot with a law degree. And sacrificing one of its own, if not done carefully, could create dissension within the cult that could eventually tear it asunder.

The leader could use the charges against the brother to give his acquiescence a favorable spin. He could tell his followers he had done nothing wrong. The sect had just run afoul of technicalities in laws made by nonbelievers who couldn't be expected to understand the righteousness of its actions. Returning the money was the right thing to do to save a beloved follower.

After a long mediation before retired Judge William Hogoboom, who had presided over the trial of the Synanon members who attempted to murder me, we reached what I felt was a satisfactory settlement on Ronald's inheritance. But the cult's leader insisted that we agree to never discuss the facts of the case publicly. I resisted surrendering my first amendment rights. If we held firm, I was sure the sect's lawyers would back down. We slowly walked down the stairs as if we were leaving, all the while hoping they would ask us to return. They did, and I finally agreed to a limited gag order that only covered the identities of the defendants and the amount of the settlement. At the time, I rationalized that the sect's leader should get some consideration for doing the right thing at such an early stage in the case, saving everyone a lot of time, money and aggravation. Besides, this was a small cult unlikely to survive past the leader's lifetime.

So why did this little Seaside Sect case bother me more than many of my other cases, even the whoppers against bigger, more violent cults?

I still think about that 10-year-old boy, suffering over the loss of his parents, being told that their deaths were destined, that by turning over his inheritance, he was assuring them a happy new life in their next incarnation. In totalistic societies, the ends justify the means. The Moonies call it "heavenly deception," meaning that any lie that benefits the group is justified. But I couldn't imagine how people could be so completely devoid of conscience, guilt or regret. Yet, in the twisted, brainwashed minds of these true believers, they were being compassionate, honoring Ronald by allowing him to donate to a holy cause and providing his parents with a better life in their next go-round. Certainly, there have been far worse crimes committed against children.

What troubled me most was my role in this farce. With the settlement, I had given this sect an easy out for its cruel deed, allowing its leader to explain away the settlement internally as a necessary action to protect the group and keep the facts out of the public record. And by agreeing to the gag order, I may have made it easier for them to do it again, to another child. Hopefully, they knew that if they did, I would be back to sue again. And next time, there would be no gag order.

Ever since then, before accepting a case, I make it clear to everyone involved that, unless warranted by extraordinary circumstances, I won't accept restrictions on my right to speak freely.

I never again heard from Ronald. Nor did I hear again of the Seaside Sect. I like to think that the case changed the group's direction or led to its end. I want to believe that the sect's leader saw the light and realized he had done wrong.

It helps me sleep.

Chapter 15: Escape from the Love Doctor

"Are you wet?"
—John Gottuso's favorite question for patients

After agreeing to shell out $3.2 million to 11 victims who had suffered psychological and sexual abuse at the hands of John Gottuso, the insurance adjusters involved in the case did something I'd never seen before: They followed us to our private room at the courthouse and hugged each of the women who had just taken their companies' money. We had to do our job and defend, they said, but our hearts were always with you.

One of the women, a 19-year-old who had been a minor when the abuse started, burst from the room, crying. When I caught up with her, she sobbed on my shoulder. I understood. Throughout her ordeal, she had been told she was worthless. Now, in this settlement and in the gracious gesture by the adjusters, there was finally proof she wasn't a "bad girl."

*   *   *   *   *   *

John Gottuso was obsessed with sex.

One way or another, he has taken advantage of his unique position as both therapist and spiritual guide to sexually and psychologically abuse women since the 1960s. The Fellowship, a small Arcadia, Calif., church he inherited from his father in 1972, and later, the school acquired by the church, provided him with a steady supply of women—and young girls—for his "psytheosynthesis" therapy, a combination of psychology and theology with a healthy dollop of kinky sex.

In bible study classes, he told young women their biggest concern in life was sex. He chided them for guarding their vaginas instead of confronting real issues. He made snide remarks about women with small breasts and criticized the gender in general for being unable to "follow through" on relationships. Sometimes he would dismiss the class but ask one young girl to remain. In 1969, he was found naked with a student in the church office. At a party, he was caught making out in a car with his brother's wife. He hounded—and frequently forced —women in the congregation and in his private therapy sessions to have sex with him, proclaiming that it would help them break through to God's good graces by not idolizing the act of sex, but making it something meaningless and empty.

Once a licensed therapist, Gottuso lost his license in 1989 for having sex with some of his patients. That didn't stop him. In 1991, he was banned from any involvement in the church's pre-school, partly because, investigators learned, he played "sex tag" under a blanket with two young girls. That didn't stop him, either. In 1998—a month after settling my case—Gottuso pleaded no contest to charges that he demonstrated a sex act on a 15-year-old girl in front of a class; he was sentenced to 30 days of house arrest and five years of probation.

Displeased with the light sentence he got from a plea bargain, I asked to speak at his sentencing in Pasadena Municipal Court. Turning my back to the judge, I called out: "Will the victims of the '60s please stand." I continued this roll call through the '90s. In all, some 30 women that I had asked to appear—all victims of Gottuso's sexual abuses—stood up. I wanted to put him on notice: the court now knew the extent of his lechery; if more victims ever turned up, he would be put away for a long time. The stunt also proved a cathartic experience for the women, who got to stare down their tormentor in front of a judge and the media.

What I found most disturbing about Gottuso's perverted odyssey was how long it continued. He brainwashed or hoodwinked people in his own church for decades and continued to operate despite multiple run-ins with law enforcement and regulators. Like the Energizer bunny, he just kept on going, damaging countless lives.

I filed two major cases against Gottuso. In the first, settled in 1989, I agreed to a gag order on the settlement amount. That usually doesn't bother me, but in this case, the sizable amount would have garnered more attention from the media, law enforcement, regulators and insurers. When I negotiated the $3.2 million settlement nearly ten years later—$500,000 each for the five minors and $100,000 each for the six adults—I made it clear from the outset of negotiations there would be no gag order. "I don't want to be back here in another ten years," I said.

*   *   *   *   *   *

The relationship between psychotherapist and patient is a powerful and tricky thing. Therapists treat fragile people beset with psychological issues so troubling they are willing to expose their innermost fears to a stranger. To such a person, the therapist becomes the Wizard of Oz—an all-powerful, all-knowing provider of emotional support, moral and ethical guidance and a safe path through the rocky shoals of life. Patients routinely become so dependent on their therapists they transfer to them the love and affection they feel towards others, a phenomenon known as "transference."

If the therapist is wise, insightful and compassionate and maintains a rigorous moral distance from his patient, the transference can yield bountiful benefits. Weak or morally bankrupt therapists take advantage of what is inherently a totalistic environment to create an abusive, coercive relationship that never ends well.

*   *   *   *   *   *

Cases involving abusive psychotherapists intrigued me for a variety of reasons. My interest was initially piqued by a *Los Angeles Times* article about a New York psychiatrist-turned-cat burglar. He stole money and weapons because he firmly believed that the Russians were going to conquer the U.S. and execute all the intellectuals—of which, he apparently believed, he was one. The cash was needed to buy his freedom and the weapons were needed in case Plan A didn't work. I wondered what his patients thought when they read the article.

In a profession brimming with bizarre treatment theories, mental stability apparently wasn't a prerequisite for entry. Moreover, ethical guidelines were hazy. Therapists were largely free to do whatever they wanted with patients, unless you could prove they violated the American Psychiatric Association's ethics code—never an easy task. I had one case in which a therapist persuaded his non-Jewish patients to covert to the religion, claiming the Jews' history of persevering in the face of persecution proved that Judaism was the only therapy that could work.

In many cases, unscrupulous psychotherapists use thought reform techniques to control and manipulate patients into inappropriate behavior. A 1980s study estimated that 60% of all therapists had at least one sexual relationship with a patient and that the most likely to sin were the more renowned practitioners, who often felt they knew better than some ethics code what their patients needed. I have had cases involving a woman therapist with a much younger male patient, a female therapist seducing a female patient and old-fashioned male therapist-female patient sex, the stuff of many a movie fantasy. In one instance, the chairman of the Southern California psychiatric ethics committee had what he termed "a romance" with the wife of a man who had brought her to him to help repair their marriage.

Then there was L. Jerome Oziel, whose partner manipulated a female patient they treated jointly into trading stocks for him and bought into an apartment building she was buying. Both are clear violations of APA ethics codes. I had sued Oziel once before. This time he offered me a deal. Drop him from the case and he would testify against his partner; don't and he would testify for him. I told him to take a hike and won the case.

Later, while purportedly treating Eric and Lyle Menendez, the infamous brothers who gunned down their own parents with a shotgun in order to speed up receipt of their inheritance, Oziel tape recorded their confessions and offered to testify against them at trial. The judge allowed portions of his testimony, bypassing doctor-patient privilege restrictions because Oziel alleged the brothers threatened him.

While I didn't want to help the Menendez brothers, who were clearly sociopaths, I felt obligated to notify their defense lawyer, who I knew, of Oziel's shady past. She never responded to the message I left her, but Oziel was never called to the stand and the Menendez brothers were convicted. In 1997, Oziel, facing abuse charges, including sex with a patient, surrendered his license and left the state.

I guess all's well that ends well.

Such therapeutic misdeeds are always damaging to the patients. Not only will new psychological problems arise from this blatant betrayal of trust, it will make it difficult for them to seek therapy in the future and to trust anyone. And for many years, there wasn't much anyone could do legally to repair the damage and deter therapists from abusing their power.

To collect damages against abusive therapists, you first had to prove medical malpractice—which was always difficult. After seeing the horrors wrought by the therapists at the Center for Feeling Therapy, Gottuso and others, I joined with other lawyers and some activist therapists to push for a law outlawing sex between patient and therapist; eventually, California passed a law prohibiting therapists from having sex with a patient as long as they had a therapeutic relationship and for two years afterwards. A single violation would result in the revocation of the therapist's license, the state medical board declared. And no longer did we have to prove malpractice to collect damages.

The new law, combined with the medical board's strict enforcement policy, worked so well that this lucrative part of my practice quickly dried up. Frankly, I didn't mind.

*　　*　　*　　*　　*　　*

I doubt if any predatory therapist ever matched the abusive spree of John Gottuso. When he graduated from Life Bible College in 1958, he scribbled a verse from scripture in his yearbook: "And the word was made flesh and dwelt among us."

It was to prove ironic and prophetic, for all the wrong reasons.

Gottuso eventually earned his doctorate in psychology at the California School of Professional Psychiatry and got his license to practice in 1972. During his years in school, he also preached at his father's church and taught Sunday school classes where he began his sexual advances. When his father died in 1972, Gottuso assumed control of the church. He promptly sold the building and moved its operations to his home. Many of the church's congregation quit, leaving a small group of what he called "dysfunctional patients in need," culled from his counseling practice.

It didn't take long for Gottuso's predatory behavior to surface. A female parishioner accused him of seducing and molesting her. He denied having sex with her, but eventually confessed to getting naked with the woman. When her fiancé questioned other members of the church and found a dozen other victims, the couple left the church.

Gottuso explained away his behavior, insisting it was all part of his unorthodox approach to helping people. But he promised to be more careful in the future. He sang a similar tune to his future wife,

Sharron Lynne Metzler, before their 1972 marriage, warning her that he would walk where others did not in order to help people break through.

That apparently meant having affairs with a variety of patient/congregants, not all of them consensual. According to one woman, Gottuso pinned her to the floor while saying: "Don't fight... it is good for you... it is going to help." His favorite question, cited by many victims, was: "Are you wet?"

Gottuso's adult bible study classes doubled as group therapy sessions, utilizing techniques remarkably similar to Maslow's encounter groups. People were expected to present their "stuff" for the group to work on. To provide seeds for the confessions expected in these sessions, Gottuso would frequently divulge personal information revealed in private counseling. If he wasn't satisfied with the confession, he would accuse the speaker of not being straight with the group. He alternated insults and ridicule with occasional praise. He kept them off balance, kept them seeking his approval, which would constitute a "breakthrough."

While men were dismissed as "heroes," "fools" or "jocks," women were particularly targeted, with sexist observations and advice. They weren't allowed to use makeup, or wear red or black, especially if it was dressy, as they needed to battle against their desire for "ass power" or "penis worship." All women wanted to control and manipulate men. A woman's worst problem was the belief that a man fulfills her. At the same time, it was a woman's role to keep quiet and submit, first to Gottuso, then to her husband.

Everything swirled around sex. If two women were having problems, the cause had to be sexual jealousy over Gottuso. When a man confessed that he wanted to beat his wife for leaving water in the sink, Gottuso mused about how enjoyable it would be for the man to have sex with his wife right after he beat her.

Personal counseling was even more explicit. One woman who filed suit against Gottuso said her sessions began with him talking seductively while hugging her and grinding his pelvis against hers. He prodded her to talk about her sexual fantasies. "What would you want to do if you and I were alone on a deserted island?" he asked. He urged her to lie on the couch and spread her legs—for her own growth—then started kissing her hand and cheek. He held her in his arms and asked her to remove her clothes. As was his pattern, he followed suit. He lay on top of her, engaged in vaginal foreplay and eventually penetrated her. Once, he forced her head down on his penis, proclaiming that she loved that appendage more than she loved Christ.

He explained that all this was necessary "to get through sexual stuff to get to God." To do that, women had to realize sex was nothing, so meaningless you could do it with people other than your spouse. All could be his "covenant wives." He would sacrifice himself to sex with the women in order to "teach" them not to practice "idolatry." What about his wife? "It doesn't matter what she thinks," he told the women. "It matters what Christ thinks."

As time went on, The Fellowship evolved into a full-fledged cult. Gottuso encouraged members to move near the church and live together. They were to date and marry other members and avoid outsiders. The church bought a mansion and many members lived there, although their identities were kept secret. Just to visit required permission. Gottuso controlled all church activities and instituted a dress code. Rock and roll was banned as "jungle bunny music." And through all of it, Gottuso aggressively pursued sexual liaisons with the young women of his congregation.

"If you cannot submit totally to my authority," he preached to them, "how are you going to submit to God's?"

*   *   *   *   *   *

Gottuso's house of cards started to crumble in 1981, when he was invited to participate in a training program with the Campus Crusade for Christ, which later asked him to give a workshop in the Philippines. There, he recruited many young Christians who were working for the Crusade. When Campus Crusade's Warren Willis discovered how Gottuso was using women at the Fellowship to satiate his sexual appetite, he led a rescue mission there and left with 35 members—almost half the church's congregation.

When remaining members went to Gottuso for an explanation, he chastised the departed as liars who were hostile to him and to God. He said they didn't want to be functional, preferring "ass power" and "sinful-self ways."

Gottuso's explanations were growing more desperate and bizarre. To some, he denied everything; to others, he claimed he was "walking where others will not" to help people. Others got the version where all women wanted him and would spontaneously strip naked and jump in his lap.

Eventually, former members started handing out flyers and letters detailing Gottuso's abuses. The Board of Medical Examiners brought an action against him for his sexual abuse of patients, based on complaints filed by nine women. The board received phone calls from women claiming abuses dating back 20 years.

In June of 1985, Gottuso, as he had done several times before, confessed an unidentified "indiscretion" to his congregation. He cried, and announced his decision to step down as the head of the church, but still maintained that he was "trying to reach these women" through "acts in love."

The group forgave him and he continued running the church. He was preaching again within three months. My first lawsuit against him was settled in 1989, the same year the medical board revoked his license to practice psychology. He was expunged from the rolls of the American Psychological Association. He told his followers he settled to protect the privacy of the congregation and his license was unimportant.

*   *   *   *   *   *

I hoped the lawsuit would end Gottuso's abusive practices. With no liability insurance and little prospect for getting a new policy, how could he weather future lawsuits? But losing his license, I eventually realized, may have actually unleashed him.

Now, whatever he did was based in religion and, he could argue, was protected by the First Amendment. Now, he had no pesky code of ethics dogging him. Further, I never considered that in applying for liability insurance for the church, Gottuso and his followers might conveniently forget to mention the actions taken against him as a secular psychologist. For this oversight, I would eventually be thankful.

He continued as if nothing had happened. He still provided counseling, claiming it was a combination of dogma and science. He told some followers that he hadn't lost his license. He told others he could get it back whenever he wanted. He said he still was a doctor of psychology, a professor who read dissertations.

The hubbub over his behavior prompted the Association of Christian Schools International to cancel the membership of Holly Oaks, the pre-school to fourth grade school acquired by the church in 1983. To end litigation with the state, the church stipulated to a revocation of Holly Oaks' license and the withdrawal of an application to run a child-care center. Further, Gottuso was banned from owning, operating, influencing or even visiting the school when children were present.

The publicity that accompanied this action prompted the church to rename the school Christ-Bridge Academy and drop the pre-school program, which meant the school was no longer subject to state licensing provisions. I guess the legislature decided that private-school kids were safe once they reached kindergarten. As a result, Gottuso continued to run everything.

He also continued teaching his morning bible study class.

Gottuso had decided that the younger the child, the easier it was to convert her to Christ—or at least his version of Christ. He focused on children ranging from ages 7 to 16. After that, he said, it was too late.

In his class, he demeaned girls as sluts and whores who only wanted sex from boys. If this verbal assault reduced them to tears, they were ridiculed. They needed to be free, to see sex was really nothing. They were encouraged to tell sexual fantasies. He demonstrated the sex act by shoving a pen into a cap. He insisted that all girls craved lesbianism, bestiality and necrophilia. He warned the boys about being manipulated by females.

In 1992, Gottuso was arrested at the school for child annoyance. Under terms of another plea bargain, he pleaded guilty to one count of assault and agreed to do 50 hours of community service and six hours —SIX HOURS!—of psychological counseling.

And still he continued to browbeat and brainwash girls into believing they wanted to have sex and wanted to have it with him. Like the people in the Las Vegas ads, students were told that what happened in bible class stayed in bible class. They were not to tell outsiders, including their parents. "Such people will not understand and will confuse you," he told them.

During all this, he made only one concession to propriety: He wouldn't consummate the sex act with any of the girls until they turned

18. Of course, that undoubtedly had more to do with statutory rape laws than propriety.

Two girls who resisted were kept out of bible class for an entire semester. During class and recess, they were confined in separate rooms and ordered to continually copy scriptures from the bible. They were shunned by other students and not allowed to attend field trips or special events. Gottuso even convinced their parents to ground them after school. Eventually the girls came to Gottuso and said they would do anything to make the punishment stop. He ordered them to drop their pants and kissed and fondled them.

Soon after Gottuso's arrest, Greg Humbles, a former board member, Ted Martin and seven former members circulated a letter detailing the church leader's shameful history and recent events. In 1990, Gottuso provided marriage counseling to a young couple without revealing that he had lost his license; the wife stated she felt sexual pressure from him. A child sleeping over at his house reported seeing his "thing" as he walked around naked. A substitute teacher reported a game of tag between Gottuso, his daughter and another child where an item of clothing was surrendered when caught. A volunteer teacher said she had sex with Gottuso while his children slept in the same room. Four teachers at the school, the letter reported, had admitted having sex with Gottuso. One stated it took place at the school.

*   *   *   *   *   *

The five minor girls I represented in the second Gottuso suit suffered through terrible childhoods. In essence, they were being raised to have sex with Gottuso when they turned 18.

Monica James never wavered in her belief in Christ, even as she was being demeaned by Gottuso in front of her classmates as a slut, a whore, a prostitute. From the eighth grade through high school, he continually groped her, touching her rear, cupping her breast or kissing her on the mouth. Once, while on probation the day before the end of the school year, she was summoned and ordered to remove her pants and underwear. She did. When the sobbing girl refused his request for sex, he told her she wasn't ready to return to her class.

Monica finally told her story to her mother. who also had been seduced by Gottuso. They talked to the Rodan family, whose three daughters, upon hearing Monica confess, told their own stories to shocked parents.

Soon, my phone started to ring.

When Monica's younger sister, Lisa, was 7, Gottuso said she was an ugly child and would never grow out of it, so "get used to it." He repeatedly demeaned her as fat and told her she was "conceived in sin" because her parents weren't married when she was born. Further, he said, she would never be accepted by anyone because she came from a mixed-race family. He called her "beaner" and "dumb Mexican," half-breed" and "half-and-half." Eventually, she confessed to suicidal feelings. His response: Offering her instructions on how to do it. Don't use pills. Put a gun in your mouth, not under your chin. Before slashing your wrists, drink red wine and cough syrup and sit in a tub of warm water so you'll fall asleep. His preferred method: Jump off a building, so, for at least a few seconds, you can experience flight.

Gottuso started talking to Tris Rodan about sex when she was 11 years old. During five years of therapy, Gottuso convinced her that without his help, she would end up having sex with anyone. Her guilty feelings, he said, were caused by her desire for sex. At age 13, he began prompting her to fantasize about different people she would like to have sex with. If she left out his name, he would badger her until she confessed her desire for him. He then insisted she describe their fantasy assignation in vivid detail and wouldn't quit this verbal stalking until she acquiesced.

He also urged her to fantasize about sex with her father, the devil and Jesus. During family therapy sessions, he urged her father to confess incestuous feelings towards her. Once, Gottuso sat next to her at school and put his hand on her knee and thigh. Another time he squeezed her buttocks while she was in line at the drinking fountain. The most humiliating incident came in class, when Gottuso asked if she would be more desirable if her vagina was on her forehead, then drew one there—complete with pubic hairs—with a red marker. He called her "vagehead" and told her she couldn't wash it off. Later, she was found curled up in the bathroom, sobbing.

"I ... detest when you, D.J.(Gottuso), tell me I'm a heartless and self-centered girl who believes her only goal in life is to have sex with every guy she sees," Tris wrote in her diary in 1993. "No, D.J., you're not going to control me anymore! I won't be one of those starry-eyed, adoring females who always sits at your feet and laughs at your stupid jokes and giggles and blushes when you harshly make fun of their 'big butts.' I've put up with that too long. And I don't have a big butt. I'm not fat. I wish I could just move away, move away from this madness. Leave the perverted, twisted world of The Fellowship and lead my own life. But you know what they say. When life is hard, you have to change. And that's what I'm going to have to do. Goodbye world of religious hypocrisy and psychological torture, I'm moving on."

Elaine Rodan, the youngest of the three sisters, suffered almost identical abuse, from ages 7 to 14. Gottuso brainwashed her into believing she was a budding nymphomaniac who couldn't be happy until she had sex. He once asked if she would rather have sex with him or a monkey.

Gottuso told both Elaine and the oldest sister, Tracey, that they would wind up in mental institutions. Elaine's psyche was so battered, she created Jane, an alternate personality, who could help her avoid being torn down by Gottuso and reassure her that she was a good person. She also started cutting herself.

With Tracey, Gottuso asked if she was having sex with animals and discussed necrophilia. "I see a lot of you in" these subjects, he told her. The relentless abuse drove Tracey, too, to start cutting her hands and arms by age 12; she eventually attempted suicide by chugging pills.

But she never gave in to Gottuso's demands, even after he convinced her parents to ground her and her classmates to shun her. One day, she confronted him in the courtyard. "I know what you have been doing to Tris," she said. "You touch my younger sister Elaine and I will kill you."

Davy Crockett would have been proud.

The cracks in the Fellowship's shaky foundation were starting to widen. When Theresa Chessir, an outsider who had two children and two young nieces at the school, heard of Gottuso's improprieties, she did some checking, learning that he had lost his license, had been arrested and that the school wasn't accredited, as she had been told. Incensed, she removed her children from the school and started handing out flyers to other parents. Gottuso followers confronted her in a church parking lot and told her she would be punished if she didn't stop. Soon, she started receiving threatening phone calls. A dead cat was left on her porch.

More people came forward to complain. More parents started suspecting sexual improprieties. When member Glen Little, one of my adult clients, confronted Gottuso, he trotted out his old "walking where others won't walk" line, which apparently included sticking his tongue into the mouths of young girls, pinching their breasts and pulling where "the hair is short" to get them past "idolatry." But he insisted he wasn't some monster using mind control to lead people to sin. There was no fornication, he explained, so there was no adultery.

When Little told all this to his wife, another of my adult clients, she confessed to being sexually intimate with Gottuso as part of her therapy. Gottuso admitted it, but said it was Glen's fault for ignoring her; he was only trying to "cheer her up."

In the end, the adults in this tragedy awoke from their denial, only to find guilt, shame, depression, plummeting self-esteem, difficulty in trusting anyone again and the perpetual, hammering recriminations: How could they let this happen, not just to themselves but to their children? It is the perpetual lament of the brainwashed when finally released from totalistic environments.

The damage wreaked on the children was even more poignant. The molding of their minds began at such a young age, they had little to relate to or fall back on once it ended. Lacking experience, maturity and self-confidence, how could they adjust to the real world?

And still, John Gottuso's aberrant behavior continued unabated. He remained in charge of the church; he continued his bible study classes. And soon, he was arrested again. In bible class, he instructed Melanie Gold to "drop her pants" and then wrapped his arms around her and pantomimed an elaborate pelvis grind to demonstrate how people got orgasms.

After his arrest, Gottuso pulled Melanie out of a car and urged her to change her story to the police. She wouldn't; in fact, she added his attempt to intimidate her to the litany she recited to police.

*   *   *   *   *   *

One day in 1996, a caller with a youthful-sounding voice told me I was going to die. It was strangely comforting. I hadn't gotten a death threat, once as common as morning dew, for a few years. Obviously, a new cult case must be coming my way.

The next day, I was asked to represent the five girls and six adults victimized by John Gottuso. The adrenaline started to flow. I didn't care if Gottuso had no insurance or assets to make the case economically worthy. There were still wrongs to be righted and I was going after him.

*   *   *   *   *   *

Epilogue:

In 2003, a psychotherapist I knew referred a young patient to me. I'll call her Susan. She was a very attractive young blonde hooked on prescription drugs who committed herself to a drug rehabilitation program that used ex-addicts as counselors. Susan's counselor seduced her, abusing his position of trust and leaving deep emotional scars.

Sound familiar?

Yes, I told my prospective client, I had a passing familiarity with drug rehabs and abusive therapists.

The case wasn't a slam dunk, since ex-addict counselors weren't licensed practitioners, and thus weren't subject to the law forbidding sex between psychotherapists and their patients.

That's the position the adjuster for the center's insurance company took when he called to discuss the case. Ah, I replied, but doesn't the rehab employ doctors? Aren't they responsible for the well-being of the center's patients? If they haven't properly trained the ex-addict counselors, educated the patients to beware of sexual advances and monitored therapy sessions to prevent inappropriate sexual behavior, aren't they guilty of malpractice?

Further, I explained, what if the whole operation is basically illegal? When Synanon started, it was clearly illegal because it was providing therapy by unlicensed individuals. Then-Gov. Edmund G. Brown, Sr., pushed through a bill exempting from licensing requirements drug rehabs that used ex-addicts as counselors and didn't involve medical doctors—as long as they didn't use prescribed medications. It was basically the Save Synanon bill.

But the bill did require the Board of Medical Examiners to establish rules of conduct for these new non-doctor drug rehabs and issue permits only to those who complied with those rules. After a prolonged period of negotiation with Synanon, which kept rejecting proposed rules, the board just quit trying and everybody simply ignored the fact that Synanon was operating illegally.

Still, while the law wasn't enforced, it remains on the book and with this case, I told the adjuster, I was going to make everyone realize that every unlicensed drug rehab in California was operating illegally. This felt good. I was warming up.

I told him it was a little-known fact that all drug rehabs used some form of brainwashing to accomplish their goals, which meant patients were even more susceptible to abuse and thus, required even more protection. I noted the seminal 1963 study of Synanon by Daniel Casriel, a New York psychiatrist who concluded that a majority of the addicts the group claimed had been cured still tested antisocial behavior. They hadn't changed, he concluded, they had just been conditioned to parrot the behavior of their counselors.

That he learned from Synanon's mistakes was evident when he founded his own drug rehab operation, Daytop Village. Among his treatment upgrades were the use of professional therapists and the installation of a rigorous follow-up care program for graduates.

This was important, I told the adjuster, because it showed that unsupervised ex-addicts couldn't be trusted to use thought reform regimens ethically. Whether the counselor has a medical degree or tattoos covering old needle marks, transference of a patient's affections for others to the therapist is bound to happen. If the ex-addict counselor reverts to antisocial behavior and abuses his position, it will undoubtedly cause psychological harm to the patient. This is what happened to Susan.

My rant was finished; the adjuster asked how a lawyer could possibly know so much about such an obscure subject. So I told him a tale about a long-ago drug rehabilitation center—the first ever to be run by ex-addicts—and a rattlesnake and a mailbox.

He fell silent for what seemed like a long time before speaking. "How much do you want?" he said, finally.

If that was to be my last case, I thought, it ended pretty good.

But in November, 2011, another case showed up at my doorstep, involving, naturally, a charismatic cult leader and an impressionable young woman. I returned her—and a goodly sum of money—to her family.

So now I really am finished. I think.

Postscript: Escape from the Present—To What?

"Be Always Sure You're Right, Then Go Ahead."
                    —Davy Crockett

My recent struggle with health issues has given me ample time to ponder what is happening in the world these days and much of it, frankly, isn't particularly good.

My father was part of the so-called Greatest Generation that saved the world from the Nazis; my generation tried to beat back the Communists. In those heady days, singers crooned about their undying love for the girl next door or their yearning for that doggy in the window. Movie stars like John Wayne and Gary Cooper built their careers around portraying heroic figures. *Father Knows Best* and *The Life of Riley*, gentle comedies about loving, if slightly scatter-brained, families, ruled TV. Our interactions with others were governed—for the most part—by Love Thy Neighbor and the Golden Rule. The post-war economy thrived and we all believed we would hand over a better world, filled with opportunity, to all those lucky children we were raising in all those cute little gingerbread houses surrounded by white picket fences.

Those days seem so idyllic now. Today, the world seems to be in shambles. Threats of terrorism and war boil up from every corner of the globe. Many of our cinematic heroes are in rehab. Movies and TV seem mesmerized with violent, amoral characters like the *Sopranos* and *Dexter*, a serial killer who kills other serial killers. Reality shows feed on dysfunctional families and personal humiliation. Songwriters seem obsessed with crime and violence. Sex and nudity pervade everything. The Golden Rule has been supplanted by the rule of gold and road rage has replaced Love Thy Neighbor. Economic disruption and globalization have stripped many of secure, reliable livelihoods. No longer does the United States lead the world in education and our standard of living seems to be in steady decline.

In times of turmoil like these, people reach out for alternative solutions to their problems. In the 1930s, the lingering anguish of a World War, a stock market crash and the Great Depression stirred greater interest in "isms"—unionism, socialism, communism and nazism. Generational schisms, an unpopular war and the fear of nuclear holocaust gave us the Me Generation of the '70s and the wave of spiritualism and cults that provided me with a career.

And in our current desperation, I keep seeing the specter of totalist thinking in everything from would-be self-help books to religious extremism to the over-reaching fiats of our last two Presidents. The banners and slogans may be somewhat different, the proponents may seem shockingly mainstream, but in their words I hear the chilling echoes of Skinner and Maslow and Mao.

*   *   *   *   *   *

In the traumatic aftermath of 9/11, this country experienced a period of mass panic and fear unmatched in its history. While Pearl Harbor was horrifying, it was still a military attack on a remote garrison that couldn't possibly deliver the breath-taking solar-plexus blow of those monstrous assaults on our most-populous city and the hub of our military machine. And the Japanese assault wasn't instantly—and endlessly—broadcast in all its surreal horror by countless media outlets to nearly every frightened soul in the country.

As the twin towers melted away like the wicked witch in *The Wizard of Oz*, a new reality gripped the country. We were vulnerable to cult fanaticism. When would the next attack come and how many would die? To quell that terrible feeling, we were willing to do almost anything, sacrifice almost anything—even our beloved personal liberty. We had no choice. What's more, our then–President, George W. Bush, said that he was on a mission from God to avenge the dead and the world was either with him or against him.

So we looked the other way when government agents discarded the presumption of innocence and herded suspected terrorists—both real and imagined—into Guantanamo Bay for "aggressive" questioning. As the populace rallied around the flag and hailed the war on terrorism, those who spoke against torture and a war in Iraq built on lies and deception were vilified, an eerie echo of the "love it or leave it" '60s. Never mind that free discourse, dissension and debate are the irreplaceable building blocks of democracy.

It was a form of brainwashing, plain and simple. Peer pressure was applied to dissenters to conform and a dazed and confused nation complied—for a time. Not until the administration exposed an undercover spy because her husband dared to criticize the war in Iraq did the media wake up and take back its mandate to question government actions, leading in short order to what amounted to a mass deprogramming of the American people.

Behind these actions, certainly, were agonizingly real concerns about the state of the union that went far beyond the war on terror. As political polarization and gridlock grew, our government no longer seemed to work. The abandonment of the work ethic and family values that sustained us in simpler times prompted many to draw comparisons to the fall of the Roman Empire.

The complacency and moral decay that followed an era of unprecedented military and economic power eventually toppled the Romans, according to 18th century British historian Edward Gibbon's six-volume, *The History of the Decline and Fall of the Roman Empire.* A bored populace spent its days seeking entertainment and diversion in the Coliseum. And like today's box office-and-ratings-obsessed entertainment moguls, a succession of Roman emperors continually amped up the blood and gore and sex in order to retain the public's attention and approval. Simple gladiator fights evolved into grisly, bloody spectacles, with Christians being fed to lions and slaves tied to chariots being pulled in opposite directions, while spectators voted on who lived or died when they weren't engaging in very public sex in the stands to celebrate the blood-letting. It was like an ancient, NC-17 version of *Survivor.*

Gibbon's compelling chronicle stands as a vivid warning that we must do something to change or this empire is likely to topple. But what should we do? And how can we accomplish such monumental change without sacrificing the independence and personal freedoms this nation was built on?

It's a troubling conundrum, especially since many of the misguided cures envisioned come with a heavy dose of thought reform and social engineering. I've spent a good chunk of my life studying these grand designs to reprogram social, political and religious organizations, so trust me on this: No matter how well-meaning, or ambitious, they are, they never turn out good.

*   *   *   *   *   *

The phenomenon of thought reform has always tantalized philosophers looking for ways to improve the human condition. Emerson, Thoreau and Skinner certainly weren't evil men for trying to impose order on a chaotic world, the dream, however unrealistic, of all utopian philosophers. Maslow and Rogers, co-founders of the humanist movement, desperately wanted to believe in the innate goodness of man. Skinner believed that one innately good man, trained in behavioral engineering and social planning, could change the behavior of the masses and create a more functional and contented society.

Like Don Quixote in *The Man of La Mancha*, they were dreaming the impossible dream.

Unfortunately, Utopian communities remain an impossible dream and these feverish vision quests have led the ambitious dreamers helming them to some tragic results. Maslow told people that if you really wanted to see psychology at work, go see what Charles Dederich was doing at Synanon. But that once-hailed program eventually devolved into paranoia and violence. Rogers' belief that in the new age of therapy, practitioners could literally try anything, led him to defend the Center for Feeling Therapy, later exposed as perhaps the most brutal and damaging psychotherapy center in history.

Today, churches proselytizing for new members and political parties seeking to sway voters are obvious examples of thought reform. So are advertising and marketing, the massive economic engines that seek to mold our consuming habits in a variety of subtle and not-so-subtle ways. Any group whose members share a deep bond—including associations of police, firemen, doctors and college fraternities—utilize some form of thought reform to forge a common identity. Without peer pressure and an aggressive type of brainwashing enforced in training, how could the military get accountants and stockbrokers to charge up hills to bayonet enemies they didn't know they had?

Cults are really a study of society in microcosm. It's part of our human nature to seek out common cause through groups of peers. But it's also human nature to over-identify with these causes. In times of social upheaval, a public desperately seeking clarity attaches itself to the appealing messages of fanatics and, in our fervor to create a better world, vilifies doubters as enemies who need to be conquered. Such zeal makes us vulnerable to manipulators.

While doing research for my legal battle with the Center for Feeling Therapy, I came across an essay written by John Hart, ironically the brother of the Center's imperious and brutal leader, Joseph Hart. In it, he concluded that behavior modification applied through peer pressure and thought reform could be implemented if some sort of civilian oversight board was employed, similar to a police commission. The board members would presumably be independent, unbiased and free from peer pressure. They would have a clearer mindset and prevent abuses.

Unfortunately, adding bureaucratic layers to a bad idea doesn't turn it into a good one. The belief that police commissions aren't subject to peer and other pressures is naïve at best. And this still means turning over to a select few the responsibility for deciding how we think and act. And that's a recipe for totalist disaster.

That brings me to Tina Rosenberg.

In 2011, the Pulitzer Prize-winning New York Times columnist offered the country a "social cure" for what ails it in her book, *Join the Club*. In it, she advocates peer pressure applied by various sociopolitical and religious groups as a way to restore our nation's core values. The book opens with a description of life in a community church that guides members into forming "new identities" and brings them "nearer to God." Ms. Rosenberg hails the power these groups have to force personal transformations and identity changes as if it's a good thing.

But if I've learned nothing else from my years fighting cults, it's that there are no guarantees that the leaders of these "clubs" will make the right choices. To believe otherwise blithely ignores the lessons of Charles Manson, Jim Jones, Werner Erhard, L. Ron Hubbard and so many others who, in my opinion, lured the unsuspecting into their "clubs" with promises of a better world. It ignores the fact that Mao used peer pressure groups to indoctrinate a nation to Communist controls or that peer pressure turned Patty Hearst into a gun-toting bank robber.

Certainly, not all clubs are a threat to our cherished freedoms. We are by nature a nation of joiners and most of the organizations we join are pretty benign. I'm not particularly worried that the Boy Scouts are going to start earning merit badges for building dirty bombs—at least, not until they grow up and start joining extremist militia groups in the wilds of Montana. But Ms. Rosenberg's proposed use of social and religious groups to engineer behavioral change on a societal level goes way over the top. While she acknowledges that peer pressure has led to cults and other tragic social blunders, it doesn't seem to bother her much. Like Maslow and Rogers, she seems convinced that somehow, we will all make the right choices in the end.

In her review of the book, Annie Murphy Paul, a former senior editor at *Psychology Today* magazine who writes about the biological and social sciences, points out the fatal flaw in Ms. Rosenberg's thesis: Peer pressure can be a powerful force, but that power can be used to promote both good and evil. "How can bureaucrats decide whose values are virtuous?" she asks.

In a world more often governed by chaos theory and the Peter Principle, Ms. Rosenberg is tragically naive. She should consider doing with her Pulitzer what Reggie Bush did with his Heisman trophy —give it back.

*   *   *   *   *   *

Billionaire Philip Anschutz has also taken time out from his busy life to tell us how we should live ours. He put up $700 million of his money in 2000 to endow the Foundation for a Better Life, which puts up billboards, posters and signs nationwide advocating values such as "unity" and "courage." Its website solicits stories of heroes.

It seems harmless, but Mr. Anschutz, a staunchly conservative Republican and evangelical Christian, worries me. Already he has put out short videos intended to indoctrinate. In one, a woman tells her hospitalized father that he did a good job of raising her, but that she can take care of herself now and that it is all right for him to stop fighting and die.

Is that compassion or a subliminal message about rising medical costs? Is he really saying that if you have a serious illness, you should do your family a favor and just die already? This will save them—not to mention taxpayers—a great deal of time and money. Mr. Anschutz certainly has a right to contribute to the public debate on this sensitive issue. But these kinds of decisions are strictly an individual choice. And what values will Mr. Anschutz be plugging in the future? He opposes gay rights, favors television censorship and has criticized those who believe in evolution.

*   *   *   *   *   *

This kind of social engineering has picked up a surprise advocate— Barack Obama.

On June 10, 2010, Pres. Obama enacted Executive Order 13544, creating the National Prevention, Health Promotion, and Public Health Council, a collection of cabinet officers and staffers charged with promoting a healthy America. The President has issued a variety of executive orders, which don't require Congressional approval, on topics ranging from torture at Guantanamo Bay to succession within the Department of Agriculture. They don't usually kick up much of a stir.

And this one seems pretty harmless on the surface, focusing on efforts to encourage people to eat better, exercise and stop abusing drugs, alcohol and cigarettes.

Who could possibly object to that? In a country overwhelmed by obesity and substance abuse, everyone favors better health. And in tough economic times, it makes fiscal sense, too. As a nation, we spend $150 billion a year treating obesity-related health issues, another $185 billion on smoking-related problems and $53.1 billion trying to lower our soaring national cholesterol count.

I don't quibble with these goals, but the execution concerns me. The president's order talks of an "advisory group" that will develop behavior modification tactics to induce better health among U.S. citizens. What that means isn't exactly clear, but it smacks of thought reform. Pres. Obama has already passed Anschutzian legislation that requires insurance companies to pay for a medical consultation to help decide whether terminal patients should live or die, which raises the scary specter of death councils. How far is he willing to intrude into such intensely personal areas?

Slapping up billboards or mounting TV ad campaigns to promote healthful habits is one thing. Using thought control and peer pressure to force change is quite another.

Can we risk this cure?

Thought reform techniques initially will produce results—and fast. It is powerful enough to change values, get people off drugs and convince them to live healthier lives. It has been done before. Long before such programs were fashionable, the head of a well-known drug-rehabilitation center used peer pressure to hector patients to stop smoking, eliminate sugar from their diets, consume more fiber and exercise more.

That was Charles Dederich of Synanon. You know where that led. Jim Jones did it, too. They proved—as did Mao, Stalin and countless totalitarian leaders—that thought reform is the quickest method to induce behavioral change and the most likely to succeed as long as the manipulative pressure continues to be applied. But they also proved it can be used to persuade people to switch spouses, abort fetuses, attack dissidents, rob banks, commit suicide or murder innocents.

Yet people still hold out hope that, with some creative tweaking, thought reform programs can be adapted to cure real-world problems. Consider the growth of "troubled teen" programs. In *Help at Any Cost: How the Troubled-Teen Industry Cons Parents and Hurts Kids*, author Maia Szalavitz traces many of the "emotional growth boarding schools," wilderness camps, and "tough love" antidrug programs that make up the billion-dollar teen residential treatment industry back to Synanon and the Synanon Game. And, inevitably, these clones have created problems of their own.

First, it has never been proven long run that these thought reform programs work. Current research indicates that 40% of alcoholics recover without any interventions, a record that even AA probably can't match. Moreover, programs based on confrontational thought reform monitored by nonprofessional therapists nearly always prove dangerous.

A program called Elan, for example, used many Synanon techniques--the confrontational "game," the humiliating verbal "haircut"—to treat troubled youths, and to that added a boxing ring, where reluctant participants were beaten until they confessed. A former member of Elan described it as a, "sadistic, brutal, violent, soul-eating hellhole" where "twenty men and women beat a 14-year-old girl in what we called a 'cowboy ass-kicking.'"

The Seed, a Fort Lauderdale, Fla., teen treatment program partially funded by a $1.8 million grant from the National Institute on Drug Abuse, featured a "Spanking Machine." The fathers of residents were required to use it to whip their children in front of a large peer group. In 1974, Congress opened an investigation into such behavior-modification programs, finding that The Seed had used methods "similar to the highly refined brainwashing techniques employed by the North Koreans." And a Jan. 26, 1988, article in Time magazine chronicled three dozen deaths that occurred in "wilderness camps" in the previous ten years due to extreme conditions, neglect and abuse.

Thought reform is like nuclear energy: it may be the most efficient way to keep the lights burning, but inevitably , there is a catastrophic price to pay. Once started, thought reform processes can't be controlled and eventually end in ruin.

I'm sure Pres. Obama has only the best intentions here. But like nuclear energy, who can guarantee the long-term stability of the program? Will the advisory board be hijacked by thought reformers, social engineers or radical religious leaders with much broader agendas? What happens if our next president is a Richard Nixon or George W. Bush clone? Or worse—the mind reels—a Tea Party extremist?

*   *   *   *   *   *

So now, let's tackle the elephant in the room: organized religion, certainly the largest and most influential peer pressure group on the planet.

Despite my personal misgivings about religious doctrines, I am not anti-religion. As a die-hard, rock-solid supporter of the First Amendment, how could I be? Whether we worship single or multiple deities, Mother Nature or the Church of the Divine Meatloaf, our populace seems hard-wired to believe in some greater force.

What I object to is abuse—physical abuse, psychological abuse, abuse of power. When groups use the power of peer pressure and brainwashing to control people and make them surrender their autonomy, their money or their moral compass, I feel compelled to step in. The constitution shouldn't protect those who use the banner of religion to shield themselves from criminal prosecution for heinous acts.

To me, stepping between abusers such as Synanon and the Center for Feeling Therapy and those they abused was an easy call. And in my impetuous youth, I applied a scorched-earth policy to my encounters with these groups. For obvious reasons, fighting Synanon became a personal campaign. I felt I wouldn't be safe again until its doors were finally closed.

But as the years have passed, my views have mellowed somewhat. I can't help thinking: What if? After Charles Dederich was removed from Synanon's management structure, for example, it is possible that those who remained might have returned it to its original mission of healing and charitable deeds—if they realized the dangers of Dederich's "game" and abandoned the practice.

Ironically, I started pondering this issue because of a thought-provoking statement by, of all people, a Scientologist.

Many years ago, Heber Jentzsch, then the public voice of Scientology, contended that the group shouldn't be forever condemned for its past actions. All religions had gone through stages where they persecuted others in an effort—however misguided—to ensure their survival, he said. After all, Christianity has survived its not-so-proud history of inquisitions, holy wars, witch burnings and child abuse.

Now Heber was a major league spin artist, but on this point I agreed. Even if the religion started as a fraud designed to make L. Ron Hubbard rich and powerful, and committed a host of crimes, it doesn't mean that the organization's future members couldn't eventually formulate a sincere religious belief. It doesn't mean we should punish future members for the sins of their past leaders.

We may mock Xenu and the nuclear holocaust-in-volcanoes tale, but is it much more outlandish than giant salamanders, burning bushes, angels of death, or the spontaneous parting of a giant body of water? Or how about this one: God sent his own son to Earth to be tortured because the first woman—who he made from a rib—listened to a snake and took a bite from a forbidden apple.

Consider the Mormons, a religious group with considerable blood on its hands. In its early days, the sect certainly acted like a cult, with its allegiance to polygamy and its paranoia about enemies. In 1857, the U.S. sent troops to Utah to quell a rumored Mormon rebellion. In the midst of skirmishes between the troops and a Mormon militia, the Baker-Fancher wagon train innocently wandered into the battle zone. The paranoid Mormons somehow saw them as a threat and instigated a five-day siege by a Paiute Indian band (Mormon militia members dressed as Indians joined in). After offering a truce and safe passage, the Mormon troops ambushed the defenseless settlers and killed 120 men, women and children in what became known as the Mountain Meadows Massacre. Brigham Young later said that God had taken his vengeance on the Baker-Fancher party.

Since then, the Church of Jesus Christ of Latter-Day Saints, the largest Mormon sect, has abandoned polygamy, amassed great wealth and grown into the nation's third-largest religious sect. In 2011, two of the leading Republican presidential candidates were Mormons. Should we condemn today's Mormons because Joseph Smith, the founder, and Brigham Young used to decapitate thieves? Should we dismiss it because splinter groups like the one run by Warren Jeffs, still practice polygamy—and with under-aged girls?

In 1979, Synanon opened a facility in Lake Havasu, Nevada. Angry residents were ready to pick up pitchforks and torches and storm the castle as if Dr. Frankenstein was building his monster there. I was asked to address the community about Synanon. They were surprised by my message: The Synanon clan had the right to live wherever they wanted, as long as they obeyed the law. Most of the residents there were good people who joined Synanon to get help or give it. If you treat them politely and courteously, you might get the same back.

I would give the same counsel today about Scientology. Like any group, they should be given a chance to evolve into a better organization. Can they? I guess it's possible. To become mainstream, Scientology would have to stop its war against other forms of therapy, stop abusing "squirrels," end Fair Game and acknowledge Hubbard's true past and mental state. It would certainly have to stop making outrageous scientific claims about the capabilities of its e-box and viewing members not as worshippers but revenue streams.

But then again, Heber Jentzsch has been missing for several years and according to some former Scientology officials, was imprisoned by the church. As long as the organization hides the truth and punishes detractors, it will never win public acceptance or trust.

A good start would be to produce Heber.

*   *   *   *   *   *

To be fair, there have been peer pressure groups that have succeeded at behavior modification without spinning out of control, but they are few and far between. Perhaps the best example is Alcoholics Anonymous, which heads Tina Rosenberg's list of values-improving peer pressure groups.

AA's 12-step program is clearly a form of thought reform. It uses confession and peer pressure to keep people from drinking. It requires lifelong reinforcement to be effective. It often induces a sense of "us vs. them" among followers, as well as the familiar "double bind"— imposing a sense of moral superiority in the group while forcing the individual to recognize his fragility without the group.

And by any reasonable measure, it has been a rousing success, without exhibiting the excesses and narcissism that mark many peer-pressure groups. But there's a reason for that. AA's operational structure was specifically designed to prevent the hijacking of the program by some charismatic, but psychologically warped leader. Just such a leader once broke away from AA to form his own drug rehab empire—Charles Dederich.

AA was an offshoot of Great Britain's Oxford Group, which was formed to provide gentlemen with a place to obtain cathartic relief by confessing their slights of others. American Bill Wilson, an alcoholic for 17 years, realized the experience might help people quit drinking. Out of this idea, AA was born in 1925. But the little organization didn't go national until 1940, when industrialist John D. Rockefeller, the head of Standard Oil, staged an AA fund-raiser. Impressed, he set up a trust for the group and—in a stroke of incomparable foresight—limited Wilson's salary to $30 a week; any more, he deduced, would corrupt the egalitarian structure that sustained AA. Wilson, recognizing Rockefeller's wisdom, went even farther, establishing rules prohibiting any accumulation of power or money. For example, no member was allowed to contribute more than $1,000.

Within the organization, Wilson referred to himself as Bill W., no better or worse than any other of the group's anonymous members. He refused money for counseling, refused to accept any rewards or titles, including an honorary degree from Yale, and turned down any personal publicity (he refused to appear on the cover of *Time*). At an AA convention in St. Louis in 1955, he quashed any temptation to accumulate power in the future by turning over leadership to a General Service Board. No one person would ever control the organization.

Call me cynical, but in today's celebrity-and-media soaked charitable world, how many organizations could remain so selfless? Had Dederich stayed in AA and risen to power, he would have loved a generous salary and the perks of power. He certainly would have hungered to be on the cover of *Time*. His reign at Synanon proved the old axiom that absolute power corrupts absolutely.

As long as I'm in a contemplative mood, have you wondered lately what the future might hold? Unfortunately, the forecast calls for cold and blustery days, a perfect storm of political and socioeconomic turbulence leading to the formation of dark and threatening cults.

However, given the tenor of the times and new technology, they may look quite different. The Maslow-inspired encounter group represented by everything from AA's meetings to Synanon's "game," has now gone virtual, gathering in the hidden nooks and crannies of internet chat rooms. Now, the abusers and thought reformers have a global reach, bullying and bending minds in these online forums and discussion groups. And the anonymity promised in this new cyber-world often shields them from having to be accountable for their actions.

But the solitude and physical separation inherent in the internet may provide some hope. Part of a charismatic cult leader's power stems from his presence, his ability to influence with a glowering look, a threatening gesture or a seductive manner. In the virtual world of chat groups, he has only his type-written words. Will that prove as effective in shepherding his flock into coordinated actions promoting his warped agenda? And will fanatical underlings prove as intimidating in applying peer pressure when separated by thousands of miles as they did when forming a tight circle around a prospective recruit in some isolated indoctrination camp?

Probably not, but much depends on how desperate people become for new solutions and instant gratification. The more fragile we become, the more vulnerable we are to the manipulations of a zealot.

And the inexorable march of technology also worries me. As machines take over more of the functions once supplied by man, will we lose what has always been our purpose in life? What will we seek to fill a void that will grow ever larger as science continues to build new toys and extend life through powerful new medicines, stem-cell technology and cloning. Some respected scientists and futurists even talk of immortality as an achievable goal. What will we do for all eternity?

I'm not a visionary. I can't predict the future. But some of this is bound to happen, creating a vacuum that will be a fertile breeding ground for cults and thought reformers of many stripes. And I'm not alone in my concerns. Theodore John Kaczynski, a child prodigy who was accepted to Harvard University at age 16, also frets about the future. He argues that the Industrial Revolution has been a disaster for the human race, creating power groups that pay no heed to the psychological consequences they impose on individuals.

The replacement of human effort with effortless machines not only robs man of his true nature and his autonomy, Kaczynski wrote, but of his need to contribute, which will inevitably lead to a totalistic, Orwellian society where humans are viewed as cattle to be herded. This transformation has already begun, as so much of our workforce has been made obsolete. This has led to mass depression, which is treated by drugs, while the entertainment industry serves up large doses of sex and violence as a means of escape from stress and dissatisfaction. Sound familiar?

Of course, few people listen to Mr. Kaczynski these days. Perhaps it's because he has always been a bit of a recluse, living for years in a tiny, remote cabin outside Lincoln, Nebraska. Or maybe it was his method for solving the problem. As his alter-ego—the Unabomber—he mailed exploding packages to technologists he felt contributed to these troubling developments, killing three and injuring 23 others over a 20-year reign of terror.

I certainly don't endorse his methods, but let me offer my own modest warning. If, as some say, we may someday be able to merge human consciousness with a supercomputer-controlled robotic body, I strongly recommend against it. Just imagine downloading all that screwed-up human psychology, with all its weakness, guilt, shame and often, the need to manipulate and control others, into a virtually indestructible mainframe. Presto, James Cameron's next movie.

Let's concentrate instead on solving the very real, monumental problems we're facing today and do it with reason. Understand the forces that can shape us and put a stop to the worship of sociopaths. Be Davy Crockett. Make sure you're right, then go ahead.

I wouldn't want the next Charles Dederich's last words to be, "I'll be back."

*   *   *   *   *   *

Final Epilogue:

I've never quite understood how I stumbled into this strange life I've led. Some of it was accidental. I knew a guy who knew a guy who got me into the decade-long battle with Synanon. Some of it stemmed from my attempts to be practical. Law school seemed to be a good Plan B if my writing career didn't pan out (also, I didn't mind spending three more years amid a sea of lovely coeds).

It certainly wasn't because of my fascination with the law. To me, the adventure of freeing people—especially children—from captivity was always more satisfying than the monetary victories won in court. Storming into Golden State Manor to demand the release of T.B. Renfroe, spiriting Terry Raines away from Synanon in Santa Monica and planning with local police the siege of Synanon in San Francisco that rescued Ernestine White's grandchildren were highlights of my life. These were my versions of those old war movies I grew up watching where a small squad rescues prisoners out of an enemy compound.

A client once asked me to help him get custody of his child, who was with his estranged wife in an encampment of followers of a female guru in the Santa Monica Mountains near Malibu. While drawing up options for pursuing a custody battle in court, it dawned on me that since there was no custody order in place, my client had just as much right to custody as his wife at this time. Instead of going to court in a suit and tie, we dressed in plaid shirts and knit caps to blend in with the followers and infiltrated the campground late one evening. We strolled around casually until we spotted the wife and the little girl. While his wife chatted with another group member, we picked up the kid, signaled her to be quiet and strolled out of the camp. If the mother wanted to regain custody, she would have to be the one to instigate legal action; with the girl by then enrolled in school and in a stable environment, I felt it unlikely a judge would return her to the campground. I never saw my client again, so I assumed the plan went well. I didn't even bill him. The adventure had just been too much fun.

I was recently asked by an interviewer whether I ever considered pursuing a safer, calmer line of work. There was a moment. After a production company decided to make a   movie of my magazine article about Jan and Dean, my dream of writing success was right there, just inches away. I would dump the tedium of the law and instead concentrate on my shiny new future crafting scripts for the Spielbergs and Lucases of the film world.

But then Synanon entered my life and I knew someone had to do something about it. This was my crucible. Like the reluctant hero of a Hitchcock spy thriller, I had to rise to the occasion, marshal resources I never knew I had and save the day. As I became more and more immersed in this strange new world, I passed the point of no return in my career and writing moved permanently to the back burner of my life.

As time wore on, my sense of outrage grew and I saw this cause as my purpose in life. The roots of this evil were buried deeply in our society, giving us generations of manipulative totalistic movement leaders and self-help profiteers babbling nostrums for what ailed us. They were in the books we purchased and the TV programs we watched. People were suffering severe psychological damage, and in some cases, death, because of them.

That interviewer also asked the inevitable question: If I had it to do again, would I do anything differently? Of course, I've given much thought to how much happier and healthier my life might be if I'd never made the acquaintance of that rattlesnake—its venom may have spawned my illness. But in that alternate universe, I probably would have married Trudy, raised her kids, and never had Chaz. If I had known all that at the moment, I would have voluntarily stuck my hand in the mailbox.

No matter how much one might wish it so, this war hasn't ended. It's human nature to want to rid ourselves of pain as quickly as possible and that makes us vulnerable to charlatans promising quick fixes.

As the man at the licensing board said, "people want their gurus." I'm tired now, and my war has ended. I hope others will pick up the reins, because the battle against charlatans and con men requires eternal vigilance.

In the end, I can't imagine my life traveling down a different road. It is in my personality to idealize my heroes and seek justice for the underdog. And once engaged in a good battle, I become a bulldog, obsessively pursuing the truth, no matter the personal cost. Somehow, some way, I would have ended up racing down this path—or something similar —eagerly following my curiosity and outrage. It is my nature.

Acknowledgments

1. My thanks to those in law enforcement who have provided me with so much help over the years: Jerry Rodgers, Marv Enquist, Lynne Cottle, Dale Hollis, Art Disterheft and Jeanette Prandi.

2. To Hal Lancaster, who has edited my work for more than 40 years with no other payment but my friendship and who single-handedly prevented this book from exceeding 1,000 pages.

3. To the lawyers—the true unsung heroes—who circled the wagon (me) and fought off the Indians (Synanon). My thanks to Tris Brown, Bob Fremlin, Tsutsumi Sakamoto, Tim Stoen, Ford Greene, Kent Richland, John Van DeKamp, Mike Carroll and John Watson. I also want to express my admiration for Phil Bourdette. Even though he eventually failed, he did all that was humanly possible to save Synanon from the misdeeds of Dan Garrett and Howard Garfield, the latter of whom may have proved that even a genius can be brainwashed. Even though Phil destroyed evidence, I forgive him.

4. To the victims who stood by me: Joey Butler, Ben Parks, Dottie Parks, Bernie Kolb and the Rowe and Murillo families. I will never forget you.

5. To the reporters who believed me and spread the word: Cathy Mitchell, Narda Zacchino, Connie Chung, Lois Timmick, Carol Mithers, Dawna Kaufman, Lisa Sweetingham, Liam Scheff, Karen Jackovich and those at *Readers's Digest* and *Time* who pursued the stories despite lawsuits. Narda and Connie are forever in my heart. And a special thanks to Dave Mitchell. In my obviously biased view, never was a Pulitzer Prize winner more deserving.

6. Appreciation is also due to the many experts who helped educate me: Robert J. Lifton, Frederick Hacker, Jolly West and, especially, the late Margaret Singer, the wisest woman I have ever known.

7. A tip of the cap, also, to those who taught me in a very different sense: Linda Hager, Tex Watson, Patty Hearst, Mao Tse-Tung, Dr. Timothy Leary and Abraham Maslow.

8. To the members of the "Bailors," my law school teammates on a USC intramural championship basketball team: Pat Neal, Wally Rosevall, Steve Brandt, Barry Currier, Jim "Hondo" LaBlanca,

Mike Wool, Alex Glasser, Mark Meadows, Mike Epstein and captain Jim Zorigian. They were my law school role models, who pushed me to study and keep up and they are friends I can never forget.

9. I would also like to acknowledge Rod Janzen for his grossly inaccurate book on Synanon and Tina Rosenberg for her misguided tome on thought reform as a force for positive social reform. They made me so angry I felt I had no choice but to write this book.

10. To my brother Lewis, who I miss so much.

11. To Trudy, who shared with me an experience no one but the two of us could ever understand and provided me with memories that won't fade, no matter how many years have passed.

12. And most of all, to my son Chaz, who has had to suffer through my retelling of these tales his whole life. May he finally know and understand his Dad's strange life.

Oh, and I almost forgot: Charles Dederich.

He built it, and they did come... then he destroyed it.

CPSIA information can be obtained at www.ICGtesting.com
Printed in the USA
LVOW01s1138250715

447625LV00028B/1126/P